LEWIS CARROLL
OBSERVED

Lewis Carroll (Charles Lutwidge Dodgson) at age twenty-four. Photograph probably taken at Oxford on May 10, 1856, by Carroll's friend Reginald Southey, another amateur photographer. Morris L. Parrish Collection, Princeton University Library

LEWIS CARROLL OBSERVED

A
Collection
of Unpublished
Photographs, Drawings,
Poetry,
and
New Essays

EDITED BY
EDWARD GUILIANO
for the Lewis Carroll Society of North America

Clarkson N. Potter, Inc./Publisher NEW YORK
DISTRIBUTED BY CROWN PUBLISHERS, INC.

Library of Congress Cataloging in Publication Data
Main entry under title:

Lewis Carroll observed.

Bibliography: p.
Includes index.
1. Dodgson, Charles Lutwidge, 1832-1898—Addresses,
essays, lectures. I. Guiliano, Edward. II. Lewis
Carroll Society of North America.
PR4612.L454   828'.8'09   76-14836
ISBN 0-517-52497-X

Designed by Ruth Smerechniak

Contents

Preface

THIS COLLECTION OF NEW ESSAYS PROVIDES, AS MUCH BY CHANCE AS DESIGN, A reasonably comprehensive view of Lewis Carroll's art. I am quite satisfied that *Lewis Carroll Observed* is not an empty phrase but an appropriate title for a significant and variegated look at the work of a fascinating, popular genius. Here is a gathering of hitherto unpublished poetry, photographs, and drawings by Carroll and diverse commentaries on his achievements by established Carroll scholars. Treated in essays are all of Carroll's major literary books, his artwork, and his work on logic. I am pleased to add that book illustrations as well as film adaptations of *Alice* are discussed and that two important French articles are translated here for the first time. In all, this book is a mixed bag of Carrolliana from which it is hoped that no one, be they armchair lovers of *Alice* or university scholars and students, should go away empty-handed.

Lewis Carroll, as most readers will know, is the pseudonym of the Reverend Charles Lutwidge Dodgson. When writing about Carroll or cataloguing his works, one must choose repeatedly between the real name and the pseudonym. Since it is Lewis Carroll that is famous, like George Eliot and Mark Twain, pseudonyms of other great nineteenth-century writers, Lewis Carroll is used throughout this book to denote the man and the artist. Occasionally, however, it is necessary to make a critical distinction between Carroll and Dodgson. Little of the future ramifications did the twenty-four-year-old Oxford mathematics lecturer suspect in 1856 when he submitted a list of potential pseudonyms–Edgar Cuthwellis, Edgar U. C. Westhill, Louis Carroll, and Lewis Carroll–to Edmund Yates, the editor of *The Train*.

It is my pleasure to explain that this book grew out of a Carroll gathering held at Princeton in January 1974. At that time Stan Marx, a distinguished New York collector, brought together some twenty university scholars, professional writers, collectors, and book dealers to put names to faces and to discuss current interest in Carroll, including possible ways of helping to promote interest. Many of the participants expressed their eagerness to continue writing about Carroll, and by the end of the first day the possibility of producing some sort of volume, particularly one that would be suitable for the inclusion of unpublished Carroll material, had been raised. At a subsequent meeting, at the Grolier Club, I formally proposed doing a volume of collected essays. A remarkable fact about this book that reflects the current swell of interest in Carroll is that none of the articles was commissioned. Members of the Carroll group and outside friends offered to contribute pieces and mentioned other people who had papers that could be reworked for an anthology. The group has continued to meet as a literary society, The Lewis Carroll Society of North America, and paralleling the history of this book, has been enthusiastically supported and with little publicity has grown rapidly. Here and on the title page I record my debt to the group.

My most grateful thanks are due Martin Gardner, Elizabeth Sewell, and Morton Cohen; without their encouragement and assistance this book definitely would not have been produced. I am also indebted to Joyce Hines, Ruth Berman, Trevor Winkfield, Michael Hearn, Stan Marx and Peter Heath for help when help was needed. Furthermore, in putting together this volume, I have greatly benefited from the sustained encouragement and unselfish assistance of Mireille Bedestroffer. To all the contributors, named and unnamed, goes my deep appreciation.

I must thank Mr. Philip Dodgson Jaques, Executor of the Dodgson Estate, for permission to publish all the previously unpublished Carroll material in this volume. I also owe a debt of gratitude to Mr. Jaques' representative, A. P. Watt & Son.

I acknowledge the Henry W. and Albert A. Berg Collection, The New York Public Library, Astor, Lenox and Tilden Foundations for the use of the manuscript of "The Ligniad." I would like to specially thank Dr. Lola L. Szladits, Curator of the Berg Collection, for her counsel and other assistance. For the photographs in the Morris L. Parrish Collection of Victorian Novelists, Princeton University Library, I am grateful for the permission and assistance of Alexander D. Wainwright, Curator; also, Charles E. Greene, for his kind help in acquiring suitable copies of the photographs. I am indebted to the late Dr. David A. Randall, and to Virginia Lowell Mauck of the Lilly Library, Indiana University, for the sketches for the *Sylvie and Bruno* books. Finally, my thanks to the entire staff at Clarkson N. Potter.

E.G.

Laughing and Grief:
What's So Funny About
Alice in Wonderland?

BY DONALD RACKIN

GIVEN THE HUMORLESS INDUSTRY OF SO MANY MODERN SCHOLARS AND CRITICS, there is no wonder we must remind ourselves periodically that *Alice's Adventures in Wonderland* is one of the great comic works in our language—that it is, in fact, funny. The briefest survey of modern Carroll criticism quickly yields many *Alice* interpretations that seem to miss the joke entirely and many others that regard *Wonderland*'s humor and wit as mere digressions from its deeper purposes. Even those critics who fully admit and admire the book's comedy rarely attempt coherent, extended interpretations of that basic element. "Oh, yes," many seem to say, "it's also quite funny, but everyone knows *that; that* surely doesn't require extended critical attention." As if *Alice in Wonderland*'s comic qualities were somehow separate or separable from its other ingredients, as if its wit and humor were merely decorations tacked onto the "serious" matter at its heart.

In fact, the widespread tendency among Carroll commentators to lump both *Alice* books together, despite all their distinct differences in style, tone, even subject matter, betrays this condescension toward Carroll's humor. For the two books are especially different in the nature of their comedy. Like so much else about the later book, Alice's adventures behind the looking glass seem somehow forced and regimented—a product of Carroll's mirroring will rather than his free, playful imagination that created Alice's underground adventures seven years earlier and that leapt into that insane land with no notion of "where in the world" (or outside it) his leap would carry him. *Through the Looking-Glass,* as Harry Levin has remarked, "made up in systematic elaboration for what it lost in spontaneous flow." [1] So, too, its comedy made up in simple order and applicability for what it lost in free exuberance and open laughter.

I would like as much as possible to limit this discussion to that separate masterpiece of English comedy, *Alice's Adventures in Wonderland.* I propose to argue that the book's other elements of form and content cannot be properly understood without continuous reference to the comedy. For the comic modes in which all of the elements come to us, the comic ambience of their medium, and the special quality of our amusement and laughter shape all their final meanings. Moreover, I would also like to suggest where and how we might set about answering an essential yet unanswered critical question: Why is *Alice in Wonderland* funny?

That question actually involves two distinct yet interdependent issues. First, and quite simply, what makes *Alice in Wonderland* comic? That is, what incidents, characters, details, and overt strategies within the work's observable surface (as well as what satirical targets outside) create its comedy? Second, and not simple at all, why must *Alice in Wonderland* be a comic work? That question is primarily concerned with the book's metaphysical and psychological dynamics: its need to be funny and our need to find it so.

The first question—what readily observable elements make for *Alice in Wonderland*'s comedy—has been dealt with quite thoroughly by many competent scholars and critics in the past fifty years. Most of the evidence is in, and we can now reach a reliable verdict, discounting, of course, some horrendous critical lapses (one could compile a quite ridiculous "Comedy of Critical Errors" from the numerous Carroll studies published since the 1920s). Perceptive critical studies like those of William Empson and Harry Morgan Ayres [2] have shown us how rich and subtle is Carroll's general satire of Victorian thought, custom, and morality. Moreover, we can usually do quite well ourselves without the aid of scholars, critics, and footnoted editions (a fact that, in itself, reveals something important about Carroll's comedy). Except for some few scattered satirical references to clearly topical matters such as Victorian politics or particular nineteenth-century children's books and poems,[3] and some few and rather minor references to unfamiliar mathematical and logical principles,[4] we modern readers can, unaided, recognize the overt elements that continue to make *Alice in Wonderland* comic. For example, the chief and abiding objects of its best satire—the pompous and unwarranted assumptions and stances of the adult world (so often aped by children) or the truly wonderful gallery of ridiculous and humorous character types (like an abbreviated compendium of humors, archetypes, or of Dickensian grotesques)—are perennial and thus immediately operative and understandable for modern readers.

But if the objects of Carroll's comedy are plain, the dynamics of his overall comic method still require further explication. Aside from a few limited critical studies,[5] little has been done to elucidate the workings of *Alice in Wonderland*'s comedy. The most noteworthy full-fledged attempt to analyze Carroll's humor is Elizabeth Sewell's *The Field of Nonsense,* which uses the *Alice* books as prime examples of the genre.[6] As admirable and provocative as Sewell's book is, however, it remains for students of Carroll's comedy a partial study at best because it deals with the nonsense of the *Alice*s as pure *game,* having no reference to anything outside its self-contained field of play.[7]

II

A thorough investigation of *Wonderland*'s comedy might well begin by recognizing an important empirical fact: few children find the book amusing. It is not merely that the book's comic references, like youth, are wasted on the young, although the fact that children do not catch many of the best jokes and probably catch little of the humorous, avuncular tone *is* a small part of the issue here. Children are not simply bored by Alice's adventures. Often they find the book a positively frightening experience (as many undergraduates have reported to me over the years), very little relieved by the bits of comedy they manage to perceive. Katherine Anne Porter's reaction is fairly typical. She says that as a child she "believed in it entirely. The difference between it and the other fairy stories . . . is, that all this takes place in a setting of everyday life. The little glass table with the key on it, and the furniture and the gardens and the flowers . . . they were all things we knew, you see, familiar things dreadfully out of place, and they frightened me." [8]

It is significant here that the very details of *Alice in Wonderland* that so frighten children tend to have the opposite effect upon adults: what confuses and frequently repels one, amuses and attracts the other. Moreover, just below the surface of these threatening adventures lurk all sorts of threatening implications, easily identified by readers with the merest smattering of Freud. When William Empson told I. A. Richards, "There are things in *Alice* that would give Freud the creeps," [9] he employed very little ambiguity. Child readers most certainly sense those creepy things; and if they would give the terribly adult and analytical Dr. Freud the creeps, imagine what they might do to poor innocents unequipped for sorting such things out into safe, comfortable, rather dull analytic categories. Indeed, Paul Schilder, an eminent American psychiatrist of the 1930s, believed the unconscious, primitive material in the Alice books to be so threatening that he urged children be forbidden them.[10]

The important question is this: what is it about the dynamics of *Alice's Adventures in Wonderland* that makes it simultaneously a horror experience for children and a comic delight for adults? Freud's theories of jokes and the unconscious will be of some help,[11] but the whole answer cannot be found there. The complex question posed here goes to the heart of our natures, and perhaps also to the heart of that elusive genre, comedy.

Let us look for a moment at the text. Often we find "poor Alice" (the narrator's favorite epithet) crying over what we—and the narrator—find funny or at least amusing. In fact, the times Alice cries or otherwise displays her apprehensions, fears, and despair significantly outnumber those times she displays any emotion we could conceivably count as pleasure or joy. True, once during her nightmarish underground adventures she cannot "help bursting out laughing." But this very atypical reaction (here to the hedgehog turned croquet ball) can also be attributed to her nervousness, her anxiety over such devastating reversals of former aboveground "certainties" like the distinctions between animate and inanimate existence. As Alice says to the enigmatic Cheshire Cat right after that one burst of uncontrollable laughter, "You've no idea how confusing it is all the [croquet] things being alive." For Alice, as for most seven-year-olds, Wonderland's confusing breakdown of all her premises of order is no laughing matter: Lying at its center (as it lies at the center of her adventures in the middle chapter, "The Mad Tea-Party") is sheer madness. And even when the dangerous absurdity of Wonderland might tempt Alice to a bit of nervous laughter, the gravity of all the mad creatures (they never laugh or display amusement, not even the smiling Cheshire Cat—a characteristic that makes them funny for adults but scary for children), the gravity of all those creatures leads the way, indicating the proper attitude for a polite and frightened Victorian child. For example, the awarding of those silly prizes after the pointless Caucus Race:

> Alice thought the whole thing very absurd, but they all looked so grave that she did not dare to laugh; as she could not think of anything to say, she simply bowed, and took the thimble, looking as solemn as she could.

Not really an amusing situation for Alice (or for the child audience that would naturally identify with her), however amusing it might be for sophisticated adults.

Keeping in mind, then, those child readers and their identification with the confused Alice, and those adult readers who would at their most conscious levels identify with the unconfused, obviously adult narrator, let us consider Chapter 2, "The Pool of Tears." In this episode poor Alice almost drowns in her own tears—a rather delightful little joke for us, a typical Carrollian living pun, but surely no joke for most child readers. We all remember Alice's early, frightening problems with unpredictable, bizarre changes of her size and the horrifying situation in Chapter 2 when she grows too large for the space in which she is confined (a scene that occasioned one of Carroll's most ominous illustrations for his *Under Ground* manuscript—see Fig. 5). Here is the text:

> Poor Alice! It was as much as she could do, lying down on one side, to look through into the garden with one eye; but to get through was more hopeless than ever: she sat down and began to cry again.
>
> "You ought to be ashamed of yourself," said Alice, "a great girl like you," (she might well say this).

The narrator's little joke here on poor Alice's horrible size—"she might well say . . . 'a great girl like you' "—neatly illustrates an important element in the book's comic strategy. The fact that this intrusion by the narrator is, like several others, pointedly parenthetical (coming, so to speak, right in the *middle* of Alice's thoughts) symbolizes graphically the close relationships between adult and child, narrator and Alice, comedy and horror that make *Alice's Adventures in Wonderland* a very special kind of comedy.

For one thing, this gently joking little remark mirrors the dominant surface tone of the entire book: although the narrator soon stops making such intrusive jokes and returns to them only at the end of the adventures, he remains constantly present through the agency of a distinctly adult prose style and tone. That style and tone—lucid, calm, faintly amused, rather snobbish, sometimes loving and indulgent but often a bit distant and even hostile—pulls deftly but dramatically against the fantastic, threatening, even horrible events it narrates. Indeed, even the laughter it might provoke is of a different sort from the laughter provoked by the adventures themselves.

When the final Kafkaesque trial of *Alice in Wonderland* begins, the narrator intrudes again. Consider this passage from that last adventure:

> Alice had never been in a court of justice before, but she had read about them in books, and she was quite pleased to find that she knew the name of nearly everything there. "That's the judge," she said to herself, "because of his great wig."
>
> The judge, by the way, was the King; and, as he wore his crown over the wig (look at the frontispiece if you want to see how he did it), he did not look at all comfortable, and it was certainly not becoming.
>
> "And that's the jury-box," thought Alice; "and those twelve creatures," (she was obliged to say "creatures," you see, because some of them were animals, and some were birds), "I suppose they are the jurors." She said this last word two or three times over to herself, being rather proud of it: for she thought, and rightly too, that very few little girls of her age knew the meaning of it at all.

This self-assured joke by the narrator, the "and rightly too" that gently, even lovingly perhaps, ridicules Alice who thinks that because she knows the names she knows the "meaning" of it all, but instead knows nothing of the meaning—this joke invites the adult reader to laugh at and, at the same time, love Alice.

Our brief glance at the text reveals several sorts of comedy operating at once and merging into that distinct Wonderland comedy we sometimes try to sum up with casual, catch-all terms like "Carrollian nonsense." The complacent adult in each adult reader smiles and laughs with the adult narrator, and yet (like that narrator) also sympathizes with "poor Alice's" consternation and fear. Why? Not simply because all adults were once children, but because a part of us all, perhaps our deepest part, remains the child, because in our deepest fantasies and dreams we too are often frightened children, unsure of and yet yearning to trust all the constructed bases of our orderly universe. Our thin veneer of rational, self-assured, sophisticated adulthood must not allow itself a full perception of its thinness and fragility. It must, among other things, employ laughter to dispel its own best (and worst) insights. Dispel them, yes, but also somehow celebrate them at the same time—an ambiguous trick of the mind, which so fascinated Freud and his followers.[12]

The dynamic tensions that *Alice's Adventures in Wonderland* establishes between these two poles—the reader as adult and that adult reader as child—create in their oppositions and interpenetrations a kind of comedy that reaches to the most fundamental incongruities in human existence, the ones that reside, paradoxically separate and yet fused, in each adult reader's multiple identities. The child side of many of us will be frightened and repelled by Alice's adventures and yet (like a bit of curious Alice herself) will be attracted, too. However, a good part of that child side, like a very good part of Alice, wants escape. Wonderland's underground world of quite probable absurdities is not at all funny to that side. Wonderland might offer a refreshing respite, a play area secure from all the constrictions and confinements of time, space, size, logic, manners, all constructed aboveground order;[13] but at the same time Wonderland presents the ultimate threat to our fragile psychological and metaphysical identities and our orderly, though synthetic, perception of our universe. Alice's escape at the end, effected by naming her very "real" experiences mere "nonsense," is certainly a comic conclusion. But it is surely not the final escape from pleasant misadventures we encounter in most comedy. Indeed, like the narrator's attitude all along, it has some whistling in the dark about it.

While Alice's last thoughts are of the "wonderful dream" she has just awakened from, one senses an unwitting irony in that "wonderful" of hers. The "wonder" in *"Wonder*land" does not connote the same things as does the "wonder" in our everyday usage of "wonderful." In fact, as I have been suggesting, it tends here to connote just the opposite. However, for Alice, as for most dreamers, many of our worst dreams must be remembered—or, more accurately, *mis*remembered—as our best, our most "wonderful" dreams, just as the necessarily sinister elements in jokes must remain submerged for the jokes to work fully and effectively.

Many small children, incapable of viewing Alice's adventures entirely as someone else's dream, no doubt appreciate those last pages of the book best and never ask their parents for this story again. Their parents, on the other hand, have returned over and over to those adventures, making *Alice in Wonderland* one of the most quoted books in our language, quoted by people as unchildish as politicians and bankers, as well as by people as childlike as physicists and poets. These adults return to Alice's adventures because, like their original dreamer, they have at one mental level categorized the threatening episodes as "nonsense," a comic dream of no referential significance. They return because they can, with the urbane and detached narrator as their guide and sometime surrogate, enter, experience, suffer, and enjoy, and then *leave* that crazy world protected from its full destructive implications.

III

Some may argue that such a grim interpretation of *Alice in Wonderland* and the book's undeniably funny atmosphere do not square. But laughter is by no means reserved for optimistic, sunny views of the world. Indeed, there is considerable evidence that nineteenth-century critics and taste-makers were keenly aware that laughter often arose from a perception of the world's disorder, discontinuity, disunity. Thus many of them stressed the view that laughter was not essential to humor, only to wit. For they saw humor as "natural, emotional, vital, organic, and in touch with the universal, and wit as artificial, impersonal, mechanical, and presumably imprisoned within finitude...." [14] This dichotomy suggests another comic tension in *Alice in Wonderland:* the tension between humor and wit, between the essentially warm, sympathetic amusement of the narrator, a humor that dissolves and merges apparent incongruities, and the rather cold, unsympathetic wit of the adventures themselves, full of inhuman and never-ending incongruities.

In any case, the horror-comedy I have been suggesting is by no means unfamiliar to us, nor was it unfamiliar to many of Carroll's original Victorian readers. One can find numerous examples or variations of it in our literature. Swift comes immediately to mind. With a little imagination we can view the Fool in *Lear* or the fantasy of some metaphysical poems as not so far off from the macabre humor of *Alice in Wonderland.* Surely, a number of Dickens's novels qualify here. Our contemporary stage abounds in drama like *Waiting for Godot,* which is at once fantastic, realistic, hilarious, frightening, and abjectly pessimistic. Twentieth-century black humorists have created a whole body of comic work based on grim underground visions of mankind's absurd condition. Even one of the grimmest of our moderns, Kafka (the author perhaps most often invoked in contemporary Carroll criticism), considered himself a *comic* writer, a writer whose most frightening works can actually provoke frequent and full laughter.[15] Indeed, contemporary comedy is sometimes directly indebted to *Alice in Wonderland:* an excellent example is Chapter 36 of Joseph Heller's *Catch-22,* a clearly deliberate adaptation of the trial scene at the end of *Wonderland.* That these post-Freudian writers are usually fully conscious of what they are doing with comedy and that the Victorian Carroll probably was not is of little concern here.

This is not to say, however, that Carroll was completely unaware of the sort of comedy he was producing. Examination of his original illustrations for *Alice's Adventures Under Ground* indicates that at some imaginative level he certainly sensed the true quality of that comedy. Unfortunately, most modern readers picture only Tenniel's illustrations when they summon up graphic memories of the *Alice* books.

And those delightful illustrations have become so integral a part of the literary experience we call "Alice," that Tenniel's rendition of the adventures has become for many the "official" one. This is a pity because Carroll's illustrations–spontaneously naïve as they are–offer a far better companion for both the original and the published text. They do so mainly because they better reflect the Wonderland horror-comedy that I have been outlining, a horror-comedy that genuinely resides in those texts. Thus Tenniel's illustrations, good as they are, might well be considered a kind of sugaring over of the threatening implications of the text, the way many daytime reconstructions of nightmares sugar over the nightmares' worst episodes. Like the shift in titles from "Under Ground" to the rather innocuous "Wonderland," this shift from Carroll's often horrifying illustrations to Tenniel's more comfortable ones fails, of course, to dispel the permanent horrors that reside in the very depths of Carroll's comic fantasy.

A few pairs of illustrations should suffice. Fig. 1 juxtaposes the *Under Ground* Queen of Hearts with the *Wonderland* King and Queen of Hearts. Carroll's drawing (the last in *Under Ground*) possesses an eerie disquieting power not at all present in the rather tame, gentle, contained comedy of Tenniel's. Although Carroll is obviously no accomplished draftsman, his picture displays something of a natural poetic talent (reminiscent of D. H. Lawrence's pictures). Here is a case of a very competent professional illustrator in contrast to the true amateur. Moreover, Carroll's illustration gains in intensity from its intimate physical relationship to its text; Tenniel's, on the other hand, stands in a formal separated relation to the text (as do all of Tenniel's

Fig. 1

John Tenniel's illustration of Alice and the King and Queen of Hearts

Fig. 1

"The Queen of Hearts she made some tarts
All on a summer day:
The Knave of Hearts he stole those tarts,
And took them quite away!"

"Now for the evidence," said the King, "and then the sentence."

"No!" said the Queen, "first the sentence, and then the evidence!"

"Nonsense!" cried Alice, so loudly that everybody jumped, "the idea of having the sentence first!"

"Hold your tongue!" said the Queen.

"I won't!" said Alice, "you're nothing but a pack of cards! Who cares for you?"

At this the whole pack rose up into the air, and came flying down upon her: she gave a little scream of fright, and tried to beat them off, and found herself lying on the bank, with her head in the lap of her sister, who was gently brushing away some leaves that had fluttered down from the trees on to her face.

Lewis Carroll's illustration of Alice and the Queen of Hearts other illustrations in the first edition). One might say that Carroll's pictures (like Blake illuminations) often grow out of the adventures; Tenniel's merely illustrate them. The same intimate relationship and the same eerie threats (especially threatening for a child reader) can be observed in Fig. 2, where the drawing underscores Alice's real misery.

Fig. 3 manifests the great and dangerous opportunities for Freudian analysis offered by the incidents in *Alice's Adventures in Wonderland.* More importantly, these three illustrations (the two on the left from *Under Ground,* of course) show how much more frightening is the story than one would guess from just the Tenniel pictures. The middle drawing is especially horrifying because of Alice's expression—an almost dreamy acceptance of the completely bizarre and extremely destructive breakdown of a crucial basis of orderly identity (one could compare here Gregor Samsa's rather phlegmatic "acceptance" of his incredible metamorphosis). The facial expression in Fig. 4, an especially moving illustration, serves the same function. Alice's dreamlike acceptance is ever so slightly funny but quite frightening as well, and Carroll's illustration is thereby so much closer to the spirit of the adventures than are any of Tenniel's pleasant confections.

Fig. 2

Fig. 3

Fig. 4

Fig. 5 perhaps best illustrates my thesis. These two pictures illustrate exactly the same incident. (Carroll's original filled an entire page, a graphic rendering of the threatening text; Tenniel's takes less than half the page, thus scaling down the implications and threats.) Carroll's Alice—in her fetal position, so horribly crowded in that womb she cannot escape—has the same dreamy look of terribly sad acceptance. Tenniel's Alice, on the other hand, tends to dispel the reader's consternation while displaying her own with a cute little pout. And of course Tenniel's little casement window offers a good deal of comfort to the unconscious of any perturbed readers (adult or child).

Fig. 6 contrasts *Under Ground*'s Mock Turtle and Gryphon with their Wonderland counterparts. In Wonderland they are thoroughly ridiculous, while underground they seem possibly menacing. In any case, Tenniel, quite famous for his animal cartoons, deftly reveals the patently *artificial* (and therefore unthreatening) nature of these mythical creatures: the oxtail and bovine head reveal the true mock nature of the imitation soup—and the false sentiment of the turtle himself, large as he is. Fig. 7, from *Under Ground,* with Alice so small in comparison to the creatures, contrasts sharply with the *pas de trois* of Wonderland in Fig. 6. Again, Tenniel sugars over the inherent horrors, emphasizing only the joys.

Of course, it is not so simple: some of Tenniel's illustrations could be viewed as a bit disturbing, and one or two might even be considered more disturbing than Carroll's counterparts. But by and large the issue, I think, is clear. Carroll's powerful, spontaneous illustrations fit perfectly the spirit and meaning of his comic nightmare.

Fig. 5

Fig. 6

it without lobsters, you know. Which shall sing?"
"Oh! you sing!" said the Gryphon,
"I've forgotten the words."
So they began solemnly dancing 'round
and round Alice,
every now and
then treading on
her toes when they
came too close,
and waving their
fore-paws to mark
the time, while the
Mock Turtle sang
slowly and sadly,
these words:

"Beneath the waters of the sea
Are lobsters thick as thick can be —
They love to dance with you and me,
My own, my gentle Salmon!"
The Gryphon joined in singing the chorus,
which was:
"Salmon come up! Salmon go down!
Salmon come twist your tail around!
Of all the fishes of the sea
There's none so good as Salmon!"

Lewis Carroll's illustration of the Mock Turtle, Alice, and the Gryphon

Fig. 6

John Tenniel's illustrations of the Gryphon, Alice, and the Mock Turtle

IV

Admittedly, this essay is tentative, merely suggesting the direction future studies of *Wonderland*'s comedy should take. My kind of curiosity, like Alice's, is a rather easy thing. Where it leads is another question. Like the beautiful garden that Alice never really reaches, the goal of fully explaining *Alice in Wonderland*'s comedy is probably unattainable. But the adventures on the way will amuse, and in some fashion instruct, that grown-up side of us that admires *Alice's Adventures in Wonderland*. As for the child side that is so frightened, it no doubt needs that fear, and it will somehow survive if left to its own devices. What I have tried to suggest, then, is how *Alice in Wonderland*'s comedy rests on a number of polarities embedded deep in its narrative technique, its verbal texture, its multiple perspective–polarities of sense vs. nonsense, consciousness vs. the unconscious, waking vs. dreaming, reality vs. fantasy, adult vs. child, narrator vs. protagonist, teller vs. doer, delight vs. fear, order vs. chaos, humor vs. wit, and laughter vs. tears. From the beginning (including Carroll's sentimental prefatory poem that contrasts so abruptly with the matter-of-fact adventures themselves), these polarities create force fields and tensions immediately disturbing but finally resolved with a dynamically comic solution.

[15]

Fig. 7

I suspect that in one of those terrible puns in Chapter 9, "The Mock Turtle's Story," Carroll himself gave us an important clue to the polar nature of his own comedy. There the Gryphon tells Alice that he went to "the Classical master" at school. "He was an old crab, *he* was," the Gryphon says (we are reminded of Charles Dodgson's own short, unsuccessful career as a crabby mathematics instructor at Oxford). The Mock Turtle answers with a sigh, "I never went to [the Classical master].... He taught Laughing and Grief, they used to say." The correspondences between "Latin and Greek" and "Laughing and Grief" are, of course, wholly nonsensical, perhaps a bit insane. But the correspondences between laughing and grief, as they manifest themselves in our waking and dreaming lives, are as organically related as the multiple, incongruous threads of our existence woven together into that whole comic fabric we so wonder at in *Alice's Adventures in Wonderland.*

NOTES

1. "Wonderland Revisited," *Kenyon Review,* 27 (1956), rpt. in *Aspects of Alice,* ed. Robert Phillips (New York: Vanguard Press, 1971), p. 189.

2. William Empson, "Alice in Wonderland: The Child as Swain," *Some Versions of Pastoral* (London: Chatto and Windus, 1935), pp. 253–94. Harry Morgan Ayres, *Carroll's Alice* (New York: Columbia University Press, 1936).

3. See Donald Rackin, "Corrective Laughter: Carroll's *Alice* and Popular Children's Literature of the Nineteenth Century," *Journal of Popular Culture,* 1 (1967), 243–55. See also *The Annotated Alice: Alice's Adventures in Wonderland and Through the Looking-Glass,* ed. Martin Gardner (New York: Clarkson N. Potter, 1960).

4. See Peter Alexander, "Logic and the Humour of Lewis Carroll," *Proceedings of the Leeds Philosophical and Literary Society,* 6 (1951), 551–66. See also George Pitcher, "Wittgenstein, Nonsense and Lewis Carroll," *Massachusetts Review,* 6 (1965), 591–611; Alexander Taylor, *The White Knight: A Study of C. L. Dodgson* (Edinburgh: Oliver and Boyd, 1952); Peter Heath, *The Philosopher's Alice* (New York: St. Martin's Press, 1974).

5. Two recent articles deserve attention: James R. Kincaid, "Alice's Invasion of Wonderland," *PMLA,* 88 (1973), 92–99; Roger B. Henkle, "The Mad Hatter's World," *Virginia Quarterly Review,* 49 (1973), 99–117.

6. (London: Chatto and Windus, 1952). Cf. Michael Holquist, "What Is a Boojum? Nonsense and Modernism," *Yale French Studies,* 43 (1969), 145–64.

7. Cf. Kathleen Blake, *Play, Games, and Sport: The Literary Works of Lewis Carroll* (Ithaca, N.Y.: Cornell Univ. Press, 1974), esp. pp. 108–31. It should be noted that Elizabeth Sewell has, in more recent pieces, developed a somewhat different view of Carroll's nonsense, one that allows for more referential interpretations. For example, see her essay in the present volume.

8. Katherine Anne Porter, Bertrand Russell, and Mark Van Doren, "Lewis Carroll: *Alice in Wonderland*," a radio panel discussion, in *New Invitation to Learning*, ed. Mark Van Doren (New York: Random House, 1942), p. 208.

9. Quoted by Stanley Edgar Hyman, *The Armed Vision* (New York: Vintage, 1955), p. 264.

10. Paul Schilder, "Psychoanalytic Remarks on *Alice in Wonderland* and Lewis Carroll," *The Journal of Nervous and Mental Diseases*, 87 (1938), 159–68.

11. See Sigmund Freud, *Jokes and Their Relations to the Unconscious*, trans. and ed. James Strachey (New York: Norton, 1960). See also Sigmund Freud, "Humour," in *Collected Papers*, Vol. V, trans. Joan Riviere, ed. James Strachey (London: Hogarth Press, 1956).

12. Cf. Freud, "Humour," pp. 216–218:

> Like wit and the comic, humour has in it a *liberating* element. But it also has something fine and elevating, which is lacking in the other two ways of deriving pleasure from intellectual activity. Obviously, what is fine about it is the triumph of narcissism, the ego's victorious assertion of its own invulnerability. It refuses to be hurt by the arrows of reality or to be compelled to suffer. It insists that it is impervious to wounds dealt by the outside world. . . . the denial of the claim of reality and the triumph of the pleasure principle, cause humour to approximate to regressive or reactionary processes which engage our attention so largely in psychopathology. By its repudiation of the possibility of suffering, it takes its place in the great series of methods devised by the mind of man for evading the compulsion to suffer. . . . Now in what does this humorous attitude consist, by means of which one refuses to undergo suffering, asseverates the invincibility of one's ego against the real world and victoriously upholds the pleasure principle, yet all without quitting the ground of mental sanity, as happens when other means to the same end are adopted? . . . If we turn to consider the situation in which one person adopts a humorous attitude towards others, one view which I have already tentatively suggested in my book on wit will seem very evident. It is this: that the one is adopting towards the other the attitude of an adult towards a child, recognizing and smiling at the triviality of the interests and sufferings which seem to the child so big. Thus the humorist acquires his superiority by assuming the role of the grown-up, identifying himself to some extent with the father, while he reduces the other people to the position of children.

13. See Kincaid's recent essay (note 5 above), where he makes a quite convincing argument for viewing *Alice in Wonderland*'s comedy as resting largely on its affirmation of the "liberating imagination" of nonsense and its subversion of the child's "callous egoism and ruthless insensitivity that often pass for innocence." Wonderland, Kincaid argues, provides an affirmation of careless anarchy in the face of dreary, careful logic and linearity.

14. Donald J. Gray, "Humor as Poetry in Nineteenth-Century English Criticism," *JEGP*, 61 (1962), 251.

15. See, for example, Max Brod, *Franz Kafka: A Biography*, 2nd edition, trans. G. Humphreys Roberts and Richard Winston (New York: Schocken, 1960).

Speak Roughly

BY MARTIN GARDNER

ASIDE FROM THE COUPLET:

> ...feeling sure that they must be
> Tweedledum and Tweedledee,

which links the uncompleted last sentence of Chapter 3 of *Through the Looking-Glass* to the title of Chapter 4, there are exactly one dozen poems in the first *Alice* book and one dozen in the second. Considering his love of mathematical order, Lewis Carroll may have intended it that way.

Of the twenty-four poems, ten are undisputed parodies of poems or songs known to contemporary readers. In all but one—"I'll tell thee everything I can..."—the original rhyme and meter are copied. In most cases the first line of the original is parodied. An eleventh poem, "They told me you had been to her...," is based on an earlier poem by Carroll that spoofs the opening line of a popular song. Four poems are unaltered nursery rhymes. Five surely are not parodies: the prefatory poem to each book, the terminal poem of the second book, the riddle poem ("First the fish must be caught..."), and the Mouse's tail. This leaves four poems that could be parodies:

1. "I passed by his garden ..."
2. "Jabberwocky"
3. "The sun was shining on the sea..."
4. "In winter when the fields are white..."

It was thought in Carroll's time that the third was intended to resemble a poem by Thomas Hood, but Carroll is on record as having denied it. John Mackay Shaw, in his monograph on *The Parodies of Lewis Carroll* (Florida State University Library, 1960), has suggested poems that 1, 2, and 4 somewhat resemble in tone, and Roger Green has argued that "Jabberwocky" was intended to copy the feeling and atmosphere of a German ballad that had been translated by one of Carroll's cousins. In all four cases, the resemblance seems to me insufficient to justify the belief that Carroll had a specific poem in mind as the basis for a parody.

None of the nonsense poems in the *Alice* books are literary parodies in the sense of an attempt to copy the style of a poet. As Dwight Macdonald emphasizes in his splendid anthology, *Parodies* (Random House, 1960), they are better described as burlesques. "He [Carroll] simply injected an absurd content into the original form with no intention of literary criticism. When he did parody serious poets, he was not very good, tending to be either too broad (as in "Hiawatha's Photographing" and his Swinburne parody, "Atalanta in Camden Town") or too fantastic (as in his parody of Tennyson's "The Two Voices"). But these qualities were just what he needed for the Alice poems, since the originals were both crude and fantastic."

It is sometimes said that many of Carroll's burlesque poems—especially "Father William," "The Crocodile," and "Speak Roughly"—were intended to deflate the pious, pompous, and hypocritical morality of Victorian times. I do not believe this. It is true that the *Alice* books are happily free of such moralizing, and that this contributed in no small way to their great and continuing popularity. But Carroll was not free of that morality. On the contrary, his moralizing exceeded that of the leading writers of his time.

For example, Carroll was so offended by the slightest impropriety in language or action on the stage that he constantly wrote to newspapers about it. He even considered editing an edition of Shakespeare for girls in which he would bowdlerize Bowdler by omitting lines that Bowdler considered inoffensive.

Exactly what did Carroll object to in the theatre? In his article on "The Stage and the Spirit of Reverence," he spells it out in detail. "O God, sir, here's a dish I love not," says Benedick in *Much Ado*. When Carroll heard this line, toned down to "O Lord," he was so upset that he thought the phrase should have been left out entirely. In *Pinafore* the Captain says, "Damn me!" and little girls in the chorus echo it by singing, "He said 'Damn me!' " "I cannot find words," wrote Carroll, "to convey to the reader the pain I felt in seeing those dear children taught to utter such words to amuse ears grown callous to their ghastly meaning. Put the two ideas side by side—Hell (no matter whether *you* believe in it or not: millions do), and those pure young lips thus sporting with its horrors—and then find what *fun* in it you can! How Mr. Gilbert could have stooped to write, or Sir Arthur Sullivan could have prostituted his noble art to set to music such vile trash, it passes my skill to understand."

The slightest jesting reference to the Devil (in whom Carroll firmly believed), whether on stage or in society, also caused Carroll much pain. "The whole subject," he declared, "is too closely bound up with the deepest sorrows of life to be fit matter for jesting."

And what did Carroll find admirable on the stage? In a melodrama called *Silver King,* a scoundrel turns out of doors a poor mother whose child is dying. "It was good," wrote Carroll, "to hear the low fierce hiss that ran through the audience. . . ." In another play, *The Golden Ladder,* a greengrocer explains why he named his child Victoria Alexandra. "And I guv her them two names because they're the best two names as is!" When Carroll saw the play, a ripple of applause greeted the line. "Yes," Carroll observes, "the very sound of those names—names which recall a Queen whose spotless life has for many long years been a blessing to the people, and a Princess who will worthily follow in her steps—is sweet music to English ears!"

Nor did Carroll confine his moralizing to articles, letters, and privately published tracts. His long novel, *Sylvie and Bruno,* is saturated with Victorian piety and rhetoric. It even contains a poem on love as preposterous as any poem by Robert Southey or Isaac Watts. When the original manuscript of *Alice's Adventures Under Ground* was published, Carroll added a preface and an "Easter Greeting to Every Child Who Loves 'Alice.'" Both are so filled with sentimental moralizing that even Victorian readers must have winced when they read them.

No, I do not think Carroll intended to puncture the *sentiments* of any of the pious poems burlesqued in his *Alice* books. He was in total agreement with their sentiments. His intent was more obvious. He chose poems so well known to Alice Liddell, and to his other readers, that they would catch at once the fun of his burlesques, and he chose poems so close to doggerel that the fun was inoffensive and even heightened. In the case of "Speak Roughly," the only additional intent is the expression of Carroll's dislike of little boys. Change the sex of the child in these verses and one cannot conceive of Carroll having written them. As they stand, they express a hostility so deeply buried in Carroll's psyche that even he did not fully understand it.

Now for a capital little mystery, although it is hard to imagine a literary question more trivial. Solving it would contribute nothing to our understanding of Carroll or his writing; indeed, it would make little contribution of any sort to literary scholarship. Nevertheless, the question is *there,* like the mountain to be scaled, and whoever solves it will earn a permanent footnote in the literature of peripheral Carrolliana.

The question: who wrote the poem that "Speak roughly . . ." parodies?

As all Carrollians know, "Speak Roughly" is the lullaby the Duchess sings to her baby before it turns into a pig. Its two stanzas, each followed by a chorus of "Wow, wow, wow!", are:

> Speak roughly to your little boy,
>   And beat him when he sneezes:
> He only does it to annoy,
>   Because he knows it teases.

I speak severely to my boy,
    And beat him when he sneezes:
For he can thoroughly enjoy
    The pepper when he pleases!

II

Before tackling the question of *who* wrote the poem that this parodies, we must consider the question of *what* poem it parodies. When Florence Milner wrote "The Poems in 'Alice in Wonderland'" (*The Bookman,* September 1903), she took for granted that "Speak Roughly" poked fun at a sentimental poem, "Speak Gently," enormously popular in Victorian England and also in the United States. "There is evidently some uncertainty as to the author of this poem," she writes, "for it occasionally appears as anonymous, but is generally credited as below." She then quotes eight stanzas (omitting the next-to-last stanza, a common practice in reprintings of "Speak Gently"), followed by the by-line G. W. Langford.

The editors of *The Lewis Carroll Handbook* (1931), and John F. McDermott in his introduction to *The Collected Poems of Lewis Carroll* (1929), also credit the poem to Langford. It seems likely they merely echoed Milner. I, too, accepted Milner's creditation in a note on "Speak Roughly" for the first edition of my *Annotated Alice.*

However, when John Shaw was writing a monograph on the parodies, he was puzzled by his inability to find a printed version of the poem, earlier than Milner's, which bore Langford's name; indeed, he was unable to find Langford. Contrariwise, *Granger's Index to Poetry* and *Bartlett's Familiar Quotations* both credited "Speak Gently" to one David Bates. Further research led Shaw to two books in which "Speak Gently" appears.

The Eolian by David Bates (Philadelphia, 1849) is a collection of poems privately published by the author. "Speak Gently," with nine stanzas, appears on page 15. *The Poetical Works of David Bates,* edited by his son, Stockton, was privately published in Philadelphia in 1870, the year the elder Bates died. "Speak Gently" is on page 18.

A brief entry in *Appleton's Cyclopedia of American Biography* (Appleton, 1888) reads:

> **BATES, David,** author, b. in Philadelphia, Pa., about 1810; d. there, 25 Jan., 1870. He was the author of numerous meritorious poems, many of which were published in book form under the title "The Eolian." ... He was the author of the well-known poem "Speak Gently," about which, shortly after its publication, there was a notable controversy and counter-claims as to its authorship. "Childhood" is another of his best-known pieces. A complete edition of his poems was edited by his son (Philadelphia, 1870).

Obituary notices were found by Shaw in the Philadelphia *Public Ledger* and the Philadelphia *Inquirer,* January 27, 1870. The second is the more informative:

> Mr. David Bates, a well-known Philadelphia broker and poet, died in this city on Thursday in the 61st year of his age. He was a native of Ohio, and came to this city many years ago, where he started in business as a banker, and was of the firm of Boyd and Bates. He was well known in literary circles. He was the author of many well-known poems, some of which are now standard literature, among these one, "Speak Gently," has a world-wide reputation—it was written for this paper. He was a contributor to *Sartain's Magazine, Godey's Lady's Book, Van Court's Magazine,* and other prominent periodicals of the day. He was a member of the Board of Brokers, in which association he was known by the familiar name of "Old Mortality." A wife and family are left to mourn his loss.

To this information, Stockton Bates, in the introduction to his father's poetical works, adds the following information.

David Bates was born at Indian Hill, Hamilton County, Ohio, March 6, 1809. He lived on a farm until he was fourteen, when he set out to seek his fortune. He had learned to play the flute, and apparently tramped about on foot, playing the flute on street corners and taking odd jobs here and there. For a short time in Buffalo he was befriended by a man he had known in Ohio. The unnamed friend sent young Bates to school for a few months, then died. Bates walked from Buffalo to Indianapolis where he got a job with a mercantile firm, and eventually rose to the post of buyer. His job required frequent visits to the East where he "became acquainted in Philadelphia and subsequently made it his home."

Stockton goes on to state that his father "wrote for most of the prominent magazines and periodicals, and enjoyed the confidence and appreciation of men of letters." But no mention is made of where a single poem in *The Eolian* was first published. "Speak Gently" is singled out as the book's best-known poem, and "Childhood" is cited as the only other poem to have attained a "world-wide reputation." Because of its translation into other languages, Stockton adds, "Speak Gently" has become "almost a universal hymn." He praises his father as a man with "high regard for the beautiful and good," whose prose was never marred by "a single impure or profane word," and who "sought not fame, but wrote for the pleasure it gave him, and for the good he hoped to do."

When I learned of David Bates, from Shaw's monograph, it seemed to me that the matter had been laid to rest. In the second printing of my *Annotated Alice* I credited the poem to Bates and reproduced the nine stanzas as they appear in *The Eolian.* Roger Green, who had discovered Bates on his own, attributes "Speak Gently" to Bates in his 1962 revision of *The Handbook.*

Then, suddenly, information about Langford surfaced. In 1969 Shaw received a letter from Frederick Langford of Pasadena, California, informing him that his great-grandfather was a brother of George Washington Langford, none other than the second claimant to "Speak Gently." Shaw's correspondence with Langford threw enough doubt on Bates's authorship to prompt Shaw to write an amusing paper on the matter, "Who Wrote 'Speak Gently'?" [1]

G. W. Langford, Shaw tells us, was born in Carlow County, Ireland, 1824. After being brought to the United States in 1835, he lived with his family on a farm in Huron, Erie County, Ohio, until 1843. From that year until his death in 1849 at age twenty-five, he was with his uncle in Schuyler County, Illinois, except for a visit to Ireland in 1845. He never married. His only other known poem, "The Absent One," has an Irish locale. There is a strong tradition in the Langford family that he wrote both this poem and "Speak Gently" during his visit to Ireland.

Florence Milner's remarks about "Speak Gently" suggest many pre-1900 references to Langford as the author, but so far only three early printings of the poem have been found with Langford's by-line.[2] The British Museum has a piece of sheet music bearing all nine stanzas (music by Mrs. Mounsey Bartholomew), with the lyrics attributed to George Washington Longford [sic]. The sheet is undated, but the Museum acquired it in 1862. Five stanzas of the poem are in J. E. Carpenter's *Songs: Sacred and Devotional* (London: Frederick Warne, 1865), credited to "G. W. Langford." The book refers to music by "Miss Lindsay," published by R. Cocks and Company, but no date is given. McGuffey's *Third Eclectic Reader* (New York, 1879) contains the poem, with the by-line "G. W. Hangford" [sic]. At the time Shaw wrote his *Jabberwocky* article, only one printing of the poem, earlier than *The Eolian*, was known. All nine stanzas appear on page 256 of *Sharpe's London Magazine*, February 1848, but no author is named.

My interest in the matter was minimal until a few years ago when I found on sale in a flea market a tiny book (4½ by 2½ inches) of temperance verse called *The Temperance Token, or Crystal Drops from the Old Oaken Bucket.* It had been edited by Kate Barclay and published by George H. Derby & Co., Geneva, N.Y., 1847. The nine stanzas of "Speak Gently" appear anonymously on pages 78–79. The book's copyright was entered in 1846. This is the earliest known book printing of the entire poem.

I was unable to find the poem in any previous anthology of temperance verse, although I had access to a very limited number of such books. Kate Barclay had earlier edited an anthology of Odd Fellows verse. It does not include "Speak Gently," but it occurred to me that Kate may have found the poem either in a temperance or an Odd Fellows periodical. A spotty search of temperance magazines failed to unearth it, but in leafing through *The Golden Rule,* an Odd Fellows weekly published in New York City, I hit the jackpot. "Speak Gently," with no by-line, is on page 120 of Vol. 2 (August 16, 1845). The volume's index lists it under "Poetry–original," so it could be a first printing. The stanzas are as follows:[3]

Speak gently!—it is better far
   To rule by love, than fear—
Speak gently—let not harsh words mar
   The good we might do here!

Speak gently!—Love doth whisper low
   The vows that true hearts bind;
And gently Friendship's accents flow;
   Affection's voice is kind.

Speak gently to the little child!
   Its love be sure to gain;
Teach it in accents soft and mild:—
   It may not long remain.

Speak gently to the young, for they
   Will have enough to bear—
Pass through this life as best they may,
   'Tis full of anxious care!

Speak gently to the aged one,
   Grieve not the care-worn heart,
The sands of life are nearly run,
   Let such in peace depart!

Speak gently, kindly to the poor;
   Let no harsh tone be heard;
They have enough they must endure,
   Without an unkind word!

Speak gently to the erring—know,
   They may have toiled in vain;
Perchance unkindness made them so;
   Oh, win them back again!

Speak gently!—He who gave us life
   To bend man's stubborn will,
When elements were in fierce strife,
   Said to them, "Peace, be still."

Speak gently!—'tis a little thing
   Dropped in the heart's deep well;
The good, the joy which it may bring,
   Eternity shall tell.

While Shaw was searching for early printings of "Speak Gently," he was struck by the number of poems he came across that had exactly the same rhyme and meter, and with opening lines that could have served just as well as the basis for Carroll's parody. For example, *The Children's Magazine* (New York, 1848) printed an anonymous poem "from the *Warder* (Irish)" called "Little Children." [4] It begins:

> Speak gently to the little child,
>> So guileless and so free,
> Who with a trustful, loving heart,
>> Puts confidence in thee.

Note that the line in the Bates-Langford poem closest to Carroll's opening line is the first line of the third stanza, whereas here the identical line opens the poem. Is it possible that *this* is the poem Carroll had in mind? To make matters worse, Shaw found dozens of other poems by English and American authors, all with appropriate opening lines, similar subject matter, and written in quatrains with the same structure as "Speak Roughly." No less than ten poems, by ten different authors, begin "Speak gently . . . ," eight start "Speak kindly . . . ," and others open with "Speak softly . . . ," "Speak not harshly . . . ," and similar phrases.

"To so perceptive a person as Lewis Carroll," Shaw concludes his article, "this deluge of didactic verse must have been apparent, and the impression grew upon me that, just as each of these variants of a common theme seems but an echo of all the others, his parody may well be an echo of all of them rather than any one of them. It is true that the Bates-Langford version shows up more frequently in this list than any other, but this may be due to the fact that this is the poem for which both Frederick Langford and I have been searching."

In the absence of evidence that may turn up in letters or missing portions of Carroll's diary, we cannot be certain that Carroll specifically had the Bates-Langford poem in mind. However, I believe it can be said with confidence this poem did exceed all the others in popularity on both sides of the Atlantic. So far, no poem on Shaw's list has been traced to earlier than 1845. It seems reasonable to suppose that the great success of the Bates-Langford poem sparked the numerous later imitations, and that contemporary readers of the first *Alice* book would have taken "Speak Roughly" to be a parody of the Bates-Langford version. [5]

The strongest evidence for the enormous popularity of "Speak Gently" is the number of times it was set to music as a popular song, or included in a hymnal. I found two musical versions published in Boston in 1846, and one in Philadelphia in 1856. [6] All nine stanzas appear on each piece of sheet music, but no one is credited for the lyrics. Frederick Langford found ten different musical versions in the British Museum, all issued in England between 1849 and 1864.

The poem's first appearance as a hymn, so far as I can discover, was in *A Book of Hymns,* compiled by Samuel Longfellow and Samuel Johnson, published in

Cambridge, Massachusetts (Metcalf and Co., 1846).[7] This is the first known book publication of "Speak Gently," although only five stanzas are given. There is no music and no by-line. The same five stanzas, credited to "Bates," are in Henry Ward Beecher's *Plymouth Collection of Hymns and Tunes* (A. S. Barnes, 1855). I have already mentioned the inclusion of the five stanzas in Carpenter's 1865 anthology, published in London, where they are credited to Langford. In 1871 stanzas 1, 3, 5, 6 appeared anonymously as hymn 33 in *Pure Gold for the Sunday School,* edited by Robert Lowry and W. Howard Doane (Biglow and Main). Three of the five stanzas entered the first *Christian Science Hymnal* (1892) and have been in the church's hymnal ever since, although the musical setting has varied.[8]

III

Why has the poem so completely vanished from the pop culture of English-speaking lands?[9] Is it because our age is not one that admires gentleness? Do we prefer to speak roughly, not just to babies when they sneeze but to everybody the poem asks us to treat with gentleness? Is it because medical science has rendered quaint the line "it may not long remain," and that references to the "good we may do here" and the rewards awaiting us in eternity have become equally anachronistic? The poem is obviously doggerel, but that is not the point. We have to ask why millions of people were emotionally stirred by the poem a hundred years ago, whereas today the poem is remembered only because Lewis Carroll probably parodied it.

Let's go back to the question of who wrote "Speak Gently." Langford's case suffers from a failure to find his name linked to any printing of the poem earlier than Bates's 1849 book. On the other hand, Langford's death in 1849 (assuming he did indeed write the poem) could explain why Bates's authorship was not immediately contested. The efforts of Langford's relatives to establish his claim seem to have developed much later. Although *Appleton's Cyclopedia* speaks of controversy and counterclaims, I have been unable to find any published record of such controversy. Is it buried in old newspaper files? Did it exist only in private letters?

The chief evidence favoring Bates is, of course, that the poem is in two of his books. But there are suspicious aspects. We know that by 1849 the poem was already famous. It had been set to music at least twice in America, it was being sung in churches, it had appeared in at least two book collections, and it had been published as early as 1845 in an Odd Fellows journal.[10] In view of the poem's popularity, one would have expected Bates to have indicated when he wrote it and where it was first published. There is not a line in his book about where *any* of his poems had earlier appeared. His son is equally uninformative. By 1870, when Stockton Bates edited his father's poems, there surely had been controversy of some sort over the authorship of "Speak Gently." Stockton makes no mention of such controversy, nor as mentioned before does he divulge when and where the poem had first been published.

One obituary of the elder Bates states that the poem had been written for the

Philadelphia *Inquirer.* If the poem could be found in this paper prior to August 16, 1845 (the date of its publication in *The Golden Rule),* with Bates's by-line, his claim would be enormously strengthened. If it cannot be found in the *Inquirer,* or if it appeared there after the date of *The Golden Rule,* his case would be enormously weakened.

A check should also be made of the periodicals mentioned in Bates's obituary to see if any of his other poems actually did appear in them. And are there surviving descendants of Bates who may own family letters or other documents bearing on the question? [11]

The odds, it seems to me, still favor Bates. But we should not forget that a respectable man, well liked in his community, is capable, under certain circumstances, of falsely claiming the authorship of a popular poem. A classic instance is provided by George Whitefield D'Vys, of Cambridge, Massachusetts, who claimed to be the author of "Casey at the Bat." The poem had been written by Ernest Lawrence Thayer and published in 1888 in a humor column Thayer was then writing for the San Francisco *Examiner.* The column was signed "Phin," Thayer's nickname.

Nobody knew who Phin was, so no name was attached to the poem when it was widely reprinted. The actor De Wolf Hopper began reciting it, and for five years even he did not know who wrote the poem. It was during this period that D'Vys proclaimed himself the author. I own a copy of a rare little booklet, *Casey at the Bat and Other Mudville Ballads,* which D'Vys had printed in Cambridge. It opens with Thayer's poem, followed by ten other ballads about Casey, all worthless. I have some letters written by D'Vys, shortly before his death, in which he speaks so convincingly of his authorship of "Casey" that one suspects the poor fellow actually believed it.

It is not hard to understand how such a deception can come about. An anonymous piece of doggerel, for reasons poorly understood and beneath the dignity of critics to investigate, suddenly becomes enormously popular. It is widely reprinted. It is set to music, almost everybody quotes it, many people memorize it, no one knows who wrote it. A humble versifier, Mr. X, who has been churning out his own doggerel and failing to get it printed, is having a few snorts in a local saloon. Someone quotes the famous poem. In a boozy moment of ego-boosting, Mr. X allows that it was *he* who penned those immortal lines. The rumor spreads. Soon the community is convinced that their local bard is indeed the author. It is too late to deny it. Mr. X is stuck with his story.

A few years later the situation has grown uncomfortable. There are doubters. Counterclaims are in the air, but no hard evidence. Finally, to bolster his shaky claim, Mr. X publishes his own book of verse for the primary purpose of including the famous poem that he did not write, and whose author he still may not know.

Is it possible that Bates was such a claimant? It is. It is also possible that neither he *nor* Langford wrote "Speak Gently." It is possible we will never know who did. On the other hand, somewhere in the dusty stacks of libraries, or recorded on the microfilm of old newspapers, there may be statements that will solve the mystery.

I would like to thank John Shaw for his great help in preparing this article. Needless to add, we would be pleased to hear from anyone who comes upon the slightest scrap of information that sheds light on this frivolous but nagging question.

NOTES

1. Shaw's paper, which first circulated among his friends in 1971, was printed in *Jabberwocky,* No. 11 (Summer 1972).

2. *The Cyclopedia of Practical Quotations,* J. K. Hoyt (Funk and Wagnalls, 1896), credits a stanza of "Speak Gently" to G. W. Langford. The 1948 edition of *Bartlett's* names Langford as the author of a quotation from the poem, but this was the result of letters from the Langford family after a previous edition had credited the line to Bates. Later editions revert to Bates.

3. All nine of these stanzas are reprinted word for word in *The Eolian,* with identical punctuation except for a comma after "kindly" (stanza 6), and after "joy" (stanza 9). Ms Barclay's version contains many punctuation changes. The third line of stanza 8 is altered to: "When elements were fierce with strife."

4. This poem is included in Mary J. Reed's *The Rosemary: A Collection of Sacred and Religious Poetry* (1848), and in many later anthologies such as Caroline May's *The American Female Poets* (1849), Thomas Buchanan Read's *The Female American Poets* (1852), and the anonymously edited *Home Scenes, or Lights and Shadows of the Christian Home* (1865).

5. In searching for book printings of "Speak Gently," not on Shaw's list, I found the following volumes of special interest:

   Heavenly Thoughts for Morning Hours, selected by Lady Catherine Long (London: James Nisbet, 1851). All nine stanzas are given anonymously. The book I checked was a twelfth edition.

   Analytical Fourth Reader, ed. Richard Edwards (New York: Taintor, 1867). "It requires soft tones and medium pitch," Edwards writes in introducing the anonymous selection, "and must be spoken slowly. . . . You also need to use clear tones, of pure quality, in reading this piece because the sentiments expressed are beautiful and good."

   The Household Treasury of Christian Knowledge and Gems of Sacred Poetry. This is a massive, anonymously edited volume of more than five hundred pages, published in Philadelphia by Carson and Simpson, 1890. "Speak Gently," with no by-line, is on p. 40.

   Heart Throbs, compiled by Joe Mitchell Chapple (Boston: Chapple, 1905). This anthology of sentimental verse was so well received that it ran through endless editions, not to mention its sequel, *More Heart Throbs.* Six stanzas of "Speak Gently," credited to Bates, are in *Heart Throbs* on p. 432.

6. One 1846 version, published by Oliver Ditson, sets the poem to previously published

music by Irish violinist and composer William Vincent Wallace, with a special arrangement for guitar by E. B. Bohuszewicz. The other 1846 version has music arranged for pianoforte by Joseph Bird. The 1856 version, published by John March, has music by G. A. Morse.

7. Samuel Longfellow, brother of Henry Wadsworth Longfellow, was a Unitarian minister. An enlarged collection of *A Book of Hymns* (Ticknor, Reed and Fields, 1848) was so well received that by 1866 it was in its fifteenth edition. "Speak Gently" (stanzas 1, 4, 5, 7, 9) is hymn 285 in all editions.

8. In the 1892 hymnal, stanzas 1, 7, 9 of "Speak Gently" are set to the tune "Evan" by William H. Havergal. No author is credited. In 1910 the same stanzas appear, set to "Sawley," a melody by James Walch, with lyrics credited to G. W. Langford. The present hymnal, first published in 1932, contains the hymn with two settings: one is the "Sawley" tune, the other "The Sarum Gradual" of 1527, arranged by Sir H. Walford Davies. Lyrics are credited to David Bates.

     Hymnal Notes (1933), a companion to the 1932 *Christian Science Hymnal,* has an informative note on "Speak Gently." After stating that the poem had appeared unsigned in *Sharpe's London Magazine,* 1848, the note goes on to say: "It has been attributed to George Washington Hangford, misspelled Langford in the 1910 Hymnal. But it was written by an American poet, David Bates." (I am indebted to A. W. Phinney, of the committee on publication, First Church of Christ, Scientist, Boston, for this information.)

9. Not entirely. The poem turns up in A. L. Alexander's *Poems That Touch the Heart* (Garden City, N.Y.: 1942) and Michael R. Turner's *Parlour Poetry: A Casquet of Gems* (New York: Viking, 1969).

10. A short story by Timothy Shay Arthur, a prolific American writer of mid-nineteenth-century pious Christian fiction, provides another indication of how well the poem was known in 1849. A story called "Speak Gently," in Arthur's *Sketches of Life and Character* (J. W. Bradley, 1850), is based on the poem and is headed by the poem's first stanza. No poet is credited. In his 1849 introduction, Arthur states that every piece in the book had appeared earlier in a magazine or newspaper, many of them anonymously, but I was unable to run down the story's earlier printing.

11. It is probably sheer coincidence, but Langford lived in Huron, Ohio, from 1835 until 1843, and Stockton Bates writes that his father, when a young man, once lived in Lower Sandusky. If this refers to an area south of Sandusky (rather than lower Sandusky County), it would be very close to Huron, an industrial suburb of Sandusky. It was in Lower Sandusky that Bates met the unnamed friend who later paid for his schooling in Buffalo. Did young Bates also meet a youth, then in his teens, named George Washington Langford?

Arthur Rackham's
Adventures in Wonderland

BY MICHAEL PATRICK HEARN

MORE THAN ANY OTHER BRANCH OF LETTERS, CHILDREN'S LITERATURE IS OFTEN dependent upon its illustrations. The author of a child's story may be restricted and even overpowered by his collaborator's conceptions. Occasionally there is a true marriage between author and artist; the text is complemented and enriched by the drawings. Lewis Carroll was fortunate in having so perfect a partner as John Tenniel to portray the odd creatures of his imagination. Carroll himself was something of an artist, but it is through Tenniel's portrayals that one best remembers the people of Wonderland.

In spite of this seemingly inseparable team, numerous newly illustrated volumes by many hands of varying degrees of skill have appeared since the first edition of *Alice's Adventures in Wonderland* was published in 1865.[1] Peter Newell, Charles Robinson, Willy Pogany, Leonard Weisgard, and Salvador Dali are just a few of the artists who have attempted to decorate Carroll. In 1907, the year the copyright expired, at least seven new editions were issued. Among these was one by Arthur Rackham. He was then enjoying remarkable success as one of the most highly respected illustrators of the day. In 1905 his *Rip Van Winkle* established him as the most exciting English contributor to the gift-book market, and he followed this volume with an even more ambitious embellishment of James M. Barrie's *Peter Pan in Kensington Gardens* (1906). Predictably, at the copyright expiration of *Alice in Wonderland,* the greatest children's book written by an Englishman, Rackham's publisher William Heinemann commissioned him to produce a new edition.

Rackham, however, was unprepared for the reactions to his obviously audacious attempt to reillustrate the classic story. He did not intend to replace Tenniel. He had great respect for the celebrated *Punch* cartoonist and admitted that he found the art for the original *Alice in Wonderland* "work which I take to be as nearly ideal in the

way of children's picture-books as anything ever achieved."[2] In his own drawings Rackham paid homage to Tenniel's contribution. In a Christmas issue of the pictorial weekly *Black and White,* Rackham drew a cartoon in which adaptations of Tenniel's depictions of Alice and the Wonderland and Looking-Glass characters dominate a book party celebrating favorite childhood illustrations. (Also included are examples from Edward Lear, Randolph Caldecott, and Heinrich Hoffmann, Fig. 1). And among

Fig. 1

Fig. 2

the figures dancing around a calendar drawn by Rackham for *Punch's Almanac for 1907* are Alice and the White Knight, who bears a striking resemblance to Tenniel himself (Fig. 2).

Rackham clearly recognized the historical importance of Tenniel's mid-Victorian woodcuts. The new Heinemann edition proposed in part to provide in color what Tenniel could only have done in black and white. This argument for the necessity of a new rendition of the classic was apparent in Austin Dobson's apologetic "proem" that introduced the volume:

Enchanting ALICE! Black-and-white
   Has made your deeds perennial;
And naught save "Chaos and old Night"
   Can part you from TENNIEL;

But still you are a Type, and based
   In Truth, like LEAR and HAMLET;
And Types may be re-draped to taste
   In cloth-of-gold or camlet.

Here comes a fresh Costumier, then;
   That Taste may gain a wrinkle
To him who drew with such deft pen
   The rags of RIP VAN WINKLE.[3]

Certainly Rackham's edition was designed not to knock Tenniel's off the nursery shelf but to give a new dress to an old favorite.

The public's response was mixed. Although acknowledged as "*the* gift book of the season," Rackham's *Alice in Wonderland* was among the more controversial offerings of the year. Some reviewers found the new work an uninvited invasion of their private nurseries; one noted that to reillustrate Carroll in a contemporary style one might likewise rewrite the text. Not everyone was offended, however. One correspondent assured Rackham, "Your delightful Alice is alive and makes Tenniel's Alice look like a stiff puppet." [4] The most damaging comment came from *Punch,* the humor weekly that had published so much of Tenniel's original work. In a cartoon, "Tenniel's 'Alice' Reigns Supreme" by E. T. Reed, the many new conceptions of Alice are paraded before the original, and at the appearance of parodies of Rackham's characterizations, Tenniel's cries, "Curiouser and curiouser!" (Fig. 3).

His fellow illustrator H. M. Brock wrote Rackham that he thought the caricature "a piece of exceedingly bad taste, to say nothing of the unfairness." [5] "Of course you were prepared for everyone to say that no one could ever approach Tenniel etc.," Brock tried to console his friend, "but it seems to me that if comparisons—always 'odorous'—must be drawn, they might be done decently. I should like too, to say how much I personally like your drawings. I would not have missed them in spite of all that Tenniel has had to say on the subject." To receive such high praise from another artist must have soothed the blows from such attacks as that from *Punch.*

Fig. 3

TENNIEL'S "ALICE" REIGNS SUPREME.

Alice. "WHO ARE ALL THESE FUNNY LITTLE PEOPLE?" *Hatter.* "YOUR MAJESTY, THEY ARE OUR IMITATORS." *Alice.* "CURIOUSER AND CURIOUSER!"

Rackham admittedly was not completely divorced from Tenniel's work. Every illustrator who has attempted to picture *Alice in Wonderland* has had in part derived some inspiration from the original depictions. So closely did Carroll work with Tenniel (at times to the point of bullying him) that his pictorial conceptions developed from conversations and correspondence with the author. Carroll in his text gives little to help the artist. His narrative is strikingly free of descriptive passages; unlike that of his many contemporaries, Carroll's style is surprisingly bare of adjectives. The most detailed description of a figure is that of "a large blue caterpillar, that was sitting on top with his arms folded, quietly smoking a hookah." For the more unusual characters (the Mad Hatter, the March Hare, the Mock Turtle) Carroll tells nothing of their physical appearance; the reader is completely dependent on the artist's renditions.

Carroll recognized the value of illustration in a child's book and consciously used them to supplement his prose. For example, in referring to the way the King of Hearts wears his crown upon his wig while in court, he suggests that the reader "look at the frontispiece if you want to see how he did it."[6] He advises at another point in the story, "If you don't know what a Gryphon is, look at the picture." This suggestion is obviously his answer to anyone who wishes to know what a Mad Hatter or a March Hare or a Mock Turtle might be.

The reader learns what each is, not through Carroll's text, but through Tenniel's drawings. Rackham's Hatter and Hare are actually Tenniel's conceptions transformed into characteristically Rackham grotesques; they remain basically the same as the originals, down to a notation on the Hatter's hat.

In addition to Tenniel's work, Rackham must have known Carroll's own sketches. Macmillan had published in 1886 a facsimile of the manuscript of *Alice's Adventures Under Ground* with all the original drawings, and it was likely still available to Rackham as late as 1907. Rackham chose to illustrate two incidents that Carroll had depicted but Tenniel had avoided. He transformed the whimsically long-necked Alice of the Carroll manuscript into his own elegant example of *art nouveau* with its curving, serpentine line (Figs. 4 and 5). This design contrasts with Alice of the big head. On eating the mushroom, the girl shrinks so quickly that her normal size head balances clumsily on her feet and hands; as in Carroll's original, Rackham portrays this incident with a curious play of distortion (Figs. 6 and 7). Rackham's point of reference is as much the art of Tenniel and Carroll as it is the actual story.

To picture Alice, Rackham had to look to other sources. Carroll typically never describes Alice; her personality is beautifully delineated, but there is never a specific reference to her actual physical appearance. As presented by the text, his heroine could as easily be Alice Liddell, for whom Carroll wrote the story, as be Mary Hilton Badcock, who reportedly was Tenniel's model. Rackham chose Doris Dormett to pose for his Alice. Rackham's work was clearly more founded in life than that of his two predecessors; Carroll's sketches were drawn from his own imagination, and Tenniel said he never drew from life. Rackham through precise detail secured many of

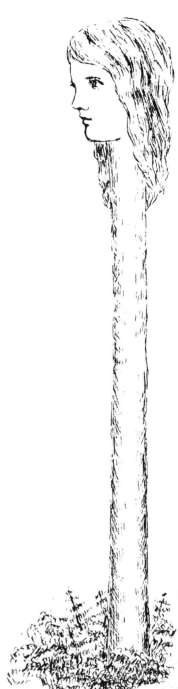

Fig. 4

Fig. 5

Fig. 6

Fig. 7

his most pleasing effects. For the Mad Tea-Party, his Alice posed in the artist's big wing-backed chair, and the table was set with Mrs. Rackham's best china. Rackham's own kitchen figured in another drawing, and his cook portrayed the Duchess. When his girl model asked if the woman would be throwing plates as in the book, Rackham assured her that that was unnecessary; he had already broken several to secure the right effect. This demand for the exact detail produced an authority and conviction of place and character in Rackham's work that is often lacking in Tenniel's and missing from Carroll's.

Rackham's style, however, cannot be called realistic. Despite the detailed material of his drawing, his illustrations are far more unearthly than those of either Tenniel or Carroll. The quality most apparent in the earlier drawings is the comic. Carroll, who was not an accomplished artist, may have admired and been somewhat influenced by the Pre-Raphaelites, but his technique is derived from popular humor prints. His style is more akin to Gilray and Cruikshank than to Rossetti and Arthur Hughes. Not surprisingly he chose Tenniel, the popular political cartoonist, to illustrate his story. Tenniel's humor relies on caricature and the incongruous; the distorted personages and anthropomorphic figures are distinctive because they are odd. His actual technique is conventional, direct without any mannerisms to distract from his statement. He displays no extravagance of style, and his comic effects are never achieved from purely pictorial means. He was in part limited by the rigid black-and-white woodcut. The original pencil drawings demonstrate a delicacy in his initial conceptions and a dreamlike quality lost in the actual printed illustrations.[7]

Rackham does not abandon the comic in his work, but this quality never overshadows his other intentions. His interpretations of the Mad Hatter, the Queen of Hearts, the Duchess, and the other characters are delineated with a radical use of distortion and exaggeration. In Tenniel's creations, one is always conscious of their physical reality. In Rackham's, one knows that they never existed except in the artist's imagination. The grotesque people of Rackham's watercolors beautifully contrast

[38]

with his depiction of Alice. She is delicately, naturalistically drawn; as in the frontispiece, she is a portrait of an actual little girl. The juxtaposition between her naturalism and the exaggeration of the other characters produces a strange, nightmarish effect. She seems to move in a different atmosphere than the other figures, and only when she undergoes the distortions of Wonderland food and drink does she actually become one of them.

Rackham's interpretation of Wonderland goes even further than that of both Carroll and Tenniel, to the landscape itself. As in characterization, Carroll does not greatly describe locale. Tenniel similarly is unconcerned with Wonderland scenery; he demonstrates no sympathy for landscape, and his few trees, bushes, and rocks are mere stage props. Rackham, in the tradition of Turner, was basically an atmospheric painter. Landscape and color often dominate his compositions. He reveals to the reader the complete character of Wonderland, not only its odd creatures but also its unique interiors and exteriors. His gnarled trees and other wild vegetation are characteristically Rackham, but they do not conflict with Carroll's intentions. His coloring further expresses his individual interpretation of Wonderland; the colorings of birds and fabrics are tonally dreamlike, and his skies cast a strange light over individual scenes. He embues the work with his own unique atmosphere.

Rackham apparently felt some restrictions in illustrating Carroll. His *Alice in Wonderland* is sparsely illustrated: thirteen color plates, three full-page black-and-white illustrations, and a handful of textual decorations. The book seems stark when compared with his two previous gift books, *Rip Van Winkle* and *Peter Pan in Kensington Gardens,* which are more like exquisite portfolios of his paintings than actual illustrated books. Rackham had the freedom in illustrating Irving and Barrie to take a single descriptive line or phrase and create an entire personal fantasy from it; thus these books are lavishly illustrated, with the color plates far outnumbering the leaves of text. Carroll was a far less conscious stylist. His unadorned prose, free of the literary conceits of an Irving or a Barrie, also displays little action. His story is a book of conversations. This conclusion is supported by Tenniel's drawings; nothing really happens in them. His figures pose stiffly; sitting or standing, Alice is shown listening to a character reciting a verse or discoursing on some point of logic.

Rackham is more adventurous in his approach. Where Tenniel is theatrical, Rackham is dramatic. For example, compare each artist's depiction of the arrival of the Queen of Hearts. With a melodramatic gesture, Tenniel's Queen confronts the stiff Alice, who is surrounded by a cold chorus of courtiers (Fig. 8). Rackham chose to show the discovery of the card gardeners by the Queen; the plate is filled with activity as the clumsy cards try to hide themselves and avoid being kicked by the Knave of Hearts (Fig. 9). Similarly, Rackham's court room is alive and tense while Tenniel's is as rigid as a wood carving (Figs. 10 and 11). In Rackham, the Knave is brutally thrust into the picture space, disrupting the court procedures; all the other figures are in agitated excitement as they await the response of the disturbed King and Queen.

Fig. 9

Fig. 8

Fig. 10

Fig. 11

What crucially differentiates the two artists is that each figure in the Rackham drawings is individually depicted, each with his own expression, while Tenniel's are not. Rackham's characters react. This distinction is nowhere more apparent than in the pictures of Alice herself. Tenniel's child is indeed a stiff puppet. In the drawing of Alice and the pig, for example, the figure stands expressionless as if to deliver a speech and holds the animal as if it were a prize ham (Fig. 12). Rackham's Alice must struggle to keep a grip on the squirming creature (Fig. 13). Rackham has instilled a rather conventional scene with his own drama.

The freedom Rackham takes with action is important in his composition. As each figure has a distinct personality, each has a specific activity. In "The Pool of Tears" the many beasts and birds struggle to keep above the calm, clear water; heads of marvelous creatures frantically jut in and out of the picture as they try to reach shore

Fig. 12

Fig. 13

(Fig. 14). In this one drawing, Rackham has encapsulated the action of an entire chapter.

The result of Rackham's labors is a remarkable interpretation of the Carroll classic. He lovingly embellished the volume with an understanding expressed by no other artist—no other artist except Tenniel. Rackham was certainly restricted in illustrating a story conceived in both word and picture as a unit. Carroll and Tenniel together kept in mind Alice's question, "What was the use of a book without pictures or conversations?"

Tenniel must remain the perfect artist of *Alice in Wonderland,* because he was the first. By being the author's choice, he received inspiration and encouragement not always evident in the actual text. No matter how fine Rackham's art is, it cannot replace the original illustrations.[8] Rackham's edition is a magnificent contribution to the illustration of children's books, but it must remain supplementary to the original.

Unfortunately, Rackham never attempted *Through the Looking-Glass.* In a gesture of bold confidence, Carroll's publisher, Macmillan, approached the artist in 1908 with

Fig. 14

an offer to illustrate the sequel for them. Rackham declined, preferring to work with his own publisher, Heinemann, who expected the copyright to expire in 1912. Parliament, however, passed a new law that extended the time of *Through the Looking-Glass*. On October 25, 1911, Rackham (with Heinemann's approval) wrote Sir Frederick Macmillan "to know whether you would consider any arrangement with him to allow him to publish an edition in the event of the copyright remaining in the hands of Messrs. Macmillan."[9] Despite the controversy his *Alice in Wonderland* had aroused, Rackham was clearly eager to begin work on the sequel. "I should add," he continues in the letter, "that I have not yet done any illustrations to the book, but that I should like to do it as the natural companion to the Wonderland that I have done, and that the friendly terms that I am with Heinemann make me wish to go on working with him." Macmillan evidently turned down the proposal. When the copyright did finally end (at least in the United States), Rackham was either too busy with other work or unable to convince a publisher to support his illustrating a new edition. His failure to interpret *Through the Looking-Glass* is regrettable; his new edition would have been a unique and delightful approach to Lewis Carroll.

NOTES

1. See *The Illustrators of Alice in Wonderland and Through the Looking-Glass,* edited by Graham Ovenden, introduction by John Davis (New York: St. Martin's Press, 1972).

2. Quoted by J. P. Collins in "The Intruding Purpose," *Pall Mall Magazine* (February 1906), p. 256.

3. From *Alice's Adventures in Wonderland* by Lewis Carroll, illustrated by Arthur Rackham (London: William Heinemann Ltd., 1907).

4. Quoted by Derek Hudson, *Arthur Rackham: His Life and Work* (New York: Charles Scribner's Sons, 1960), p. 72.

5. *Ibid.*

6. As Rackham's subject for his frontispiece was not the same as Tenniel's, this line was dropped from the Heinemann edition; this omission is the only liberty taken with the text.

7. A large selection of the original drawings are in the Berg Collection of the New York Public Library.

8. Rackham faced a similar conflict when he illustrated Kenneth Graham's *The Wind in the Willows* (1940). Although Rackham had been the author's initial choice to decorate the book, the earlier sketches by Ernest H. Shepherd are perhaps the best-known depictions of Toad, Water Rat, and Mole. Rackham, however, surpassed Shepherd in his fine watercolors, the final work of his career.

9. The letter is now in the Macmillan correspondence preserved in the manuscripts division of the British Library; it is quoted with their kind permission.

Lewis Carroll as Photographer:
A Series of Photographs
of Young Girls

BY EDWARD GUILIANO

IN THE PAST FEW YEARS THERE HAS BEEN A GREAT UPSURGE OF INTEREST IN PHOTO history in general and Victorian photography in particular. Dozens of books on Victorian photography have come on the market, and photograph exhibits have been held at many major museums and distinguished galleries around the world. With the appearance of each new book and each new exhibition, Lewis Carroll—for so many only connected with the famous *Alice* books—becomes more widely known as one of the most outstanding photographers in the nineteenth century. Deservedly so, for Carroll was one of the few early photographers who elevated picture-taking from a rather mechanical process to an art form.

The skill and beauty in Carroll's photographs has always been known to people deeply interested in Carroll's life and works. Almost every book about Carroll that has been published since his death in 1898 has contained an impressive series of photographs. However, it was not till the late 1940s that his place in the history of photography became fixed through a thorough investigation by a photo historian. At that time, the now eminent Helmut Gernsheim literally stumbled upon a scrapbook of Carroll's photographs while doing research on the photography of Julia Margaret Cameron. Not knowing anything about a photographer named Lewis Carroll, Gernsheim quickly recognized that the photographs were the product of "a genius at work," and began the first earnest study of Carroll's art. The result of Gernsheim's effort was a classic piece of photo history in which Carroll's genius is proclaimed: *Lewis Carroll: Photographer* (1949; rpt. New York: Dover, 1969).

Despite Gernsheim's work, it has taken until very recently for Carroll's photography to attract a wide following. That it is finally receiving the widespread attention it deserves is certain. In 1974 a magnificent album of Carroll's photographs of young girls was published in Italy, and in that same year the National Portrait Gallery in England mounted an exhibition (and published a catalogue) of Carroll's portraits entitled "Lewis Carroll at Christ Church." Previously, in 1972, the Arts Council at the Victoria and Albert Museum had presented a massive comprehensive exhibition, "Beginnings of Photography," featuring eighteen of Carroll's photographs. A still more telling exhibition took place in 1974 in New York City. Photographs by Carroll and by Julia Margaret Cameron, the other great Victorian amateur photographer with whom Carroll is often associated, were shown at a fashionable gallery. Many of the Carroll photographs on exhibition were not unique prints, and several had been previously published; nevertheless, the photographs sold for previously unheard-of prices ranging from $1500 to $5000 each.

II

Photography first became a popular pastime in England in the 1850s. Till then patent restrictions were rigid, and the daguerreotype process used was so involved that portraiture was almost impossible. Things changed rapidly after 1851 when the wet-plate or collodion process was developed and photography was introduced to the masses in what amounted to the first photographic exhibition, the Great Exhibition of 1851. Just five years later, in 1856, Lewis Carroll, then twenty-four years old, took up photography. For the next quarter of a century, the prime years of his life, he practiced his hobby with extraordinary devotion. In 1880 he abruptly gave up photography for reasons that are not known. His decision remains one of the mysteries in the life of this eccentric and complex man that will probably never be solved satisfactorily.

In Carroll's day photography was by no means the neat and efficient process that it has become. It was tedious, cumbersome, and messy—so messy that it was called the "black art" since the chemicals used in the collodion process left black stains on hands and clothes. Carroll's willingness to cope with all the inconveniences inherent in photography some hundred years ago attests to his passionate commitment to his hobby. His diaries are filled with records of hours upon hours spent photographing, while in the same breath he laments how time is slipping by and how his responsibilities as a mathematics lecturer keep him away from his many literary and mathematical projects.

He seemingly never questioned, at least for twenty-five years, his time in the darkroom, or time spent photographing sitters, or the hours involved in packing and unpacking whenever he took his camera along on trips. On the contrary, he went so far as to rent a studio, and eventually he had a glass house built on the roof of his rooms in Tom Quad, Oxford, so that he could have sufficient light to take photographs throughout the year. Moreover, he was more than willing to assume the arduous role of traveling photographer. When he planned a vacation, or found a particularly appealing setting for photographing, he packed up his equipment, wrapping each piece of equipment in protective paper, sent it ahead by train, employed cabs for short distances, and set up a temporary studio. The locations ranged from D. G. Rossetti's garden in Chelsea to Coniston, in the Lake District, where he photographed the Tennysons.

It is not so difficult to understand the attraction photography held for Carroll. Initially, the gadgetry of the camera and the photographic process may have attracted him. Lewis Carroll's love for gadgets is well known. His large rooms at Oxford were filled with all sorts of mechanical things. He owned a microscope, a telescope, eventually an early typewriter, and such unusual items as various musical boxes, "magic" pens, and a flying bat.

Carroll's attraction to photography obviously went much deeper than mere mechanical intrigue. Dr. Phyllis Greenacre in her psychoanalytic study of Carroll *(Swift and Carroll,* International Univ. Press, 1955) notes that one gets the clear impression that taking and developing pictures were a real triumph for Carroll. When photographing he largely limited himself to idealized subjects: little girls and famous people. "It would seem that the photographs were to capture and hold as incontrovertible fact the precious moments in time and space occupied by his ideal and adored subjects. . . ." (p. 146).

The clearest explanation for Carroll's attachment is that photography provided an accessible channel for him to express himself visually. Throughout his life he felt a need for the visually concrete. He was always interested in the visual arts, regularly visited artists and museums, and sketched throughout his life. Somewhat frustrated by his unrefined drawings, he was able to achieve fulfillment with his photographs. He attained such high-quality photographs because his approach was that of an artist abetted by a lifelong quest for beauty and perfection. He took his photographic work so seriously that he often earnestly signed his photographs "from the artist." For example, when he first approached Mrs. Tennyson in 1857, well before *Alice* was published and Carroll's fame made, he introduced himself as the artist who had done some photographs she had seen. Carroll's interest in the visual arts extended to the theater. Throughout his life he was a regular theatergoer, and in his younger days he wrote and produced some marionette plays. Costume photography also provided Carroll with an outlet for his theatrical impulses.

Carroll was an avid collector of photographs. When he died he left behind thirty-three photograph albums, the majority filled with collected prints. Twelve albums of his photographs, the result of the roughly three thousand negatives he produced in his lifetime, have survived. The bulk of these are portraits of either famous people or children, usually pretty young girls. His impressive list of portraits, the product of many uncharacteristically bold photographic quests, includes: John Ruskin, Tom Taylor, George MacDonald, many of the Pre-Raphaelites, Michael Faraday, the Crown Prince of Denmark, the Terry family, Tennyson, and, for that matter, himself. He also took some landscape photographs, buildings, paintings, sculpture, and even experimented on some skeletons.

It is his photographs of children and his handling of groups that sets Carroll apart from the rest of his contemporary photographers. In his study of Carroll, Helmut Gernsheim unhesitatingly acclaimed Carroll the most outstanding nineteenth-century photographer of children. Subsequent commentators, a group that has included such distinguished artists as Brassaï and Graham Ovenden, have repeatedly confirmed that belief.

Presented here is a series of photographs of young girls, all believed to be previously unpublished—except the fifth and sixth, which have been published in slightly different forms and have been included to make this series more representative of Carroll's photographic treatment of young girls. The photographs are from the Morris L. Parrish Collection of Victorian Novelists at Princeton University. Among the finest Carroll collections in the world, the Parrish Collection's holdings include four of the photographic albums of Carroll's work, totaling more than three hundred photographs. The prints presented are from Carroll's personal albums or from an album he prepared specially for Henry Holiday, the original illustrator of *The Hunting of the Snark.* The design and dimensions of the prints, as well as the accompanying signatures and other writing, are exactly as they appear in the albums.

The photographs will be left to speak for themselves; however, it may be profitable to briefly summarize the distinguishing characteristics of Carroll's compositions. His knack of capturing the unique beauty of each of his sitters is probably the most obvious quality of his photographs. That he had an eye for beauty is certain. One of the most haunting qualities of many of his photographs is a dreaminess and preoccupation with each sitter's private world. We are drawn to their eyes and foreheads and seek entry into their minds. Carroll's arrangements are comfortable and expressive, with everything playing a part in some decorative way right down to the trimming of the print. Figures are positioned naturally. Backgrounds are simple and economical with just a few accessories. Sitters and backgrounds are blended in natural harmonies. The subtle nastiness that is often found in Carroll's writings is completely absent from his photographs. Although it is not clearly evident in the photographs presented, Carroll's grouping of people distinguishes his work from the stiff, formal, often pompous portraits of his contemporaries. What *is* obvious here is the artistic adventurousness of many of his compositions.

Kathleen H Tidy

Kathleen Tidy, c. 1861

Lorina "Ina" Liddell, c. 1857

Alice Liddell, c. 1857

Alice Pleasance Liddell.

Alice Liddell, c. 1859

"Open your mouth, & shut your eyes" — Lorina, Alice, Edith.

Edith, Lorina, and Alice Liddell (1. to r.), *c. 1861*

ETHEL BROD⊖   *Lilian Brodie. June 21/61*

Ethel and Lilian Brodie, June 21, 1861

Amy Raikes, July 1875

Lisa Wood

Bessie Slatter "with Guinea pig"

Flora Rankin

Flora Rankin, "No lessons today"

M.A.A., "Maggie" Dodgson, c. 1857

Margaret "Maggie" Dodgson, "Reflection," c. 1857

"A maiden knight; to me is given
Such bliss, I know not fear."

Miss Laurie, "Waiting for the Trumpet," July 7, 1875

NOTES ON THE SITTERS

ETHEL AND LILIAN ("Lily") BRODIE are the daughters of Sir Benjamin Collins Brodie (1817–80), Wayflete Professor of Chemistry, Oxford. The photograph of the Brodie children, taken in 1861, prefigures the opening of *Alice's Adventures in*

Wonderland, which Carroll began writing in 1862 and published in 1865.

M.A.A., MARGARET ANNA ASHLEY ("Maggie") DODGSON is the younger sister of Lewis Carroll. Born in 1841, she was the ninth of the eleven children of Archdeacon Charles and Frances Jane Dodgson. (Charles Lutwidge was the third child and the first male.) Maggie died a spinster in 1915.

MISS LAURIE, about whom little is known, was probably first met by Lewis Carroll on a visit to the Henry Holidays at "Oak Tree House," Hampstead, in July 1875. On July 7 Carroll writes in his diary: "Photographing all day; did one of Miss Laurie in chain armour." The chain mail belonged to Henry Holiday. Several photographs of Miss Laurie and of her mother that were taken at this time are preserved in an album Carroll presented to Henry Holiday, which is now in the Parrish Collection, Princeton University Library.

EDITH, LORINA, AND ALICE LIDDELL hardly need an introduction. The Liddell sisters were the children who accompanied Carroll and his friend Duckworth on the outing up the Thames on July 4, 1862, from which *Alice's Adventures* grew. They are the second, third, and fourth children of the Reverend Henry George Liddell (1811–98), Dean of Christ Church and Vice Chancellor of Oxford. Alice Pleasance Liddell, later Mrs. Reginald Hargreaves, for whom the famous stories were written, was born on May 4, 1852. She died in 1934. Lorina, "Ina," later Mrs. W. B. Skene, was the eldest sister. Four years older than Alice, she died in 1930. Edith was about two years younger than Alice and died tragically in 1876.

AMY RAIKES, a distant cousin of Carroll, lived with her parents in Onslow Square, London, in the 1860s. Carroll probably met Amy and her two sisters, Alice (who became a lifelong friend) and Edith, in 1868 while at his Uncle Skeffington's home in Onslow Square.

FLORA RANKIN is not mentioned in Carroll's diaries and no letters from Carroll to her are known to have survived; thus little is known about Flora. A second photograph of her, obviously taken by Carroll the same day as the photograph reproduced here, is in the Parrish Collection.

BESSIE SLATTER is Elizabeth Ann Slatter, daughter of John Slatter (1818–99), successively Curate of Sandford-on-Thames, Vicar of Streatley, and Rector of Whitchurch. In 1876 he became Honorary Canon of Christ Church, Oxford. Carroll was well acquainted with the Slatters in the 1860s and photographed the entire family. Bessie survived her father as a spinster.

KATHLEEN H. TIDY was born in Athlone, Ireland, in 1851. At ten she was a member of her grandmother's household in Littlethorp (near Ripon), Yorkshire, where Lewis Carroll got to know her.

LISA WOOD is mentioned twice in the unpublished portions of Carroll's diaries. On January 14, 1858, Carroll accompanied his father on a visit to the Wood family at their home in Skelton (near Ripon), Yorkshire. At the time the family included two children, Lisa and Malcolm. Twenty-five years later, on July 26, 1883, Carroll mentions having received a letter from Lisa, then Mrs. Currie.

The Nonsense System
in Lewis Carroll's Work and in
Today's World

BY ELIZABETH SEWELL

FOR A LONG TIME NOW—PROBABLY EVER SINCE I ACCEPTED THE FACT THAT LEWIS Carroll was going to haunt me in one way or another for years to come—I have been trying to notice contexts in which writers or speakers quote from his Nonsense. Thus far, the results of my wholly unstatistical study suggest certain patterns. Such quotations are liable to appear in a setting that is educated, intellectual, professional; in English terms, upper middle class. Philosophers quote from him sometimes; so do academics; English bishops would be likely to, one feels, but that is guesswork; high-class advertising certainly does. There is no question, however, as to the fields in which such quotations are found most often and in most numbers. They are law and politics.

It is as if something in us recognizes that the *Alice*s and the *Snark* have some interpretative affinity with various areas of our lives, but most immediately with what goes on in our juridical and political systems.

"System"—a good word. There is the "digestive system" of the body, communications systems in the media world, systems engineering, the feudal system. The negative might be instructive too, for the word "unsystematic" conjures up images of randomness and perhaps disorder. I propose that Carroll's Nonsense is itself a system. First, we might pause a moment to look at the word. Perhaps a good working definition is as follows: a self-consistent set of orderly relations observed in or attributed to a particular field or class of terms. (Not exactly right—the relations may also construct that field or class, but it will do for now.) And one system, by congruence, resemblance, or contrast, may illuminate another.

When I first set out to study classic English literary Nonsense in 1949, it was Nonsense as a system that I wanted to explore, as a set of valid mental relations with close affinities to logic, mathematics, and the analytic processes of the mind. In the end I settled on the Game as the most helpful analogy to Nonsense. The cards and croquet in Wonderland, and more importantly the chess game in the Looking-Glass world, are pointers in that direction. What emerged was a vision of an autonomous enclosed field (think of a football field if the word sounds too abstract), governed by absolute rules, insulated in time and space. The units in the action, including the human units, are separate and discrete (one could add, lonely), "one and one and one and one and one" in the White Queen's words. All emotion is excluded except that appropriate to a closed world of controlled rivalry where relationships run the narrow range of argument and hostile incivility to downright heartlessness, the more telling because taken wholly for granted within the set pattern. Excluded also, needless to say, are all synthesizing tendencies such as those of imagination, dreams, sympathy, love, poetry—remember how effectively Carroll sterilizes metaphor in his parodies of poetry—and, further, excluded also are all great issues that make us human, experiences such as sorrow and beauty and God and so on. How essential these exclusions are to Nonsense can be seen in the horrid mishmash of *Sylvie and Bruno* where Carroll attempted a different kind of Nonsense [1] that could accommodate them, and failed. Given the separated units in the field, the action depends on manipulative skill, on detachment, on controlling and not being controlled.

This was how I thought about, and wrote about, Nonsense some twenty years ago.[2] There, I suppose, I might have left it, but something else happened, causing new and different possibilities to emerge: the system I had been thinking about became in its turn a system for thinking with. (The same thing happened to me in regard to poetry, it too becoming something to think with, the object of research proving to be, when explored, the method of further research.) So I began to think with my notion of a Nonsense system, using it to explore other poets, and poetic methodology.

Of more immediate concern here, however, is the impetus it gave me in another direction, toward those fields where the quotations with which we began signal enigmatically to us. My first venture here was a piece called "Dreams and Law-Courts."[3] I became fascinated by the frequency with which these two elements, dreams and law courts, occur together in literature, or rather not together so much as actually fused—law courts that are dream or nightmare, dreams that are places of formal judgment. The law proceedings that came to mind, enclosed in dreams as they were, included the Mouse's Tail, the trial of the Knave of Hearts, and the Barrister's dream in *The Hunting of the Snark*. I want to quote some pieces of what I said about them, starting with the Snark dream and then going on to the two in *Alice in Wonderland:*

The case as it proceeds becomes more and more vague, muddled and self-contradictory. What is interesting is the way in which the various functionaries of the Court abdicate one by one from their functions; the Judge declines to sum up, the Jury refuse to reach a verdict, the Judge cannot pronounce sentence, and little by little the Snark takes on one function after another, returns a verdict of "Guilty" (although acting supposedly for the defense), and pronounces sentence, "Transportation for life . . . and *then* to be fined forty pound." Only at the last is it discovered that the pig had in fact been dead for some years before the case began. . . . In the Mouse's Long Tale . . . here, too, Fury, who begins as prosecuting counsel and apparently in fun, absorbs as did the Snark the other functions in the Court, and the trial ends lamentably for the accused. . . . The trial of the Knave of Hearts at the end of Alice's story proceeds in a no less vague, muddled, topsy-turvy fashion. The jury, lizards, mice and birds as they are, are luckless and incompetent. Witnesses are threatened. The King, sitting as Judge, has no idea of procedure, and due process is subverted–"Sentence first, verdict afterwards. . . ." Where the other two trials of Carroll's emphasize the running together of roles and the condemnation of the prisoner, the main note of this one is a crescendo of hypnotizing incoherence, of which the equivalence of importance and unimportance is part, approaching closer and closer to nightmare. . . .[4]

Rereading these judicial narratives in the original, would we, I wonder, shrug them off as their author's habitual merry nonsense? Or would we recognize them, uncomfortably, for what they are, Nonsense indeed and by no means unfamiliar in our own recent experience and our knowledge of the last eighty years of our history?

In the essay I suggested we recall Dreyfus, the Reichstag trial, the treason trials in the Soviet Union in the late 1930s, the McCarthy hearings after World War II. Were I to bring that up-to-date now, I would add the trial of the Chicago "Conspirators," with its image of a defendant sitting in court gagged and pinioned to his chair and parties on opposing sides having a "pull devil pull baker" tug-of-war with the American flag, which had been draped as a cloth over the table where they sat. These are all of them trials of a peculiar nature, into which politics of a highly specialized kind obtruded. We have seen many and shall no doubt see more. What is startling, when one reads accounts of them, is the way in which reporters and participants (or historians if the events lie well behind us in time) recognize the resemblance to what went on in *Alice in Wonderland*. Quotations from Carroll turn up all over the place, along with the recognition that in such trials there is that element of dream or nightmare within which Carroll encloses all three of his imagined court proceedings.

Kafka is here too, you may be saying to yourself at this point. So indeed he is, a prophet also, and there are studies extant that deal with the relation between these two artists in regard to their visions of the law at work—frightening if we take them seriously. It is the earlier of the two prophets whom I am concerned with here, however, because *we* quote Lewis Carroll when confronted with such realities as those mentioned above, a Lewis Carroll as indigenous and Anglo-Saxon as our great institutions, parliamentary democracy, trial by jury, and so on. What he has to say to us goes beyond just the trials. We have to look at the whole Nonsense system that he elaborates with such logical and artistic consistency in his masterpieces, and to ask, from this small beginning of a resemblance, questions that may indeed come very close to home.

What Carroll indicates to us is that something imagined, be it vision or dream or nightmare, may "come true." I put that in quotation marks because again it is a phrase we may use readily without paying attention to its meaning. How and why imaginings may become actuality is a question we will hold for the moment. If these Nonsense trials are like real trials that happened a considerable time later, it seems possible that the whole Nonsense system, of which those trials are a small part, may have similar analogies with much else that we experience here and now. I believe this to be true.

Let me recapitulate some characteristics of Nonsense, as envisaged here and worked out in *The Field of Nonsense*. It appears as a system working on the principles of logic, analysis, dialectic—and resembling a game. The logic is compelling, as logic must be, even though it may mean arriving at logical conclusions from absurd premises pushed to their final term. (We should perhaps remember that not merely logicians and mathematicians are logical; small children are highly logical also.) The principle of analysis applies not merely to the thought-world of Nonsense but also to the objects and people in it. They become discrete isolated units, with which alone, incidentally, a game can be played, and they are preferably regarded as mere objects (Alice is a pawn in *Through the Looking-Glass)* or, to put it more bluntly, as inanimate or dead; the impossibility of playing a game with living and self-willed objects is demonstrated in the Queen of Hearts' croquet game. The system operates, as a game must do, within a strictly enclosed space and time. This enclosure is regulated by absolute rules (which have nothing to do with "rules of conduct," i.e., ethics), and these determine the relations between the units and the parties. All synthesizing tendencies in emotion, thought, and language are rigorously excluded from the system, including love, imagination, metaphor, and poetry. The only relations between the people or living units of the game are those of dialectic, namely rivalry and competition. The game is self-renewing—"Let's fight till six and then have dinner." The dialectical relations may appear as argument, discourtesy, even a covert and disturbing cruelty.

Already I want to ask the question that haunts this description: "Does this sound familiar to you?" A sharp-beaked head that emerges from the doorway you have just knocked at says, "No admittance till next Wednesday" and bangs it in your face. I want to say at once, "Aha! New York City . . ." and though that is not altogether fair, it is not far wrong, even though it could hold good of other cities as well.

Relations between words and their users, and between words and meaning, are also affected. Words, metaphors, and poetry are given a surprising amount of attention in these Nonsense narratives, attention directed toward shifting them from their synthetic, dream, metaphoric properties toward their containment as counters in the logical game under way. So Humpty Dumpty insists on the need to keep the mastery over words—and keeping control by manipulative skill of the objects or people you are playing with is one of the essential principles of winning a game (think how often a sports commentator will say of a basketball or football team, "They lost control of the ball"). Words also develop a curious literalness in this system, as if the implicit and human meaning becomes subordinated to the mere legalistic interpretation of a pattern taken at its face value: "Jam every *other* day." The last quality of the whole system I want to mention is its perfect self-consistency, totally insulated against the normal day-by-day experience of the universe as we think we know it.

Again, does any of this, much of it, all of it, sound familiar to you when you really look at it? The first and immediate analogy would seem to be, naturally, the vast empire of professional sport, but I do not want to stay with that one, much as it interests me. We have to move on toward those areas in which the Carroll quotations seem so recurrent. Games, game plans—is not that a phrase we have heard in other contexts than simply those of ball games? Surely that thinking, implying this same universe of discourse, turns up in political campaigns fair and foul, in the management of economic crises, in military maneuvers or war games that the great powers hold every summer. Vast enclosed systems where the system itself thrives, turning and turning inexorably on itself according to its own rules while everyone caught within it withers under a sense of fragmentation, "one and one and one and one," frustration, irritability, and profound conviction of the meaninglessness of it all, worlds of competition, of manipulative skills by which to control events and people.

We all know worlds, fields, areas like this. What I am saying is that all our great institutions, in this country and probably in the West in general, have taken on increasingly the precise characteristics of Nonsense systems. I think Carroll is truly a prophet, a diagnostic one. If his message is alarming and if I seem to you to be sullying an unworldly and rather innocent man with this kind of shadow, I can only say that prophets are to be recognized and honored, and that he may be among them.

A number of our institutions appear to resemble the bare bones of the Wonderland and Looking-Glass worlds. I have just mentioned in passing that of professional sport, and I shall similarly pass by the world of commerce and business, about which I do not know enough to write at firsthand, though one surmises that certain analogies here might be instructive. The field of juridical procedure we glanced at earlier, and since I have written about that before, I shall not dwell on it now. There remain three other pieces of the Establishment to which I want to draw our attention as these disturbing resemblances to Nonsense begin to make themselves felt. The first is religion, and since in every case that follows I am expressing my own profound uneasiness, not to say rage, at how things are, I had better cite the particular to which

I belong: the Roman Church, especially its whole operating system in regard to the attempted regulation, by fixed logical self-sufficient rules, of the area of marriage, sex, and reproduction. It is possible that this is actually a Nonsense system reaching its end, if one may judge from the massive rebellion, tacit or overt, by those within it, particularly, perhaps, women.[5] Nonsense in its own autarchic self-repetition eventually induces nightmare, and then the Alice figure breaks out—"You're nothing but a pack of cards!" or "I can't stand this any longer!"

I wish I saw us breaking out of the second Nonsense system which, I believe, figures even more largely in our Establishment today, but this has not yet happened. This second system—and again I speak of something I belong to—is education. I think particularly of university and college education, though I imagine that the Nonsense analogy applies overall. The insulation from real life and the needs and desires of those in it, the smooth logical self-justifying working of the machinery, the game playing, the competitiveness (academic politics are notoriously ruthless), the need-to-win mentality and the cheating that goes on, the steady production of teachers and Ph.Ds for whom there are now no jobs, the meaninglessness to most graduate students of what they have to do, the isolation of department from department, of specialist from specialist—it looks like Nonsense indeed, and perhaps at its best it is. At its worst it feels like nightmare, and so people "drop out."

There is a second stage to this process which we had better look at, too, for it leads into the third area I want to touch on. We educate people in a Nonsense system for (in theory) a minimum of about ten years, and something nearer twenty for those who have to run the whole course, and we do this because we need to habituate them to Nonsense worlds and practice, so that they accept status as pawns in others' games, accept alienation one from another, accept senselessness and recurring misery. I do not mean that there is a conspiracy to wreak this fate upon us all. It is simply that this is how we have come to envisage life, the universe, efficiency, and it is a self-reproducing and possibly self-intensifying state.

It leads into my third and last analogy with Nonsense—our present world of politics. Here I want to leap right away into an extreme position, then work my way back. I am going to describe something—a system, call it a political system—and ask once again if you recognize it. These are some of its traits: (1) it is ruled by an obsessive logic, starting from principles that may be inhuman or absurd but are to be rigidly followed; (2) those within the system are compelled to work with it not by external force so much as by the sheer compulsion of logic on the human mind, producing the kind of passivity produced also by dream or nightmare; (3) the system is totally insulated from all that we agree to regard as normal life; (4) it requires nonsensical tasks to be performed; (5) each individual within it is isolated from every other, by a policy of propaganda, control, and terror.

I wonder if one's first idea of this description would be prison? Possible, but it is wider than that. Whole countries have been run on such a system, although those of us in the Anglo-Saxon world think we know of it only by report and secondhand, so far. It is relevant and profitable, with regard to what I have been saying, to read Hannah Arendt's *The Origins of Totalitarianism* (especially Chapters 12 and 13) [6] with Lewis Carroll in mind. She discusses not merely the system of totalitarianism but also that of the Nazi concentration camp as the quintessence of the former. The progression through logic into something very close to Nonsense looked at in this way, and then into Hell, is clear and explicit. Hers is not solely a descriptive account but an enquiry into method, and it is here that the Nonsense analogy puts in once again so disconcerting an appearance.

We are liable, still, to think of these horrors as something distant from us, done by someone else, by "lesser breeds without the law" so to speak. I can remember an earlier and more secure period in my life when I would scoff at those who spoke of Fascist tendencies in the government of this country. I and those like me thought of such warnings as coming from fanatics or demagogues; but they, like myself, may now feel a lot less sure since Vietnam, Chile, Watergate. Yet if we have an educational system, as I believe we do, largely operating on Nonsense principles, would not its final effect be to produce material—the human material, I mean—for a Nonsense system in the state as a whole? Education is always both a reflection of current society and a forecast of the type of citizenry it deems most desirable. Perhaps, therefore, we may be training, within an apparently democratic structure, the pawns in a Nonsense game who will participate, willy-nilly, in the nightmare that any system founded upon logic, game, analysis, manipulation, isolation must lead to in the end.

And the alternative—if we still have an alternative, as all of us must sincerely hope? It may perhaps lie in another and different analogy for the great public institutions we have glanced at, which in their turn are only images outside ourselves of what we house and foster inside our own individual minds and spirits. I would suggest that the alternative to Nonsense, as a constructing principle on which to build private and public structures for living in, is poetry, with its method of metaphor, magic, dream, identification—all the things Nonsense has to rule out.

There are hints of this in the *Alice*s themselves, the notion of authority as a product of dream, of king and pawn dreaming one another mutually—that deep underlying question, "Who is dreaming whom?" that runs through the second *Alice* narrative, or the understanding reached between Alice and the Unicorn that only if each affirms the existence of the other can the pair of them maintain their fabulous/ real existence.

We do not need to be reminded, in this day and age, that we of the West have been walking ever since the time of Descartes further and further into a world constructed upon the outlook of mathematics, logic, analysis. Carroll's message is that this progression leads into a world of game-playing, Nonsense, and nightmare. His deep sense may prove to be very close to that of Blake, who sees in the logical, rational Urizen a power beautiful when balanced by other powers of the mind, lethal when developed in independence and isolation. Our institutions are the result and the exact image not merely of vague social forces at large in our history, but most essentially of the shape and nature of our thinking and our minds.

It seems likely that the new information we are acquiring about the two sides of the brain may fit here. Institutions and minds both need an element of dream, poetry, magic perhaps, as well as an element of logic. How this has been closed out—"Imagination, How Lost and How Restored" as Wordsworth says—is far too big a subject to tackle here. Such a revolution may seem dauntingly distant and vast; yet it need not, for there is good evidence to suggest that the place where such revolutions begin is in the mind, individual minds, yours and mine, and that they start small, as small as Alice with her tenacious sanity, her passage through two formal Nonsense universes, and her final determination to break their grip and wake up.

NOTES

1. According to Carroll's Preface to *Sylvie and Bruno,* the Nonsense (I use capital N throughout to denote the literary genre) element in the book, and its originality as well, consists in the work having been constructed from a large collection of his "odd ideas, and fragments of dialogue, that occurred . . . with a transitory suddenness . . . random flashes of thought . . . such, again, . . . which occurred in dreams . . . which only needed stringing together, upon the thread of a consecutive story." He adds later, "It is written . . . in the hope of supplying, for the children whom I love, some thoughts that may suit those hours of innocent merriment which are the very life of Childhood, and also, in the hope of suggesting, to them and to others, some thoughts that may prove, I would fain hope, not wholly out of harmony with the graver cadences of life."
2. *The Field of Nonsense* (London: Chatto & Windus, 1952).
3. Included in *The Logic of Personal Knowledge: Essays Presented to Michael Polanyi on his Seventieth Birthday* (London: Routledge & Kegan Paul, 1961).
4. *The Logic of Personal Knowledge,* pp. 180-181, 186.
5. From a simple reading of Carroll's three classic Nonsense works, for instance, it is evident how profoundly unfeminine the Nonsense world is. This aspect of Carroll's creation has received a good deal of attention from the psychological point of view, but it is also clearly important, perhaps much more so, from the viewpoint of methodology.
6. New edition with added prefaces (New York: Harcourt Brace Jovanovich, 1973).

High Art
and Low Amusements

BY ROGER B. HENKLE

LEWIS CARROLL WAS NOT A LITERARY FIGURE. HE DOES NOT APPEAR TO HAVE troubled himself to any significant degree over the direction of the arts during the Victorian period, nor to have entered into any dialogues with literary people. He knew a surprisingly large number of the literary eminences of his day—Tennyson and most of the Pre-Raphaelites, for example—but essentially only as social contacts and as potential photographic subjects. When we try to assess Carroll's *Alice* books as major literary events of the Victorian age, as many of us have done in the last few years, when we construe them as statements of mid-century *angst,* as oblique social commentary, as sophisticated game structures, or as quasi-mythic allusions to imagined alternative worlds, then we invariably run up against the problem of Carroll's own sense of where the books stood in the development of literary expression. Does he give us any impression of the seriousness with which he took his writing? Did he really look upon them as happy surprises, as entertainments for a private audience of child friends that inexplicably made him a minor literary lion? Did he have any conscious aesthetic at all?

These questions are all the more frustrating because Carroll's letters and diaries indicate that his most consistent and avid "literary" preoccupation throughout his life was with the most trivial cultural expression of his time: the popular theater. He loved to attend second-rate farces and burlesques. Almost every week he would take the train into London with Uncle Skeffington, or Uncle Hassard, or his cousin Frank Dodgson for an evening at the theater. The fare was a heavy consumption of creampuffs: *Hanky Panky the Enchanter, A Bottle of Smoke* and *Goodnight Signior Pantaloon* (both the same night), *The Statue Bride, The Doge of Duralto, Mazurka, or the Stick, the Pole and the Tartar, Fee Fo Fum,* and *A Sheep in Wolf's Clothing.* This was in keeping, of course, with Carroll's lifelong penchant for indulging his whimsies. But it reflected some little determination on his part; the Bishop of Oxford, Samuel Wilberforce, had declared that the "resolution to attend theatre or operas was an absolute disqualification for Holy Orders." Carroll got around Wilberforce's interdiction in a number of ways (largely by not committing himself to a religious vocation), yet all his life he felt constrained to justify his inveterate theatergoing.

The burlesques and farces were occasionally on double bills with more substantial drama. On June 22, 1855, for instance, Carroll saw the "capital farce" *Away with Melancholy* and then Shakespeare's *Henry VIII;* on a night in January 1856, *Hamlet* and *The Maid and the Magpie.* Such a jarring conjunction suggests that the great art of Shakespeare and the contemporary popular theater were so clearly in different leagues that one did not reflect upon the other. A division seemed to exist during the early decades of the Victorian period between "high" or "serious" art and popular or "light" art. Carroll's unusually strong sense of that division supplies, in his otherwise sparse commentary on art, the clearest insight into his apprehension of his own literary position.

Most of what Carroll had to say about literature can be found in his early diary entries, when, as a young man, he set himself to projects for self-improvement with what seems at times to be almost painful application. He plotted for himself "schemes," such as reading "whole poets" in order: Shakespeare, Milton, Byron, Coleridge, and Wordsworth, and for rereading all of Sir Walter Scott. He kept up with what was coming out in fiction and recorded his judgments. They reveal two insistent criteria: that art be morally circumspect and that it be true to human nature. Indeed, the two appear to be the same; once a writer undertakes to be "realistic" in his representation, then he must express the moral imperatives that are at the heart of human nature. Carroll complained of a novel called *The Bachelor of Albany,* written by Marion W. Savage, that he "found very little to like in it. In the first place, it is not written in a *healthy* tone; there is an ill-natured kind of satire running through all, and the writer seems unable to draw a really lovable character. The dramatis personae are imperfect puppets. . . ." (Diary entry of April 28, 1855.) Similarly, he recoils from *The Little Treasure,* which he attended at the Haymarket Theatre, for its attempt to elevate itself beyond the light and trivial without incorporating a sufficiently elevated vision of human nature: "A great objection to such plays is the insult they offer to human nature by simulating its noblest passions—those which redeem it from mere sensual brute life. It is a profanation of the things we would rather revere." (Diary entry of January 17, 1856.)

The moral didacticism for which mid-century Victorian fiction is infamous is directly associated with the English brand of "realism" that flourished at the same time. It is no wonder, then, that Carroll's contemporaries reacted so violently to the appearance, later in the century, of "realistic" novels as they were known among the French, in which the baser characteristics of ordinary men were graphically displayed. There is an ingenuous literal-mindedness to those earlier Victorian standards: when Carroll reads Charles Kingsley's realistic novel *Alton Locke,* a book impregnated with ethical sententiousness, he notes solemnly that "if the book were but a little more definite it might stir up many fellow-workers in the same good field of social improvement." The aesthetic explains his discomfort over Emily Brontë's *Wuthering Heights,* and helps us understand the nearly total eclipse of that mythic novel throughout the nineteenth century. "Finished that extraordinary book *Wuthering Heights;* it is of all novels I ever read the one I should least like to be a character in myself. All the 'dramatis personae' are so unusual and unpleasant. The only failure in the book is the writing of it in the person of a gentleman. Heathcliff and Catherine are original and most powerfully drawn idealities: one cannot believe that such human beings ever existed: they have far more of the fiend in them." (Diary entry of May 21, 1856.) For readers like Carroll, there is no case to be made for idealized characterization; to the extent that portraits differ from the morally neutral commonplaces of human nature, they become simply unnatural, in both senses of the word.

There was more to it than that as far as Carroll was concerned. "High" art itself ranges into areas that he found put a severe strain upon the moral intelligence. Such art creates an intensity of feeling and leads to demands upon individual spiritual judgment that the imagination does not seem capable of handling. Possibly Carroll just did not want to venture into dangerous regions of doubt; reading about them made him uncomfortable. He surely sensed that the fabric of belief had been so weakened generally that the art of the time dare not probe deeply and seriously into it, lest no imaginative synthesis prove adequate to shore up the faith. A performance of Goethe's *Faust* in Edinburgh illustrated, to Carroll's shock, the disorientation that ensues when art penetrates into dark affairs of the soul. "This was very beautiful.... Still, I think it is a play that should never have been put on the stage—it is too horrible and too daring in its representation of the spirit-world. The scene of Marguerite in prayer, writhing in despair as Mephistopheles gloats at her side, was as dreadful as anything I have seen on the stage. All the direct allusions to his demoniacal character were received by the gallery with applause: I don't think this ultra-realising of things to us (at present) abstractions, can tend to good; it must lean far more to infidelity." (Diary entry of September 16, 1857.) Safer, then, to abstain from probing such areas altogether, as did the mid-century theater, contenting itself with insignificant farcical entertainments and leaving any "serious" exploration to Shakespeare.

In a curious confession entered August 30, 1855, Carroll talked about the tension that he felt in the presence of great art:

There is a peculiar pleasure in listening to what I may call "unsatisfactory" music, which arises, I think, from the fact that we do not feel called on to enjoy it to the utmost; we may take things as they come.

In listening to first-rate music there is a sense of anxiety and labour; labour to enjoy it to the utmost, anxiety not to waste our opportunity; there is, I verily believe, a sensation of pain in the *realisation* of our highest pleasures, knowing that now they must soon be over; we had rather prolong anticipation by postponing them. In truth we are not intended to rest content in any pleasure of earth, however intense. . . .

That is a telling observation, coming from Lewis Carroll, for we recall how sensitive he was about the burdens of "serious" responsibilities. He was particularly vexed by the requirements of his adult duties and proprieties, fanatically organizing himself and his work, maintaining a prickly, prudish way when delicate matters were at stake. This would seem to supply more evidence, as if tone were not enough, that Carroll conceived of his *Alice* books as works safely within the category of light, nonserious art. He was writing a special kind of fiction in a well-defined tradition, one that we read things into only at our own risk. If substantial issues of religious belief and human morality appear to materialize out of the fantasy adventures, they must be kept in the perspective that the manner and form of the books supply; nothing is "meant" literally. Lewis Carroll would not transmit the pleasures of *his* imagination in any work fraught with anxiety and labor.

We assume that we know better now, of course, than to be put off by the apparent playful inconsequentiality of the *Alice* books. Whatever Carroll may have *thought* he was writing, the *Alice* books tap complex and deep-lying human concerns. I am convinced, and have argued elsewhere, that the two works are oblique but potentially subversive expressions of what Carroll disliked about the tenor of Victorian life. Other critics have discovered in the *Alice*s highly sophisticated game structures, psychological sublimations, and elaborations that are mythic in nature. The *Alice* books are surely "serious" in the Victorian sense, books that deal with troublesome human problems under the disguise of light literature.

They constitute, in fact, rather intriguing instances of the way in which light writing of the Victorian period was beginning to absorb the content and the attitudes that had earlier been the characteristics of high art. During the 1840s and 1850s, popular literature expanded its audience as never before. This was the consequence of several factors: the enlargement of the middle class; the growth of literacy; the expansion of leisure time; the development of means of mass production and mass distribution of magazines, newspapers, and inexpensive books; and the acquisition of a wider sense of shared cultural identity. The audience for such literature was largely middle class, including a great many people who had just ascended into the middle class and who clung to its homelier ethical values as indicia of station.

At first, Victorian popular literature simply entertained. It was humorous and playful, or extravagantly romantic and improbable. As it came to be the favorite, familiar reading material of the great mass of the literate public, however, it necessarily catered more directly to that public's inclinations and prejudices; it served as a comfortable reinforcement of the assumptions of an entire way of life—the way of life we characterize as middle class or bourgeois. The content of popular literature gradually became less exotic, shifting from vicarious adventure to domestic humor to the foibles of the ordinary man. And in the process, that literature felt itself bound to become a more aggressive supporter of the mores of its audience; it expressed not only the interests of the middle class but its values also. At the same time, the more culturally sensitive writers of the later decades of the Victorian period, the avatars of civilized, sophisticated, and militantly antibourgeois values, the George Merediths and Oscar Wildes, began to write in the humorous, evasive manner that was once the province of light, occasional art. In reaction against the sententious moralizing of Victorian serious art, and in the need to find an acceptably oblique means of delivering their own subversive or discreetly amoral points of view, the literati of the 1880s and 1890s adopted comic, deceptively nonmimetic modes. The division that Carroll apparently assumed to exist in the 1850s between serious, realistic literature and light, fanciful literature no longer held.

Carroll, in fact, did his part to break down the division, for the *Alice* books furnish one of the first instances of the manner of light, popular amusement being used to mask an intelligent man's critique of the texture of ordinary life. By the time Carroll wrote his second series of children's books, *Sylvie and Bruno* (1889) and *Sylvie and Bruno Concluded* (1893), he had made the crucial adjustments, which only financial success and complacency can sometimes enable one to make, to bourgeois culture and its cherished ideals. Consequently, as the *Alice* books show evidences of the tension of real distress and dissatisfaction caught within the mold of carefree works of humor, the *Sylvie and Bruno* books reflect the increasing burden that light literature had to bear as the expression of a relatively conservative middle-class lifestyle. The latter break loose only occasionally into the madcap irreverence of the *Alice* books, and they assume none of the earlier aplomb. For long, bleak stretches, the *Sylvie and Bruno* books are tediously "realistic" in their portrayal of facets of domestic life, and they are often tiresomely preachy.

The prefaces to the *Sylvie and Bruno* books constitute Carroll's last major written comments on art, and demonstrate an awkward combination of his earlier whimsy and his new determination to give serious treatment to estimable human concerns. In the preface to *Sylvie and Bruno,* Carroll uneasily jokes about the difficulties of stringing together his narrative material and invites the reader to find the "padding" in the text. The book proves, he says, that one can combine a few hours of thoughtless merriment with some reflections on the "graver cadences of life." At great length he descants on the mortality of man, digressing gratuitously to tell us that he thinks even Bowdler's Shakespeare is too morally offensive, and then concludes by urging us not to go to entertainments, especially the theater, in which the subject matter might be detrimental to our moral character. In an amazing argument Carroll states that "one of the best possible tests as to our going to any scene of amusement being right or wrong" is whether we would care to pass our last moments at it—whether, in other words, we would like to be caught dead there. *Sylvie and Bruno Concluded* is equally painful, meandering at times like the conversation of a man in his intellectual dotage, its preface concluding to the echoes of the Lord's Prayer.

Nothing is more offensive in Victorian culture than the inclination of some of its prominent literary figures to trivialize human spirituality by putting it in sentimental and banal terms. The justification for a notion of a solemn, decorous "high" art at the beginning of the Victorian period lay in a dread of just such a thing. It is one of the sad facets of Lewis Carroll's career that he succumbed to that invidious tendency to blend the uncritical indulgence of light humor with the moral earnestness of the mid-Victorian novel-with-a-mission. It is quite possibly a consequence of his failure to devote more critical attention to the literary issues of his time.

Assessing Lewis Carroll

BY JEAN GATTÉGNO
Translated by Mireille Bedestroffer and Edward Guiliano

It is not necessary to reestablish Lewis Carroll. Today he is neither unknown nor underrated. Yet perhaps we should try to determine his true place, which may not necessarily be the one we had thought. For those who see him only as "the author of *Alice*," the forerunner of the new and unusual, modern marvelous, it is advisable to stress, as many articles in this book have done, that he was a logician and, even in his day, a linguist, and to see his work as casting a new look at language. For those who are inclined to consider him primarily as a scientific innovator, it is wise to recall that *Alice* was considered revolutionary from the moment it was published, and that its intended audience, i.e., children, had every reason to see it as a new kind of literature written especially for them. In pointing out these two aspects of Carroll's work, the linguistic side and the child-oriented side, I do not claim to synthesize two possible interpretations of these books. Rather, I intend to underline the richness of his works, which are not reducible to just one approach.

Still, all is not said by noting these two important aspects. The technique used in the adventures in *Alice, Sylvie and Bruno,* and *The Hunting of the Snark* is not just concerned with language and childhood; the place of dream and reality also deserves careful consideration and is not limited to either one of these two aspects. Finally, we might have to think about the enigma that the Carroll/Dodgson relationship poses and which neither attempts at psychoanalysis (such as Phyllis Greenacre's) nor "historical" research (such as A. L. Taylor's) have completely succeeded in resolving.

The common point among the diverse views and readings of Carroll's work must emerge from within and appear throughout the work itself and not in some center external to it. Language is not its subject, but it is a key for deciphering it.

II

When *Alice* appeared it caused astonishment and seemed to be what it still is today, if only read without preconceived ideas: a revolution in children's literature. We must not overlook the fact that the story was told and then written down for children, and was meant to appeal to them first and foremost. In what sense is it revolutionary? First, because it was the first time that a little girl was not simply the heroine but the focal point of a story. Everything that occurs happens to Alice, and everything is understood through her. Her gaze imparts life to the entire unusual world that inhabits Wonderland and Looking-Glass land and which, at all other times, is utterly still in an eternal slumber. It animates the White Knight of the Queen of Hearts for an instant—a dream instant—and enables them to make real what was only virtual in them. Alice is half-god in her adventures. Without her, the cats Dinah, Kitty, and Snowdrop would only be cats; thanks to her, they change into characters that express Alice's secret wishes and are at the same time, in themselves, new realities. The Cheshire Cat and Humpty Dumpty are both characters and individuals—characters because they become flesh from Carroll's creative words (voicing a type of language that had in part antedated Carroll), and that it is in their speech that they are firmly delineated. They are individuals in the sense that, even a hundred years after their creation, they still seem like real creatures and can be set side by side with other real beings and people, historical or ordinary.

Alice enters this world and sets it in motion, as a collector does with his music box or mechanical toy. Berkeleyan solipsism? Perhaps in part. But it is also the magic power of children's speech, which brings to life whatever it speaks of. This is the all-powerful, eternal life-giving force of which, among mankind, the child is simply the freest interpreter and the truest. Thanks to Alice—and Carroll—the subject's unconscious desires, the childhood freedom lost then found again, the long-repressed animistic beliefs, all reemerge. And the little seven-year-old girl who strolls through these two unusual worlds carries within herself all the violence of her untrammeled outlook. In this violence the grown-ups are the clearly marked targets in an animal form that is merely the reverse side of the animal state to which they attempt to reduce the child—as is demonstrated by the scene between Alice and the Unicorn. The dialogue constantly points out the reality of this violence, which was strongly underlined in Jean Christophe Averty's admirable reading given on television [over French television, 1970—Ed.]. In spite of everything that happens to Alice, the aggravations and mishaps, she is never a victim. And although she has to wait until both her adventures are over to prove her triumph to everyone, and primarily to herself, she never lets down for a moment.

The victory of the child over the adult is attested to in all of Carroll's work; the psychological richness revealed in *Alice in Wonderland* and *Through the Looking-Glass* is sufficient proof of this victory.[1] Carroll painted his heroine from within, not that he "was" Alice, but he allowed the child within him to speak, the child that he had been and wished to be–in short, the uncensored part of him that had not been destroyed in the process of growing into an adult. Furthermore, today when we are assured that children do not enjoy reading *Alice,* we believe it since grown-ups tell us so, just as we believe the learned people who, in the seventeenth century, affirmed that fairy tales were nonsense. Indeed, nothing demonstrates the subversive nature of Carroll's work better than the insistence on the part of "serious" critics to regard it primarily as the expression of a neurotic. In this way, in order to strengthen their biographical point of view, they can rid themselves of the problem of Carroll's language, the uninhibited speech of the child that renders adult speech ineffectual.

III

All this by itself would have been enough, both in Carroll's time and in our own, to guarantee Carroll lasting value; liberated speech appeared in the nineteenth century, and he was one of its initiators. But there is more here than just uncensored children's speech. There is also a new vision of language and speech that causes the logic of wishes to triumph over the logic of words. Alice continuously runs up against a mode of speech that those with whom she is speaking consider to be "coherent," that is, logical, and which always turns into a "non-logic," another kind of logic, that Alice cheerfully names "non-sense." Little Bruno in *Sylvie and Bruno* is in this respect the reverse of Alice, a specialist in non-sense, whereas his sister Sylvie and the Professor are unable to do anything about it. The inversion of characters is not significant; only the discourse is of importance, not Alice or Bruno as speakers. The degree to which the adventures of Carroll's characters, obviously starting with Alice, are inscribed in speech and are closely dependent upon it should be recalled. One has only to consider the role played by nursery rhymes, of which certain Carrollian episodes represent the "turning into action"; the use Carroll makes of certain vernacular expressions (mad as a hatter or a March hare) whereby the unreal subject is brought to life. Alice herself asserted it even before her dream: "What is the use of a book without pictures or conversations?"

What is attested to in this language that the reader constantly comes up against in Carroll's work? First of all, the absolute arbitrariness of human language through the split in the "human" relationship signifier/signified; the signifier is a form that no man has ever consciously decided on at a particular moment. In spite of what is too often believed, Humpty Dumpty's role is not to emphasize to Alice and the reader the all-powerfulness of the speaker through his authoritative formula, "the question is [to know] which is to be master–that's all." His role is to reveal to Alice the arbitrariness of the relationship in question. The professorial assurance he shows when "explicating" "Jabberwocky" scarcely conceals the essential subjectivism of his interpretation. As Carroll himself emphasizes in the preface to the *Snark*, a portmanteau word is a personal subjective compound peculiar to the person speaking; and had Judge Shallow (in Shakespeare's *Henry IV*) chosen to say "Rilchiam" for "Richard + William," no doubt someone else could just as correctly have chosen to say "Wilchard." It is Bruno who truly expresses Carroll's viewpoint. After someone objects to his saying "a mile or *three*" since it isn't usual, Bruno replies that "it would be usual–if we said it often enough." Better still, in his *Symbolic Logic* [2] Carroll is firm on this point: "I maintain that any writer of a book is fully authorized in attaching any meaning he likes to any word or phrase he intends to use."

This is also the shattering of the opposition between "sense" and "non-sense." Gilles Deleuze has shed remarkable light on this outstanding feature of the adventures of Alice, who "undergoes and fails in all the adventures of common sense," and who "always goes in both directions at once." [3] The opposition one constantly finds in Carroll's work is not between non-sense and "sense," which would be its opposite, but between two kinds of sense, paradoxically linked, and of which it can only be said that one is the reverse of the other. To Alice's constant question, "In what sense?" Deleuze answers, "The question has no answer, because a characteristic of sense is not to have any direction, and not to make 'good sense,' but always to have both at once." The March Hare and the Mad Hatter embody this; they live in apparently opposite directions that in fact indicate the same point, the common territory of both characters. The frequent paradoxes in Carroll's work are the reverse not of sense but, at the very most, of what is erroneously called "common sense."

This is why logic is so important in Carroll's work. It is not certain, as I myself have been inclined to assert, that his theoretical works are the formalization of the richness contained in his fictional works. It is valuable to recall, in the first place, that Carroll started his research in logic seven years before he related *Alice* as a story. In fact, in 1855 he noted in his diary: "Wrote part of a treatise on Logic, for the benefit of Margaret and Annie Wilcox." His research had ample opportunity to find material for exploration and discovery in the adventures of a little girl outside the universe of "common sense." How would it be possible not to discern, from the constant presence of intuitions relating to methods of reasoning which one finds in all the work from *Alice* to *Sylvie and Bruno* (from 1865 to 1893), the persistence of a thought process about which we may certainly say that the unconscious speaks more freely through it than in a treatise on logic, but not that its expression needs a particular emotional environment in order to emerge? It is true, as Ernest Coumet points out in his article in this book, that it is the paradoxes and even Carroll's conception of symbolic logic that anticipate certain discoveries of modern logic. But the whole Carrollian mode of expression attests to the existence and strength of another kind of logic, no longer that of "sensible" expression but that of the unconscious, and therefore of desires. Carroll was one of the first to allow these to emerge and to assert themselves.

It is perhaps in this respect that the surrealists, in considering Carroll as one of their distinguished forerunners, had true insight. Carroll's writing deals with dreams in a way that has nothing in common with the dream literature of which Coleridge and De Quincey are the most famous examples in England. It is true that Alice's adventures are two "dreams," whose dream nature is described, affirmed, and authenticated at considerable length by the author at the end of *Alice* and at the beginning and end of *The Looking-Glass.* It is also true that the structure of various episodes, as well as the nightmare atmosphere of several scenes, become intellectually satisfying once one knows that it was a dream. However, this is not what is essential, but rather the digressions that Carroll permitted himself reveal more than an intention to reproduce a state of almost complete freedom. For example, when Alice dreams about characters who are dreaming about her, this is not another paradox but the expression of a consciousness trying unceasingly (and in vain) to look on itself objectively, at the same time that it feels and knows it is caught in its own subjectivity; not a triumph of solipsism but, on the contrary, an effort to escape from it. Or when in *Sylvie and Bruno* the character that is the Narrator sees two forms of the same character: Sylvie, who belongs to what he calls the dream-world, and Muriel, who belongs to his real world; and when he feels tossed between the two universes, the characters of the one progressively invading the other, we are not simply witnessing a game the schizophrenic allows himself to play. Rather, we see in this process (even if both interpretations are compatible) an effort to express the infinite richness contained in each word, each meaning, each reality. Sylvie is Muriel, although each one is exclusively herself. In the same way, little Bruno points out to his father that the two jewels he had offered to Sylvie to choose between were only one and continues: "Then you choosed it from *itself.* . . . Father, *could* Sylvie choose a thing from itself?" She certainly could in a world where the identity principle would not be the norm of norms, where A could be A and *also* non-A. And, for the moment, only the world of wishing, and of absolute contradiction, permits it.

IV

At least one other problem still has to be raised: who is speaking in *Alice* or in the *Snark?* In *Sylvie and Bruno* it is an "I" who tells the story, at times as an all-knowing novelist and at other times as an actor and character within the "story" that is told to us. Should we think it is the same person as the one who tells, and lives, Alice's adventures, but asserts himself more freely? And what should we think of the person who states in the *Symbolic Logic:* "If I find an author saying, at the beginning of his book, 'Let it be understood that by the word *"black"* I shall always mean *"white,"* and that by the word *"white"* I shall always mean *"black,"'* I meekly accept his ruling, however injudicious I may think it"?

The question is not purely rhetorical. Especially in the last example, the "I" cannot be simply the "author's," but necessarily encompasses a number of persons who share the attitude defined by the sentence in question. This attitude, we have seen, is also found in *Alice.* The spoken words therefore refer back to a person who might well be the same. However, this evidence has not yet been proved. Too often a distinction is made between Dodgson the mathematician, whose logic has become the sole interest of academicians, and Carroll the author of *Alice* and the *Snark,* concerned about preserving anonymity in his "private" life and growing angry at any intrusion by one world on the other, to the point, during the last year of his life, of refusing to accept any mail sent to "Lewis Carroll" at Oxford. We have seen that this necessary overlapping of two worlds is the very same problem the Narrator in *Sylvie and Bruno* has. Therefore no one will question that an element of schizophrenia is always present. But it does not divide two entities, "the man" from "the writer," or even the "serious writer" from "the writer of nonsense." On the contrary, it is their point of encounter because it is the point at which the Carrollian mode of expression (Dodgson's or Carroll's) surges forth. Indeed, in his treatise on Euclidian geometry *(Euclid and his Modern Rivals),* signed "C. L. Dodgson," Carroll does not say much and is generally satisfied with paraphrasing Euclid, at the most with humor. However, here and there are characteristic Carrollian sentences, typical attitudes of "Lewis Carroll," such as this warning in the "prologue" (preface):

> I have not thought it necessary to maintain throughout the gravity of style which scientific writers usually affect ... I never could quite see the reasonableness of this immemorial law: subjects there are, no doubt, which are in their essence too serious to admit of any lightness of treatment—but I cannot recognize Geometry as one of them.

The sharp distinction between style and content leads us unerringly to a constant of which there are frequent examples in *Alice.* All the same, Carroll spoke out elsewhere; as soon as censorship could be at least partially lifted, thanks either to the anonymity of the numerous pamphlets Carroll produced in Oxford over a few years,[4] or to his pseudonym, it was the Carrollian *essence* that truly began to speak out. This [unconscious] essence could be either a subjective carry-over from childhood or, more profoundly, that which it expresses in a quasi-phylogenetical manner. It is neither accident nor neuroticism that in these circumstances there would be no human being corresponding to "Lewis Carroll" and that C. L. Dodgson still maintained this even shortly before his death. It is, rather, the expression of the intangibility of the speaker, who is not a person but the speaking subject. The language in Carroll's writings is that of the Subject and not of a subject, whose mode of expression is outspoken and which Deleuze, in discussing humor, calls the "fourth person singular," a subject associated with "esoteric language, which in each instance represents the overthrow, deep down, of ideal language. . . ." It is to this language that we should listen.

NOTES

"Pour Lewis Carroll" appeared in *Lewis Carroll,* ed. Henri Parisot (Paris: Éditions de l'Herne, 1971), pp. 35–40. It is translated with the permission of the author and the publisher.

1. See my *Lewis Carroll* (Paris: Corti, 1970), second part.
2. 1896 (rpt. New York: Dover, 1958), p. 166.
3. In *Logique du sens* (Paris: Editions de Minuit, 1969), throughout but especially pp. 92–114, 273–278.
4. See "The Vision of the three T's . . ." and "The New Belfry of Christ Church, Oxford."

Carroll's
"The Ligniad":
An Early Mock Epic in Facsimile

With an Introduction
BY ROGER LANCELYN GREEN

WE KNOW ALL TOO LITTLE OF LEWIS CARROLL'S, THAT IS CHARLES LUTWIDGE Dodgson's, years as an undergraduate at Christ Church, Oxford–from January 1851 until he took his B.A. degree in December 1854. Unfortunately the first volume of his diary, which covered all or most of this period, is one of the four lost sometime between 1898, when Stuart Dodgson Collingwood (his nephew) used the complete set in writing the *Life and Letters of Lewis Carroll,* and their rediscovery in Wilfred Dodgson's cellar sometime before the celebrations and exhibitions in 1932 in honor of the hundredth anniversary of Dodgson's birth.

In his undergraduate days those dining in Hall at Christ Church were divided into "Messes" of half a dozen or so, apparently with a postgraduate student in charge of each–Dodgson was "caterer" of the Bachelors' table in 1855, as described in the earliest extant volume of his diary.

One member of Dodgson's "Mess" in their undergraduate days was the Reverend C. J. Cowley-Brown, who published his recollections in *The Scottish Guardian* on January 28, 1898, immediately after Dodgson's death:

> Members of "The House," whose memories can carry them back to the
> period, will call to mind the batches of half a dozen undergraduates who

dined together at different tables in the hall, and the disgraceful way the dinner at that time was served. The hour was then five. Though the spoons and forks were silver—some of them very old, the gift of former members of The House—the plates and dishes were pewter. The joint was pushed from one to another, each man hacking off his own portion, and rising from the table without waiting for one another, without even waiting for the ancient Latin grace. . . .

In Dodgson's "mess" were young Philip Pusey, whose crippled frame enshrined a pure soul and a cultivated intellect; the late Rev. G. Woodhouse; the present rector of St. John's, Edinburgh [the author of the article] and others equally unknown to fame. . . .

"Of all the friends I made at Christ Church," wrote Dodgson on August 2, 1898, to Mrs. Woodhouse, "your husband was the very *first* who spoke to me—across the dinner-table in Hall. That is forty-six years ago, but I remember, as if it were only yesterday, the kindly smile with which he spoke."

George Girdlestone Woodhouse (1831–98), in whose honor "The Ligniad" was written, was the eldest son of George Windus Woodhouse, Vicar of Albrighton, Shropshire. Apparently Dodgson got to know the family well enough to visit them sometime before January 7, 1856, when he mentions in his diary after describing Kingsley's *Alton Locke* (1850), which he had just read, that the song contained in it, " 'Mary, call the cattle home'—a wild and beautiful bit of poetry . . . I remember hearing it sung at Albrighton: I wonder if any there could have entered into the spirit of Alton Locke—I think not. . . ."

Young Woodhouse followed his father to Christ Church in October 1850, took his Bachelor of Arts degree in 1854, was later ordained, and became Perpetual Curate of Upper Gornal, Staffordshire, 1861–67; and later became Vicar of Yealhampton in Devonshire.

What suggested that Dodgson should write a mock epic in honor of Woodhouse, we shall probably never know. But "The Ligniad" was written and signed by Dodgson, dated May 23, 1853, and the poem in his writing is here published for the first time. In comparison to the rust-colored (faded black) ink of the text, Dodgson's monogram and the date appear in a fresher black ink. Perhaps they were added in 1897 when Dodgson gave the poem to Mrs. Woodhouse after her husband's death. According to Falconer Madan, "it has twice occurred in sales, and twelve lines are printed in the sale catalogues (1922 and 1927)." In the latter sale it was purchased by Owen D. Young, was exhibited in the Columbia University Centenary Exhibition in 1932 (No. 392 in the catalogue), and is now in the Berg Collection in the New York Public Library.

The poem is called "The Ligniad," from the Latin *lignum* meaning wood, and is in general a parody of the epic style. Dodgson, of course, wrote many parodies, from the earliest examples in his family magazines through his writings as Lewis Carroll till the end of his life. Mock epics of this sort were not uncommon in the eighteenth and early nineteenth centuries—for example, *The Dunciad* (1728) by Alexander Pope.

The first lines of "The Ligniad" echo the opening of *Paradise Lost:*

> Of Man's first disobedience and the fruit
> Of that forbidden tree . . .
> Sing, Heavenly Muse . . .

But after the opening there is little direct parody, though occasionally there is an echo of Milton, as in the lines about the "tricksy fairies," which seem to be based on Book I, lines 780–788, of *Paradise Lost.* Other odd lines echo other poets, as for instance the fifth line from the end, which is based on Coleridge's *Christabel,* "A sight to dream of, not to tell."

The only sustained parody seems to be in the four lines that are described as "adapting . . . a fragment from our Poet Laureate," which are very close to the penultimate stanza of Tennyson's "Edward Gray" (1842):

> Love may come, and love may go,
>   And fly, like a bird, from tree to tree;
> But I will love no more, no more,
>   Till Ellen Adair come back to me.

It is also possible that the lines beginning "Glory of the ancient time" parody some Pindaric Ode that I have been unable to identify. The general manner is of Wordsworth, especially in his "Ode on the Intimations of Immortality"—but there were many other odes in this type of meter, such as Coleridge's "Dejection" and various well-known examples by Keats.

We may presume that Woodhouse was good at Greek, and would have known the actual Odes of Pindar on which the English Odes are based. He was certainly studying the Greek dramatists: the Greek quotation ὤμοι, πέπληγμαι—"Ah me, I am smitten!"—is from Aeschylus, *Agamemnon,* line 1343. The reference to the lost plays of Euripides (seventy-three in number) must have some topical relevance. There is also a reference to "Ainsworth's *Dictionary,*" which was the Latin-English dictionary by Robert Ainsworth (1660–1743), revised by B. W. Beatson and W. Ellis in 1829, and still in use until superseded later in the century by "Lewis and Short."

The most puzzling reference is to "Scapula": It is mentioned as a companion to Ainsworth's *Dictionary,* and must be a book, since there is also the reference to "a fly-leaf of Scapula." It may have been some Greek lexicon preceding Liddell and Scott. "Scapula" means a shoulder bone, which does not seem to have any connection with Dodgson's reference. I have been unable to find any book with that name, although I have long "sought it with thimbles and sought it with care, and pursued it with forks and hope!"

THE LIGNIAD, IN TWO BOOKS.

BOOK I.

Of man in stature small yet deeds sublime,
Who, even from his tender toothless years,
Boldly essayed to swallow and digest
Whole tomes of massive learning, ostrich-like,
Sing, classic Muse! and speed my daring quill,
Whiles that in language all too poor and weak
For such high themes, I tremblingly recount
To listening world's an hero's history.
    Nursed in a cradle framed of Doric reeds,
In a fly-leaf of Scapula enwrapped,
Fed on black-broth ~~and~~ (oh classic priviledge!)
Seasoned with Attic salt, the infant throve.
Small taste had he for toys of infancy;
The coral and the bells he put aside;
But in his cradle would soliloquise,
And hold high commune with his inner man
In Greek Iambics, aptly modified—
A smile sardonic wore he in his joy;
And in his sorrow shed no mawkish tear;
'ὤμοι, πέπληγμαι was his only cry,
And with much "smiting of the breast," he wrestled,
And would have rent his hair, but that he had none.

Note: Lewis Carroll's draft measures 8⅞″ x 11″; it is reduced slightly
here to 8¼″ x 10″.

The Ligniad, in two Books.
Book I.

Of man in stature small yet deeds sublime,
Who, even from his tender-toothless years,
Boldly essayed to swallow and digest
Whole tomes of massive learning, ostrich-like,
Sing, classic Muse! and speed my daring quill,
Whiles that in language all too poor and weak
For such high themes, I tremblingly recount
To listening world's an hero's history.

Nursed in a cradle framed of Doric reeds,
In a fly-leaf of Scapula enwrapped,
Fed on black-broth and (oh classic priviledge!)
Seasoned with Attic salt, the infant throve.
Small taste had he for toys of infancy;
The coral and the bells he put aside;
But in his cradle would soliloquise,
And hold high commune with his inner man
In Greek Iambics, aptly modified—
A smile sardonic wore he in his joy;
And in his sorrow shed no mawkish tear;
ᾤ μοι πεπλήγμαι was his only cry,
And with much "smiting of the breast," he wrestled,
And would have rent his hair, but that he had none.

A merry boy the infant hath become;
He leaps and dances in the light of life,
With his shrill laughter rings the ancient house,
The stairs reecho to his tread, as light
As when beneath the solemn oaks at eve
The tricksy fairies in their revelry
Wheel in wild dance, nor mark the dewy grass.
Yet even now upon that chiselled brow,
Lately so bright and fair, a Shadow dwells;
It is the Ghost of Latin yet unlearnt,
And dark forebodings of the Greek-to-come!
What can his grief be? he has all he loves,
A Scapula, an "Ainsworth's Dictionary",
And "all the Greek, and all the Latin authors—"
Then wherefore, moody boy, that crystal tear?
"It is the thought," methinks <u>I</u> hear him moan,
Clasping with quivering hands his aching brow,
"That certain Plays Euripides hath written
"Are lost, are lost, and I shall never see them!"
  "Homer may come, and Homer may go,
    "And be shifted, like lumber, from shelf to shelf,
  "But I will read no Greek, no Greek,
    "Until the Lost Dramas I've found for myself!"
Thus, all unconscious, rhymed his agony,
Adapting to the anguish of the hour
A fragment from our Poet Laureate.

2

A merry boy the infant hath become;
He leaps and dances in the light of life,
With his shrill laughter rings the ancient house,
The stairs re-echo to his tread, as light
As when beneath the solemn oaks at eve
The tricksy fairies in their revelry
Wheel in wild dance, nor mark the dewy grass.
Yet even now upon that chiselled brow,
Lately so bright and fair, a Shadow dwells;
It is the Ghost of Latin yet unlearnt;
And dark forebodings of the Greek to come!
What can his grief be? he has all he loves,
A Scapula, an "Ainsworth's Dictionary",
"And "all the Greek, and all the Latin authors" —
Then wherefore, moody boy, that crystal tear?
"It is the thought," methinks I hear him moan,
Clasping with quivering hands his aching brow,
"That certain Plays Euripides hath written
"Are lost, are lost, and I shall never see them!"
          "Homer may come, and Homer may go,
          "And be shifted, like lumber, from shelf to shelf,
          "But I will read no Greek, no Greek,
          "Until the Lost Dramas I've found for myself!"
Thus, all unconscious, rhymed his agony,
Adapting to the anguish of the hour
A fragment from our Poet Laureate.

THE LIGNIAD, IN TWO BOOKS.

BOOK II.

Sing ye, who list, the deeds of ancient might,
In tournament, or deadlier battle-fray:
Sing ye the havoc and the din of war,
A nobler and a gentler theme be mine!
Through twice nine years eventless passed his life,
Save that each day some large addition brought
To that vast mass of learning stored within.
But now bright Fancy thrilled his raptured mind,
And poised her wings for flight, yet ere she rose,
With ponderous Sense he loaded her to Earth;
And the full flood of Poesy within
He primly tortured into wooden verse:
  "Glory of the ancient time,
   Classic fount of other days!
  How shall I, in modern rhyme
   Fitly sing thy praise?
   It chanced, the other day,
A tattered beggar asked an alms of me:
"Bestow a trifle, sir, in charity!"
   I turned and said
 ~~I have~~ "Good man,
  I have but sixpence in my purse
   Yet rather than
   In hunger you should pine,

3

The Ligniad, in two Books.
Book II.

Sing ye, who list, the deeds of ancient might,
In tournament, or deadlier battle-fray:
Sing ye the havoc and the din of war,
A nobler and a featler theme be mine!
Through twice nine years eventless passed his life,
Save that each day some large addition brought
To that vast mass of learning stored within.
But now bright Fancy thrilled his raptured mind,
And poised her wings for flight; yet ere she rose,
With ponderous Sense he loaded her to Earth;
And the full flood of Poesy within
He grimly tortured into wooden verse:

"Glory of the ancient time,
Classic fount of other days!
How shall I, in modern rhyme
Fitly sing thy praise?
It chanced, the other day,
A tattered beggar asked an alms of me:
"Bestow a trifle, sir, in charity!"
I turned and said
I have "Good man,
I have but sixpence in my purse
Yet rather than
In hunger you should pine,

"And so your misery grow worse,
          It shall be thine,
If you'll be only good enough to say
          That, in
          Latin."
Was this encouragement to classic lore?
          Say rather, more!
So may my course for ever smoothly run,
          And onward swell
In that smooth channel where it hath begun:
     Still climbing, climbing up the classic heights
          Where Fame doth dwell
               And still
               I will
     From month to month, from week to week,
Devote my drowsy days and wakeful nights
          To Greek"
Such were the fancies of his lighter mood—
His lighter mood, which very seldom came:
But now my Muse, approaching higher themes,
Shrinks from the task in trembling, for the field,
Green & smooth-shaven, spreads before her sight;
The wickets pitched, the players ranged around;
And he, the hero, in his glory there;
A sight to dream of, not to write about!
Then fare thee well, greatest of little men,
In Greek, in Latin, in the cricket-field:
Great as a bowler, greater as a bat,
But as a "short slip" greater yet than that!
                    FINIS   CLD. May 23. 1853.

4.

"And so your misery grow worse,
  It shall be thine,
If you'll be only good enough to say
    That, in
      Latin."

Was this encouragement to classic lore?
    Say rather, more!
So may my course for ever smoothly run,
    And onward swell
In that smooth channel where it hath begun:
    Still climbing, climbing up the classic heights
      Where Fame doth dwell
        And still
          I will
    From month to month, from week to week,
    Devote my drowsy days and wakeful nights
      To Greek"

Such were the fancies of his lighter mood —
His lighter mood, which very seldom came:
But now my Muse, approaching higher themes,
Shrinks from the task in trembling, for the field,
Green & smooth-shaven, spreads before her sight;
The wickets pitched, the players ranged around;
And he, the hero, in his glory there;
A sight to dream of, not to write about!
Then fare thee well, greatest of little men,
In Greek, in Latin, in the cricket-field:
Great as a bowler, greater as a bat,
But as a "short slip" greater yet than that!

FINIS

CD. May 23. 1853.

Hark the Snark

BY MORTON N. COHEN

A HUNDRED YEARS (OR SO) AGO, THE VERSE OF THE SNARK WAS, FOR THE FIRST TIME, heard in the land. A hundred years is a long time for readers to ponder a piece of nonsense poetry, and one might think that by now we would have covered the *Snark* landscape and come to terms with it. But Lewis Carroll and his work have never been easy to pin down. Both have, to some extent, eluded literary historians and critics alike, even though Carroll's life is fairly well documented and critical comments abound. A century has clearly not been long enough for us to discover all there is to know about this man and this poem.

Actually we do know a great deal about *The Hunting of the Snark*. We know, for instance, that on July 18, 1874, Dodgson took a solitary walk across the Surrey Downs, and that on that walk a single line of nonsense—"For the Snark *was* a Boojum, you see"—flashed through his mind like a lightning bolt. We know, too, that there then followed a long period of gestation, over twenty months in fact, before the poem saw the light of day. Martin Gardner has assembled these and other facts in that handsome book *The Annotated Snark,* recently reprinted by Penguin and soon to be published in a new and revised hardbound edition by Kaufman. And it is more a comment upon Lewis Carroll, perhaps, than the biographers and critics that, after a hundred years, something remains to be said.

To begin with, there are still some biographical data hovering about Lewis Carroll that ought to be brought to ground, events occurring during the summer of 1874 that can perhaps help us infer something more about the inception of the *Snark*. These events can be seen as setting the stage for that flash of imagination. And there are also some reactions the poem received in the press that have not entered the historical or critical literature on Lewis Carroll. Let us look first at the biographical setting from which the poem emerged.

We have seen and heard a good deal about the *Snark*'s meaning, much of it amusing and some of it tedious, but very little helpful for understanding Dodgson. Search as one may, one finds few comments upon that inspirational walk across the Surrey countryside. Why did it happen at all, and why did it take place when it did? Ready answers have not come along, nor, to be sure, is there a conclusive one. We haven't begun to understand the workings of the imagination, and Dodgson's particular kind of genius will always elude easy formulae. But one can seek understanding through biographical facts, and an examination of what we know of Dodgson's days in the summer of 1874 may tell us something important.

We know that Dodgson invented *Alice in Wonderland* to amuse the Liddell girls on a golden summer afternoon (also on a day in July, incidentally, a dozen years before he invented the Snark). The value of that audience is immediately apparent to anyone who has taught, lectured, or performed in any way before an audience. One is required to perform and one does: the imagination takes wing and soars higher in response to such demands than at other times. But Dodgson was walking by himself. There were no external demands, no deadlines, none of the conventional requirements, not even a plan to write a new long poem. What, then, moved him? Was it perhaps an internal necessity, an emotional demand?

The spring of 1874 was a busy time for Dodgson, so busy that he neglected to write in his diary for three whole months, from March 28 onward, an exceptional lapse for this man who valued record-keeping so highly. Then, on June 22, having escaped Oxford and gone to Sandown on the Isle of Wight for a seaside holiday, he sat in his room at the King's Head Hotel and, conscience-struck, tried to record the important events of the last three months. That lost quarter of a year had been filled with his usual activities—appointments with his speech correctionist, lunches and dinner parties in London, theater performances, correspondence, Christ Church chores and involvements—plus a few special needs, such as efforts to supply Lord Salisbury with the name of a possible mathematical tutor for his elder daughter, Maud; efforts to find an illustrator for *Phantasmagoria;* and plans for reprinting some of his mathematical writings.

Dodgson spent the last twelve days of June at Sandown, enjoying reunions with old friends, traveling around the island, sketching some of his young friends on the beach. But on the last day of the month, he left and joined the Dodgson family circle at The Chestnuts in Guildford. He records no particular reason for going then; he went presumably because it was his habit to pay a visit home from time to time. On this visit, though, a large number of the family were on hand, and Lewis Carroll and his brother Edwin had to take beds at a Mrs. Carter's at the Old Rectory. As was his fashion, Carroll enumerated in his diary all the family members he found present at Guildford. Among them he noted "C. Wilcox, who is ill (inflammation of the lungs)."

Recorded at first only in passing, Wilcox's illness soon enough became a compelling force. We do not know very much about Charles Hassard Wilcox, born in 1852, the seventh son of the Whitburn Wilcoxes, the Dodgsons' cousins. We do know that through the years the Dodgsons and the Wilcoxes remained on excellent terms and frequently visited one another. Lewis Carroll's diary contains many accounts of such visits, and indeed he must have had many memories of happy days spent in Whitburn on the Wilcox hearth. But Charles Wilcox was more than just a cousin—he was Lewis Carroll's godson: for that reason, if for no other, Carroll would take a special interest in him.

We might well ask, why would a man in his early twenties, suffering from inflammation of the lungs (a euphemism for tuberculosis or consumption), be sent away from his own home to stay with cousins? The answer could be that Guildford, over 250 miles south of Whitburn, enjoys a milder climate and therefore, with the ensuing autumn and winter in mind, was thought in 1874 to offer more hope of a complete recovery. Guildford's proximity to London and London doctors may have been another consideration.

Although Carroll returned to Oxford on July 2, only two days after going to Guildford, he did not stay away long. He must have asked his Guildford relations to keep him informed about young Wilcox and his medical progress. Carroll, titular head of the family, would feel a deep responsibility for all that ensued at The Chestnuts, even apart from his personal concern for his godson's welfare.

The reports that came to Oxford from Guildford could not have been happy ones, and on July 14, less than a fortnight after he had returned to Oxford, Carroll recorded concisely in his diary: "Wrote to Fanny, offering to come over to take a share in nursing Charlie Wilcox." Three days later, on the 17th, he left Oxford to return to Guildford. Charlie Wilcox's condition, which had deteriorated during the previous fifteen days, undoubtedly shocked Carroll. Once on the scene, he immediately assumed the task of nursing the invalid through the long nights that followed. He took up his first vigil on the night that he arrived, the 17th. It could not have been a pleasant experience, and the patient's condition must have weighed heavy on his heart and been etched deeply in his mind.

On the very next day, after only three hours of sleep, Lewis Carroll went for the memorable walk on the Surrey Downs. Concerned with the tragedy being acted out at The Chestnuts, perhaps because of it, his walk could have served as an escape, at least a temporary one, into a brighter and healthier world, a world of natural beauty. Certainly it enabled him to put some distance between himself and the painful reality at The Chestnuts. A man of sensitive, artistic temperament, he needed time to assimilate the facts, to master them. How natural, then, for deep personal defenses to come to his rescue. His feet carried him through the rolling countryside, and his mind responded as well, by producing the flash of inspiration, seemingly from nowhere, to carry him off to fairyland, to limbo, to a world of nonsense: "For the Snark *was* a Boojum, you see." And as he entered the world of the imagination and dwelled upon the meaningless line, he enjoyed a brief respite from the bleak reality that lay behind and before him at The Chestnuts.

When he returned he resumed the nightly vigils. During all these long, sad hours, Dodgson undoubtedly pondered that light, nonsensical line that had whipped him away from his surroundings in mid-July, and he started to build the structure that became one of his longest poetic efforts. Surely it is not entirely accidental that *The Hunting of the Snark* moves away from the world as we know it into a mythical, unreal world, that it destroys the natural succession of things, renounces logic, and violates all reasonable expectations. Just as Dodgson's first inspiration is the last line of the poem, so he builds the work of art, as it were, backwards. And with parallel illogic, the ship that takes the band of eccentric creatures on their Snark hunt also makes its journey backwards. Time, place, purpose are irrelevant; meaning there is none; all that matters is relief, which Carroll achieves through suspense and laughter.

Out of the nightmare of Charlie's illness, perhaps, Dodgson built a fun-giving work of art; perhaps it was his way of demonstrating a superior logic, the logic of artistic survival.

The Charlie Wilcox story ends sadly: He died of his ailment on November 10. Later that year, on December 20, writing to one of his favorite young friends, Edith Jebb, Dodgson explains why he had been such a poor correspondent that summer and autumn: "I have been again and again intending to write to you," he tells her. ". . . I wanted to say how much I should have enjoyed coming to visit you in the summer, if I could have managed it conveniently, but all my plans for visiting and photographing were knocked on the head by the illness of a cousin (and godson) of mine, who was laid up ill at Guildford, and I went home to help . . . to nurse him, and stayed there 6 weeks, and afterwards went down with them to the Isle of Wight, where he died, after 5 months' illness." No outright evidence exists that Lewis Carroll himself made any connection between the *Snark* and the tragic case of Charles Wilcox, but surely one there is.

I I

The Hunting of the Snark appeared in March 1876 and was in due course reviewed. But one cannot today go to any single source to read the reviews, and surely that lacuna should not survive the *Snark*'s centenary. A number of studies do say that the poem got "mixed" reviews; it clearly was not at first as popular as *Alice*. *The Annotated Snark* pins down two notices for us and gives brief summaries of both: a negative comment by Andrew Lang in the *Academy* (he objects to the medium of verse over prose and suggests that if the book "is rather disappointing, it is partly the fault of the too attractive title") and the anonymous one in the *Athenaeum* (it has nothing good to say about the work, calling it "the most bewildering of modern poems").

Recent examination of some twenty contemporary papers has turned up four more reviews of the *Snark*. The *Spectator* called it "a failure"; the *Saturday Review* approved of it hedgingly; the *Graphic* printed a rave notice as a feature set quite apart from its regular book reviews, asserting that "everybody *will*" read the book and "will scream with laughter"; and *Vanity Fair* disapproved, stating that Carroll had gone from good *(Alice)* to bad *(Looking-Glass),* and from bad to worse *(Snark).* The Snark hunt that produced these reviews also turned up an ingenious "explanation" in verse of the true meaning of the poem, written by one "Frumious" and printed in the *Wykehamist,* the Winchester School paper. Appended here are the *Snark* reviews and the "Frumious" verse explanation. The reviews were indeed mixed, but as for a delicious salad or delicate soufflé, it is good to know the ingredients precisely.

THE ACADEMY, 9 (APRIL 8, 1876), 326–27

The Hunting of the Snark.   By Lewis Carroll.
(London: Macmillan & Co., 1876.)

Someone has said that it is very difficult to write in a Rabelaisian tone about Rabelais, and the remark is true about the criticism of nonsense in general. It is impossible to analyse in cold blood the impressions which ought to be given and received in high spirits, and high spirits are even more necessary in the person who is to appreciate than in him who makes the joke. The clown is successful, in spite of the fact that he has just had an execution, a fire, a death, and so on, in his house, as we have very often been told. He is sure to get a laugh from the part of his audience that is in the vein, but he only makes the melancholy soul more morbid. But though it is hard to write boisterously about the pantomime, and in a Rabelaisian tone about Rabelais, it is only too easy to write snarkishly about *The Hunting of the Snark.* One of the features of this mysterious creature was, to put it mildly, its uffishness—

> "Its slowness in taking a jest—
>   Should you happen to venture on one,
> It will sigh like a thing that is deeply distressed;
>   And it always looks grave at a pun."

To tell the truth, a painful truth it is, this quality of the snark has communicated itself to the reviewer.

In the first place, he is disappointed to discover that the *Hunting* is written in verse. Why did not Mr. Carroll stick to what Walt Whitman calls the free heaven of prose? The details of the chase would have made an episode in some nonsense epic very admirably, but as a mere fragment of poetry the *Hunting* is not so satisfactory. The effect of Alice was got—I only put this forward tentatively, as part of a "Theory of Nonsense considered as a Fine Art," which will be elaborated when the new University Commission establishes a chair in that branch of aesthetics—much of the effect of Alice was got by the contrast of her childish niceness and naturalness with the absurd and evanescent character of the creatures in Wonderland. Now there is no sense in the territory of the Snark at all, except that mature and solemn experience of life which the reader brings with him. He is introduced to a bellman, a butcher who can only kill beavers, a beaver which makes lace, a banker, a barrister, a baker who can only make bridecake, a bonnet-maker, and so on, all just landed in the isle where the Jubjub bird sings to the Jabberwock. He sees them in themselves, he does not see them with the eyes of the child who, as in *Alice,* takes them as natural persons in a world not understood.

This is the sad position of the elderly reader, and, looking at the nonsense as nonsense for children, one does not think they will see much fun in the Barrister's dream about "Ancient Manorial Rights," "Alibis," "Insolvency," "Treason," and "Desertion," or in the Banker's presenting the "frumious Bandersnatch" with a crossed cheque for seven pounds ten. But to return to our Snarks.

The Bellman, who was captain of the host, had once occasion to remark:—

> " 'That, although common Snarks do no manner of
>   harm,
>   Yet, I feel it my duty to say,
> Some are Boojums——' the Bellman broke off in
>   alarm,
>   For the Baker had fainted away."

The Baker was revived, by suitable remedies, and explained the cause of his emotion:—

> " 'A dear uncle of mine (after whom I was named)
>   Remarked, when I bade him farewell——'
> 'Oh, skip your dear uncle,' the Bellman exclaimed,
>   As he angrily tinkled his bell.
>
> 'He remarked to me then,' said that mildest of
>   men,
>   'If your Snark be a Snark, that is right:
> Fetch it home by all means—you may serve it with
>   greens,
>   And it's handy for striking a light.

.   .   .   .

> But oh, beamish nephew, beware of the day,
>   If your Snark be a Boojum! For then
> You will softly and suddenly vanish away,
>   And never be met with again.' "

This fearful revelation, as the Bellman justly said, should not have been kept back till the Snark was at the door, and it was in vain that the Baker pleaded that he had already mentioned the fact in Hebrew and Dutch, in German and Greek. When people start together on a voyage in unknown seas, they cannot be too explicit in stating the conditions of the adventure. The awful fate of the Baker should be laid to heart by everyone who goes out to look for Snarks, Happiness, an Eastern Policy, and other such mysterious matters in general request. Omitting the touching episode of the reconciliation of the Beaver and the Butcher, a reconciliation effected by the tender influences of instruction kindly imparted, and gratefully received; omitting the doom of the Banker in the clutches of the Bandersnatch, I hurry to the terrible conclusion. The Baker had gone off on a quest of his own, when:–

> " 'It's a Snark!' was the sound that first came to their ears,
>   And seemed almost too good to be true.
> Then followed a torrent of laughter and cheers:
>   Then the ominous words, 'It's a Boo–'
> Then, silence. Some fancied they heard in the air
>   A weary and wandering sigh
> That sounded like 'jum!' but the others declare
>   It was only a breeze that went by.
> They hunted till darkness came on, but they found
>   Not a button, or feather, or mark
> By which they could tell that they stood on the ground
>   Where the Baker had met with the Snark.
> In the midst of the word he was trying to say,
>   In the midst of his laughter and glee,
> He had softly and suddenly vanished away
>   For the Snark *was* a Boojum, you see."

What became of those who

> "down the trees
> Followed the dark effigies
> Of the lost"

Baker, Mr. Carroll has declined to tell. Since Sophokles wrote the closing scene of the Oidipous Koloneus–for in writing nonsense surely we may put in the k's–since the lurid fancy of Mr. Robert Buchanan uttered the wild "Songs of Corruption"–a very nice poem–nothing more weird than this conception of the Baker's doom has purified humanity through pity and fear. Shadows we are, and Snarks we pursue, is the moral; only, unluckily, we don't vanish away when the Snarks turn out to be Booja.

The pictures in the *Hunting of the Snark* deserve a few words. Mr. Holiday's Inventions (inventions seems to be the right word at present in art-criticism) are not all remarkable for Vision. The Bellman in the frontispiece is an excellent ancient mariner, but there is no sort of fun in putting a bell into his left hand and a mannikin into his right. Incongruous the picture is, but grotesque is just what it is not. On the other hand, the drawing of the Beaver sitting at her bobbins is very satisfactory, the natural shyness of the Beaver in the presence of the Butcher being admirably rendered. In a sketch of the whole crew there is a really graceful half-draped female figure with an anchor and a trident, who may or may not be the Bonnet-maker, but who would deeply shock the Banker at her side. If the book is rather disappointing, it is partly the fault of the too attractive title. "We had a vision of our own," and it has proved somewhat of a Boojum.

A. LANG.

THE **ATHENAEUM**, 67 (APRIL 8, 1876), 495

The Hunting of the Snark: an Agony in Eight Fits. By Lewis Carroll. With
    Nine Illustrations by Henry Holiday. (Macmillan & Co.)
It may be that the author of 'Alice's Adventures in Wonderland' is still suffering from the attack of Claimant on the brain, which some time ago numbed or distracted so many intellects. Or it may be that he has merely been inspired by a wild desire to reduce to idiotcy as many readers, and more especially reviewers, as possible. At all events, he has published what we may consider the most bewildering of modern poems, not even excepting that which is said to have induced a convalescent to despair of his wits, and a coroner's jury to modify a verdict. A most singular ship's company goes forth to hunt a Snark:—

> To seek it with thimbles, to seek it with care;
>   To pursue it with forks and hope;
> To threaten its life with a railway-share;
>   To charm it with smiles and soap.

Two of the oddly assorted crew hear a Jubjub sing, and are strangely affected thereby; another is attacked by a Bandersnatch, and the fright turns him into a minstrel of the Negroloid species; the most ill-starred among them "softly and suddenly" vanishes away, having fallen a victim to the absorbing powers of a Boojum—which appears to be a monster somewhat akin to the terrific Caledonian Bore, which has played so great a part in the drama of human sorrow. What a Snark is seems to be one of those problems which no fellow—not even a mathematical Student of Christ Church—can solve. On its nature the author throws little light. By way of making amends, however, he explains in his Preface that "the 'i' in 'slithy' is long," and "the first 'o' in 'borogoves' is pronounced like the 'o' in 'borrow.'" He also contributes an interesting philological *excursus* on the vexed adjective "frumious."

Mr. Holiday's drawings are excellent. We may take the dream-picture, for instance, in which a legal Snark is

> Defending a pig
> On the charge of deserting its sty,

and mark how admirably the effects are produced. We may admire, too, the utter absurdity of the illustrations at pp. 30 and 75, replete with humour akin to that which makes Mr. Samborne's fun (though quite different in expression) so cheery. And we may guess, from the grace of the principal female figure at p. 40, how well Mr. Holiday could copy an artistic model if he chose; from the life-like look of the beaver at p. 11, how thoroughly he can enter into the lower phases of animal existence. Particularly good, we may observe, is his drawing of hands and feet, parts of the human frame too often maltreated in art.

That the author, when not driven wild by the modern improvements on ancient Oxonian architecture, or by the eloquence of irrepressibly bellowing barristers, can write seriously, intelligibly, and sympathetically, is proved by the dedicatory verses, "inscribed to a dear child, in memory of golden summer hours and whispers of a summer sea":—

> Girt with a boyish garb for boyish task,
>   Eager she wields her spade: yet loves as well
> Rest on a friendly knee, intent to ask
>   The tale he loves to tell.
>
> Rude spirits of the seething outer strife,
>   Unmeet to read her pure and simple spright,
> Deem, if you list, such hours a waste of life,
>   Empty of all delight.
>
> Chat on, sweet maid, and rescue from annoy
>   Hearts that by wiser talk are unbeguiled:
> Ah, happy he who owns that tenderest joy,
>   The heart-love of a child!
>
> Away, foul thoughts, and vex my soul no more!
>   Work claims my wakeful nights, my busy days;
> Albeit bright memories of that sunlight shore
>   Yet haunt my dreaming gaze!

THE SPECTATOR, 40 (APRIL 22, 1876), 527–28

"THE HUNTING OF THE SNARK."

We regret that "The Hunting of the Snark" is a failure, for it is a failure, partly because a very little more pains might have made it a success, and partly because we have a certain delight in its author's special faculty. Mr. Lewis Carroll, as it pleases the author of "Alice in Wonderland" to call himself, is one of the few humourists among us who is also an artist in nonsense, who can pour out words without meaning which make us laugh, and write songs without sense, or indeed intelligible words, which nevertheless give us pleasure from the associations they awaken. He is the only man who can make readers feel that they are asleep and irresponsible for their thoughts, and yet pleasantly conscious all the while. Nothing in literature ever was so like a pleasant dream as "Alice in Wonderland," or "Alice in the Looking-Glass," with their endless absurdities, each of which woke up some comic association; their preposterous card dignitaries and chess powers, all vivified by a child's imagination; their proverbs turned into personages, till we dine with the March hare, and listen to the mad Hatter; and their incidents and speeches and songs, which, as you wake—that is, close the book—you cannot recollect, because the dialogues have all faded away into a vague reminiscence of absurdity, and the songs live in the memory only as sounds with associations, but without meaning; and the figures die away till, like the Cheshire Cat, nothing remains of them but a diabolical and slowly-vanishing grin. Nothing could be more perfectly like a dream after seeing a pantomime than the scenes between Alice and the Queen of Hearts, who is always ordering somebody's head off, or between Alice and the Duchess, who tells her that, if you take care of the sense, the sounds will take care of themselves, unless it be this song, which Mr. Carroll obviously wrote while asleep after a supper following an evening of opéra bouffe:—

> " 'Twas brillig, and the slithy toves
>   Did gyre and gimble in the wabe;
> All mimsy were the borogoves,
>   And the mome raths outgrabe.
>
> 'Beware the Jabberwock, my son!
>   The jaws that bite, the claws that catch!
> Beware the Jubjub bird, and shun
>   The frumious Bandersnatch!'
>
> .   .   .   .
>
> And as in uffish thought he stood,
>   The Jabberwock, with eyes of flame,
> Came whiffling through the tulgey wood,
>   And burbled as it came!

.   .   .   .

'And hast thou slain the Jabberwock?
  Come to my arms, my beamish boy!
O frabjous day! Callooh! Callay!'
  He chortled in his joy.

'Twas brillig, and the slithy toves
  Did gyre and gimble in the wabe;
All mimsy were the borogoves,
  And the mome raths outgrabe."

We believe, and are sad to believe, that there are Scotchmen in the world to whom that song is "just silly," as we believe, and are sad to believe, that there are children who get quite angry when told to learn the lovely bit of incoherence by which Foote tested a boaster's memory, and which has lived 120 years, and will live a thousand:—

> "So she went into the garden to cut a cabbage-leaf, to make an apple-pie; and at the same time a great she-bear, coming up the street, pops its head into the shop. 'What! no soap.' So he died, and she very imprudently married the barber, and there were present the Picninnies, and the Joblillies, and the Garyulies, and the grand Panjandrum himself, with the little round button at top; and they all fell to playing the game of catch as catch can, till the gunpowder ran out at the heels of their boots."

The majority of men, however, are not Scotchmen, and it is creditable to the world, so stupid as it sometimes is, that nonsense like that we have quoted, artistic nonsense intended to produce without words the impression that humour produces with them, should have touched its fancy till Alice's two series of adventures were translated into half the tongues of Europe; till the Jabberwock passed into the English language, as a person who might be sketched; and till thoughtful essays were written— at least, we have read one—to explain the principle on which Mr. Carroll invented his wonderful words. Children worshipped the books, luxuriating for the first time in a form of grotesquerie which they could understand, and their elders were often amazed to find how heartily they had laughed over stuff the charm of which, all the while, they could not analyse. They said they laughed too, which was another triumph for Mr. Carroll, for there are comic things—some of Cruikshank's fairy drawings, for example— which men will laugh over with internal laughter, without ever fairly acknowledging their child-like enjoyment. The art of those two books—the sustained power with which reason is set aside, and as in dreams everything happens because it happens, and not because there was any reason why it should happen, the thoughtful breaking of connecting-links, the studious defiance of expectations, is amazing, and the more so because there is in the book so little rollick. Nonsense is generally amusing, because, besides waking up that sense of incongruity which is the cause of laughter, it suggests high spirits and devil-may-careishness and *abandon*—a state of mind, in fact, which is for a moment a relief from a too serious world; but Mr. Carroll's writing does not suggest this mood at all, but another and much quieter one. Tickling, not horse-play, is his forte, and he writes often as Lamb might have talked aloud in a dream, saying things that somehow make the reflective side of men chuckle as Lamb's wit does. Not that there is a "purpose" in Alice's adventures, for there is none, any more than in an ordinary dream; Mr. Carroll's art is too good for that. He relies sometimes on mere oddities, a mere reversal of the expected sentence, but generally he produces the effect of reflection by touching an association, as, for example, in introducing the Hatter, which makes the reader remember the element of absurdity in something quite familiar to his mind, like the proverb vivified in that personage. He writes, in fact, artistic nonsense, and is master in that high art.

He does not show himself master in "The Hunting of the Snark," and we have puzzled ourselves for some time to comprehend precisely the cause of failure, and are not sure even now that we have caught it. We thought at one moment that we had it, fancying, doubtless in a crass mood, that Mr. Carroll had been weak enough to work out an idea, to try to extract his special fun, the fun outside reason, the fun of no sense, from the drama of human life. That hunting of the invisible object which when gained may be a boojum, and not only disappear, but make the hunter vanish too, in the moment of seizure, is a little like human life; the Bellman who steers the ship, only ringing his Bell, which wakes attention, but gives the helmsman no course, standing for Conscience; and the Chart without land in it, and therefore blank, representing the Future; but we speedily gave that up, as a fancy fit only for that commentator of the future, who will one day, we suppose, evolve from the depths of his moral consciousness the meaning of the allegory under which Mr. Carroll veiled his secret wisdom. Such a purpose would, of course, involve failure, for though the human journey, the Quest of the Sangreal, on which every man consciously or unconsciously engages, admits of humorous treatment, it must be the humorous-pathetic or the humorous-sardonic, and not the humorous-nonsensical. The man who enjoys Mr. Carroll is sure to have too much of Omar Khayyám's *motif* about his mind, too deep a sense of the apparent failure in human destiny to endure seeing it all turned into pure nonsense. But as we have said, there is no reason for accusing Mr. Carroll of consequence in his thought, even in "The Snark," and we must seek another reason for the failure. Humour is not absent, except from the pictures—and one even of them, the beaver who is "shy," because the butcher, who only kills beavers, is looking at her, is very comic—while the line, "For the Snark *was* a Boojum, you see!" is better than anything in "Alice," and may pass into a proverb. The description of the landless chart is delicious:—

"The Bellman himself they all praised to the skies—
    Such a carriage, such ease, and such grace!
Such solemnity, too! One could see he was wise,
    The moment one looked in his face!

He had bought a large map representing the sea,
    Without the least vestige of land:
And the crew were much pleased when they found it to be
    A map they could all understand.

'What's the good of Mercator's North Poles and Equators,
    Tropics, Zones, and Meridian Lines?'
So the Bellman would cry: and the crew would reply,
    'They are merely conventional signs!

Other maps are such shapes, with their islands and capes!
    But we've got our brave Captain to thank'
(So the crew would protest) 'that he's bought us the best—
    A perfect and absolute blank!' "

And we do not know anywhere a more original kind of fool than this:—

"This was charming, no doubt: but they shortly found out
    That the Captain they trusted so well
Had only one notion for crossing the ocean,
    And that was to tinkle his bell.

He was thoughtful and grave—but the orders he gave
    Were enough to bewilder a crew.
When he cried 'Steer to starboard, but keep her head larboard!'
    What on earth was the helmsman to do?

Then the bowsprit got mixed with the rudder sometimes:
    A thing, as the Bellman remarked,
That frequently happens in tropical climes,
    When the vessel is, so to speak, 'snarked.' "

Nothing, moreover, can be more perfect in inconsequence than some of the scenes—for instance, the effort to teach the Beaver to add two and one together—and nothing more comically ridiculous than some of the single thoughts:—

"But the valley grew narrower and narrower still,
    And the evening got darker and colder,
Till (merely from nervousness, not from goodwill)
    They marched along shoulder to shoulder.

Then a scream, shrill and high, rent the shuddering sky,
    And they knew that some danger was near:
The Beaver turned pale to the tip of its tail,
    And even the Butcher felt queer.

He thought of his childhood, left far, far behind—
    That blissful and innocent state—
The sound so exactly recalled to his mind
    A pencil that squeaks on a slate."

The whole, however, falls flat, and we suppose the reason is that the nonsense is not artistic, that it does not wake as the nonsense in Alice's two adventures did the chain of association. We can be amused by the Cheshire Cat, but not by the Beaver; by the Queen of Hearts, but not by the Bellman; by the mad Hatter, but not by the Baker who could only bake bride-cake, and whose uncle gave him the wisest of rules, as the Bellman admits, for the hunting of the Snark:—

"You may seek it with thimbles—and seek it with care;
    You may hunt it with forks and hope;
You may threaten its life with a railway-share;
    You may charm it with smiles and soap."

We do not expect anything, and have therefore no sense of oddity in the unexpectedness of what we get; there is no Alice to stand as central figure, serenely puzzled and fearless, and there is no dialogue full of quirks, and oddities, and little turns that force out laughter against our will. The total effect is not one of humorous nonsense, but of tiresome nonsense, exciting only regret that Mr. Carroll should have wasted his powers on a book in which only a single line comes up to his usual level:—

"For the Snark *was* a Boojum, you see."

THE SATURDAY REVIEW, 41 (APRIL 15, 1876), 502–503

The author of that delightful bit of fun, *Alice's Adventures,* has just produced another specimen of his peculiar humour. The *Hunting of the Snark* is shorter and slighter than his former efforts in this way, and it is perhaps doubtful whether a form of nonsense which depends in a great measure on being surprising can be kept up successfully when its novelty has passed away. The reader is then too well prepared for the absurdities which await him, and their effect is consequently weakened. Nevertheless there is in this case a fascination in the familiar matter-of-fact way in which the most ridiculous and incoherent things are strung together which it is difficult to resist. The story is in verse, and describes an expedition of various lunatics, conducted by a mad bellman, in search of a mysterious object, of doubtful place in natural history, called the Snark, which, it appears, is sometimes a Boojum, and when the latter is encountered dreadful things happen. It would be unfair to disclose the secret of the five unmistakable marks by which one may recognize the 'warranted genuine Snark,' but we may say that they afford materials for endless speculation as to what it is. There is a touching passage descriptive of the difficulties of navigation which irresistibly recalls some recent incidents in real life. The bowsprit, it seems, 'got mixed up with the rudder sometimes,' and the captain bewildered his crew by such orders as 'Steer to starboard, but keep her head larboard.' It may be mentioned that in the end the Snark does turn out to be a Boojum, but readers had better go to the work itself to learn the details of the catastrophe. The illustrations display that same want of any sense of fun which distinguishes most comic draughtsmen in these days.

THE GRAPHIC, 13 (APRIL 15, 1876), 379

THE HUNTING OF THE SNARK

All the lovers of 'Alice,' that is to say, all reasoning beings, must have looked out eagerly for anything more about her doings. Now, although it may be slightly disappointing not to meet with our favourite in 'The Hunting of the Snark,' by Lewis Carroll (Macmillan), it must always be a consolation to think that had she gone on that grisly quest, she might, like the Baker, have met a Boojum, and the consequences would have been too deplorable. Seriously, we are glad to meet with the author again, and in a new vein, so to speak; much as we admired his former works, we should have been half afraid had his new one been in the same vein, for fear he should overdo it, and we cannot afford to lose 'Lewis Carroll.' It would be as impossible as absurd to try and analyse this glorious piece of nonsense; but we may remark on the singular facility of verse which it shows. Also upon the extraordinary power of gravely reciting circumstances, wildly impossible, in a way which commends them to mind and memory as historical fact. The enmity and subsequent reconciliation of the Butcher and the Beaver are quite as moving as many episodes in contemporary literary biographies, and when the former was upset by his dread of the exigencies of society, could there be a more perfectly human touch than—

> The Beaver went simply galumphing about
> At seeing the Butcher so shy:

Spiteful triumph personified! Time fails us to tell how the Bandersnatch was proof against commercial blandishments; of the highly unpleasant note of the Jub-jub bird; the mathematical and ornithological lectures of the Butcher; and, last, but not least, the mysterious fate of the only man who really met a Snark. As for that beast, judging from analogy, we presume it had a strong element of the 'Snob' in its composition; the five points of its character seem to point to this—but it would be hard to say whether the male, female, or purely 'society' type predominated. Everybody ought to read the book—nearly everybody *will*—and all who deserve the treat will scream with laughter. Finally, may we be serious for a minute, and say how tender, how beautiful in its English, how truly religious in the best sense, is that affectionate Easter appeal 'To every child who loves Alice.' It has passages that might be written in letters of gold, and we hardly envy the reader who can read it without some queer sensation in the throat. Mr. Holiday's illustrations are good in their way—best where they borrow most from Mr. Tenniel.

VANITY FAIR, 15 (APRIL 29, 1876), 248

The author of 'Alice in Wonderland' should be made by reason, or, failing reason, by force, to content himself with that greatest of all triumphs. He goes from good to bad, and from bad to worse. 'Through the Looking-glass' was not nearly so good as Alice, yet it had some exquisite fooling in it; but this book has little to recommend it beyond the name of the author, and that little is to be found at the end of the preface. The rest is not worthy the name of nonsense, as Alice and the Knight knew it, but deserves only to be called rubbish; while a letter to every child 'who loves Alice,' which is thrown in, is a simple piece of impertinence.

THE **WYKEHAMIST,** MAY 1876, PP. 2–3

THE HUNTING OF THE SNARK.
ἐς τοπὰν ἐξμηνέων χατίζει—*Pind. Ol. 2, 152.*

You ask me, Mr. Editor, to state
Views on a problem mooted much of late:
What is the Bellman? why he rings the bell?
And what the Banker and the Beaver tell?
And what the Butcher? and, O save the mark!
Who, what, or which, the mischief, is the Snark?

Brothers! a moment leave the ice half done:
Forsake the jamless tart, the sanded bun!
And listen, while I struggle to expound
The sense that Nonsense hideth underground.

Well then, so far as I can yet descry,
The Snark they seek is Popularity.
The shapeless, nameless thing, that seems so grand,

Sought upon height, in depth, by sea and land!
—How many flowers arise around our feet
Here in the world, and every flower is sweet!
'Tis sweet to don the last new thing in dress;
Sweet—I am told—the lady's faltered "yes";
And sweet to contemplate the gimcrack robe
With which our modern priest converts the globe;
And sweet to sing, in proud anticipation,
"God save the Empress of the Jewish nation";
Sweet to the patriot, foaming o'er his ale,
The sacred relic of a Hyde Park rail!
Sweet are these things, and others, each and all,
But nought can match the time ineffable,
When, in the middle of our work, we pause
To hear five hundred asses bray applause.

As onward o'er the sea of Life we wend,
Cant rings his blatant bell—"attend! attend!"
I spread my vacant chart before your eye,
And, if no strength, I have authority!
Hap what may hap, I proudly strike my bell,
"Hush! who said 'humbug'? hush! we meant it well!"
With such a Captain, o'er the boundless seas,
We drift, a motley crew, before the breeze,
Before the world's uncomprehended wind;
And, at the limit of our course assigned,
Mere crags and chasms—ne'er a Snark,—we find.

Stand forth the Banker! what is here implied?
Surely, the power of Cash personified:
He scatters thimbles, lest the fingers ail,
Whereby the shirts are made, and profits fail!
And strives to prove how popular a neighbour
Is bloated Capital to hungry Labour:
Thus, as he seeks the Snark with pious care,
Appears the Bandersnatch of Strikes or War,
—Black with asphyxia, behold him lie,
While Bellman Cant proclaims a homily!
Then, galvanized to action by despair,
He calls a meeting and assumes the chair!
And, as in curst monotony of bones,
Wails "peace" and "progress" in distracted tones;
Then fall'n from favour and from high estate,

With broken mutterings, he yields to fate.
"Trust all your country unto Manchester,—
The policy of profits cannot err;—
Bury, O bury me by Irwell's side,—
Black in the face, but rich in funds, I died."

Next, in the forefront of the sacred quest,
The Barrister sniffs, stalks, and yelps his best:
All wig and gown; but, underneath and really,
The actual, unadulterate, Kenealy!
Ex-Advocate, Ex-Lion, and Ex-Bencher,
And Ex-M.P. when Stoke repents its venture;
Heedless that from his ostentatious stride,
Hope, with her anchor, smiling, turns aside,
Heir of the Barons, how he stalks away,
And scents the looked for Snark in Notoriety!
Mark too his dream . . . The Snark, with glass in eye,
(Vox parùm discernentis populi)
Shall settle all things underneath the sun,
As Counsel, Judge, and Jury, all in one!

The Butcher, wondrous wight! whose one remark
And single aim was just the magic "Snark";
Here, as a pikestaff, manifest to all,
Stands out our modern hustings Liberal!
Born in the world to kill, not make alive,—
The drone-destroyer of the human hive,
And called by Cant unto the place he fills,
Link-boy, to bear his blazing principles!

Opposed to him, but in no lasting schism,
The Beaver of our modern Toryism;
He, artful builder of a noted name,
Rears his clay home within the house of Fame;
He weaves new lace, and, marvel to relate,
Affirms thereby that he has saved a State!
And thus with quizzing-glass, and tongue, and pen,
In cool contempt, instructs the Upper Ten.

These, feigning each the other not to see,
Slip into one harmonious policy,
And, in the grotto dark of Parliament,
They seek the Snark and call it Government!
"How feed with buns the new enfranchised mass,

Keep Tripe and Onions for the Middle Class,
Yet save the Upper their *vanille de glace,*"
Such is the problem ... Sudden through the sky,
Resounds the Jub-Jub song—the maddened cry
Of foodless, creedless, homeless Poverty;
Straight, into utter amity combine
The sham Aristocrat and Philistine!

Then, next, what signifies the sum absurd,
"Take all from nought and then subtract one-third";
—In other words, the cure they vow will fit us,
Is, just a hair from off the dog that bit us;
And, just to raise the Red Sea stock from zero,
They set about re-organizing Pharaoh!
And, all the while, around them soar and range
The creepy creatures of the Stock Exchange;
The Press pours ink upon their high design,
Toad, newt, and monkey, Bull and Bear, combine
To grind the music of the—nether—spheres,
And Irish Members trumpet in their ears!
While Rothschild pins the Tory by the tail,—
"Now, cent. per cent.! or let the Khedive fail!"

Lastly, the Baker.—Here we seem to see
Th' epitome of poor Humanity!
—How many coats we start in life withal!
The Coat Religious, Coat Conventional,
The Coat of Health, the Coats of Circumstance,
Time, Temper, all beneath the over-Coat of chance!
And thus equipped, and gay, in Youth's glad morning,
We start in life, with just our Uncle's warning!
And, somehow, leave our boxes all behind,
Use the wrong tongue, and never speak our mind,
Deceive our comrades, wrestle long with fate,
And find the Snark arises far too late;
Apt to begin when Life's sun sinks away,
Apt to be fullest on the following day;
Thus we go on, and friends begin to doubt us,
And we, to feel the world gets on without us:
Once more, with pains, some petty height we gain,
And shriek for recognition—all in vain!
Then in a moment, softly, suddenly,—
So like the Baker, vanish we away!

FRUMIOUS.

Whale or Boojum:
An Agony

BY HAROLD BEAVER

Is it that by its indefiniteness it shadows forth the heartless voids and immensities of the universe, and thus stabs us from behind with the thought of annihilation, when beholding the white depths of the milky way?
HERMAN MELVILLE, *Moby-Dick,* Ch. 42.

IT WAS A FRENCHMAN WHO FIRST PROPOSED THAT LEWIS CARROLL MIGHT OWE A literary debt to Herman Melville. W. H. Auden had earlier juxtaposed *The Hunting of the Snark* with *Moby-Dick.*[1] Robert Martin Adams, more recently, discussed both works within the context of a single study.[2] Marcel Marnat not only confronted but directly compared the two masterpieces: Whale and Snark, White Whale and Boojum, the majestic prose saga and the inconsequential-sounding ballad. "A passionate parody was it," he asked, "or merely a teasing echo, dimly caught—with no formal parallelism in mind, of course—just for the fun of it, as a game?"[3]

Thus what was raised as speculation inevitably hardened in the presentation: Carroll was either adapting, or maybe countering, or even parodying, *The Whale.* "Symbol matches symbol and the Boojum is all the more horrible for remaining unseen."[4] J. M. Barrie, Carroll's heir as children's favorite, for one, had certainly read his Melville. Much in *Peter Pan*–above all, the clock-devouring crocodile in pursuit of Captain Hook–ultimately derives from *Moby-Dick*. The hallmark of Carroll's style, though, is an unselfconscious-seeming display of his own darkest designs. If he had read *Moby-Dick,* it is true, "he could only have done so with head spinning. Thrilled, yet at the same time feeling a profound unease...." [5] But had he?

Like Melville, of course, he was a master of mirror imagery. With Melville, too, he shared a wide-ranging passion for burlesque of standard authors as well as biblical sources. But where Melville was consciously manipulating his parodies, Carroll remained untouched by, even oblivious of, his deeper inversions and radical skepticism. Or so it seems. While Melville could exultingly boast of *Moby-Dick,* "I have written a wicked book, and feel spotless as the lamb," [6] Carroll's diary reveals his ambition to publish *The Snark* as a Christmas poem. The strain was marked, however. Years later, introducing *Pillow Problems, and other Mathematical Trifles,* he owned:

> ... There are mental troubles, much worse than mere worry, for which an absorbing subject of thought may serve as a remedy. There are sceptical thoughts, which seem for the moment to uproot the firmest faith; there are blasphemous thoughts, which dart unbidden into the most reverent souls; there are unholy thoughts, which torture, with their hateful presence, the fancy that would fain be pure. [7]

Bedeviled by insomnia, he would worry away all night over his mathematical teasers to keep worse anguish at bay. But the inversion, twenty years earlier, had seemed merely lighthearted, surfacing backwards from the final line to a final stanza to fit that line to a finished sequence to fit that stanza. Had not "Lewis Carroll," his very pseudonym, been assembled by a deliberate inversion of his Christian names, "Charles Lutwidge"?

The odd bolt of inspiration came on July 18, 1874, near Guildford:

> I was walking on a hillside, alone, one bright summer day, when suddenly there came into my head one line of verse–one solitary line–"For the Snark *was* a Boojum, you see." I knew not what it meant, then: I know not what it means, now; but I wrote it down: and, sometime afterwards, the rest of the stanza occurred to me, that being its last line: and so by degrees, at odd moments during the next year or two, the rest of the poem pieced itself together, that being its last stanza. [8]

The poem was not out in time for Christmas 1875. In March 1876, therefore, he added a small pamphlet, "An Easter Greeting to Every Child Who Loves Alice," not "to lose the opportunity of saying a few serious words to (perhaps) 20,000 children."

> To rise and forget, in the bright sunlight, the ugly dreams that frightened you so when all was dark–to rise and enjoy another happy day, first kneeling to thank that unseen Friend, who sends you the beautiful sun....

Cardinal Newman, for one, was quite captivated by this reversal of tone. He wrote to the daughter of the Dean of St. Paul's:

> The little book isn't all of it nonsense, though amusing nonsense; it has two pleasant prefixes of another sort. One of them is the "inscription to a dear child"; the style of which, in words and manner, is so entirely of the school of Keble, that I think it could not have been written, had *The Christian Year* never made its appearance. The other "the Easter Greeting to every child etc." is likely to touch the hearts of old men more than of those to whom it is intended. . . .[9]

But how far was Dodgson—as Charles Lutwidge or Lewis Carroll, turn him inside out or outside in—ever aware of his own envelopes and smoke screens? That initial dedication to Gertrude Chataway:

> Girt with a boyish garb for boyish task,
>   Eager she wields her spade: yet loves as well
> Rest on a friendly knee. . . .

for all its echoes of *The Christian Year* and self-conscious acrostic riddling, suggests a deeper, unconscious level of inchoate lusts and fears of self-destruction—some covert sexual trauma turned to a mimic tea with muffins, jam, and conundrums.

For unlike his poetic alibi, the Baker—with his "forty-two boxes, all carefully packed," inside the *Agony*—we should rouse Charles *from* muffins, we should rouse him *from* ice, should rouse him *from* mustard and cress, should rouse him *from* jam and judicious advice, and *probe* his conundrums and *press*. The obvious place to start is the "Preface"—which, like most prefaces, was written last. On Thursday, February 10, 1876, between composing his first and third diatribe on *The Professorship of Comparative Philology,* Dodgson records in his diary: "At night wrote a new Preface for *The Snark."* That preface begins:

> *If*—and the thing is wildly possible—the charge of writing nonsense were ever brought against the author of this brief but instructive poem, it would be based, I feel convinced, on the line, "Then the bowsprit got mixed with the rudder sometimes."

As Lewis Carroll, that is, he opens on a pause—that lingering lilt on *"If"*—then takes us straight to "The Bellman's Speech," confronting the blank "Ocean chart":

> He was thoughtful and grave—but the orders he gave
>   Were enough to bewilder a crew.
> When he cried, "Steer to starboard, but keep her head larboard!"
>   What on earth was the helmsman to do?

> Then the bowsprit got mixed with the rudder sometimes:
>   A thing, as the Bellman remarked,
> That frequently happens in tropical climes,
>   When a vessel is, so to speak, "snarked."

The paralysis—the loggerhead self-contradiction—of the poem is essential. Every positive will be negated: forwards is backwards; earth is ocean; east is west. This is to be the first and prime lesson, literally, of "non-sense." He continues:

> I will not (as I might) point to the strong moral purpose of this poem itself, to the arithmetical principles so cautiously inculcated in it. . . .

Secondly, it appears, "The Beaver's Lesson" is essential. Number and nonsense, when merged in the self-reductive algebraic equation:

$$\frac{(x + 7 + 10)\ (1000 - 8)}{992} - 17 = x$$

might seem to underlie the bowsprit/rudder entanglements, leading investigation nowhere. Yet arithmetical principles somehow persist. Just as the Grand Geometrician of a Masonic universe reigns in *Moby-Dick,* through all the global circuits of sun and whale and *Pequod,* through all Melville's pyrotechnic displays of contrary ebbs and flows in chapters, sentences, even phrases, so too Carroll's miniature universe, he claims, rests on number.[10]

Dodgson, of course, was an eminent mathematician. He was also forty-two years old in 1874 when he began the poem. But far from "Call me Ishmael" or, rather, "Call me Baker," Carroll merely intrudes "Rule 42 of the Code" at the opening as emblematic clue. (In Holiday's illustration the number is clearly marked on one of the Baker's many boxes on the quay outside his uncle's bedroom window.)

> *No one shall speak to the Man at the Helm.*

Which the Bellman himself had completed:

> *and the Man at the Helm shall speak to no one.*

An untouchable privacy must enshroud the captain/poet/town-crier, as he paradoxically tolls his bell, with an "oyez, oyez." The poem is to be locked in silence as the Baker's adventure ends in "silence." That is the third essential lesson: the clam of contradictory, destructive pressures inside the "Agony" is to be impenetrable. What next then? A few deliberate false trails, expected of the author of *Jabberwocky,* on portmanteau words. But even here the most relevant portmanteau remains, so to speak, "snarked." Is it some maritime snail-cum-shark?[11] Or, as has been suggested, is it snarl-cum-bark?[12]

No answer. Instead, elsewhere, Carroll privately echoes the question: "Of course you know what a Snark is? If you do, please tell *me:* for I haven't an idea what it is like."[13] Or again: "Are you able to explain things which you don't yourself understand?"[14] So he plays at allegory. Melville, far more obviously attracted to such

[114]

learned mirror-writing, shuddered at the idea that *Moby-Dick* might be deemed "a hideous and intolerable allegory." [15] When Sophia Hawthorne followed her husband's congratulatory letter with more prying formulas, Melville replied offhandedly:

> I had some vague idea while writing it, that the whole book was susceptible of an allegoric construction, & also that *parts* of it were—but the speciality of many of the particular subordinate allegories, were first revealed to me, after reading Mr. Hawthorne's letter, which, without citing any particular examples, yet intimated the part-&-parcel allegoricalness of the whole.[16]

Carroll, too, appears puzzled by the allegorical potential of his eight "fits." "Periodically I have received courteous letters from strangers," he sighed,

> begging to know whether *The Hunting of the Snark* is an allegory, or contains some hidden moral, or is a political satire: and for all such questions I have but one answer, *"I don't know!"* [17]

In 1896, twenty years after publication, he saw published in a newspaper (so he claims):

> ... that the whole book is an allegory on the search after happiness. I think this fits beautifully in many ways—particularly about the bathing-machines: when the people get weary of life, and can't find happiness in town or in books, then they rush off to the seaside to see what bathing-machines will do for them.[18]

This is his most perverse evasion, his final smoke screen to blot that craggy landscape. For how call a work "allegory" if it contains merely a blank map—that is to say, no map, no complex interpretative guide, but (as in Kafka's *The Castle)* their very antithesis? If anything it seems a kind of allegory *à rebours*—a clue to the impossibility of any final map, a clue to mysterious, pervasive, and malicious *dis*order—that heralds the end of all formal allegorical vision. We gaze at our own risk till "the palsied universe lies before us a leper"! Till blinded by "the monumental white shroud that wraps all the prospect around" the dazzled reader.[19]

So allegory, with Ishmael, we must reject. We would do better to follow the acrostic advice given to Marion (one of Carroll's many little friends):

> Maiden, though thy heart may quail
> And thy quivering lip grow pale,
> Read the Bellman's tragic tale!
>
> Is it life of which it tells?
> Of a pulse that sinks and swells
> Never lacking chime of bells?[20]

"Read the Bellman's tragic tale!" But who *is* the Bellman? His hand-bell, in Holiday's realistic representation, has suggested curious thoughts to one commentator:

> It has apparently escaped notice that the Bellman's bell is an ordinary school-bell of the type used before electric bells came into use. It seems to me that Dodgson quite consciously derived his Bellman from the new secular state education of which so much was hoped.[21]

What satisfies one reader may raise a smile in others. For our analogue—that "wicked book" surreptitiously riddling and jesting with sacred texts (Moses striking water "upon the rock in Horeb"; or glimpsing the "back parts" of God)—suggests other clues. Is the Reverend Dodgson imposing the same inversion on his "tragic tale" that opens with a Bell-man and closes with the picture of a tolling bell-buoy? Is the whole *Hunting of the Snark* perhaps playing a deliberate (or is it unconscious?) parody of that traditional English carol popularly known as the "Bellman's Song"?

> The moon shines bright, and the stars give a light:
>   A little before it was day
> Our Lord, our God, he called on us,
>   And bid us awake and pray.
>
> Awake, awake, good people all;
>   Awake, and you shall hear,
> Our Lord, our God, died on the cross
>   For us whom he loved so dear.
>
> O fair, O fair Jerusalem,
>   When shall I come to thee?
> When shall my sorrows have an end,
>   Thy joy that I may see?
>
> The fields were green as green could be,
>   When from his glorious seat
> Our Lord, our God, he watered us,
>   With his heavenly dew so sweet.
>
> And for the saving of our souls
>   Christ died upon the cross;
> We ne'er shall do for Jesus Christ
>   As he hath done for us.
>
> The life of man is but a span
>   And cut down in its flower;
> We are here to-day, and to-morrow are gone,
>   The creatures of an hour.[22]

"Our Lord, our God, he called on us": or transposed from church bells to hand-bell:

> The Bellman himself they all praised to the skies—
> Such a carriage, such ease and such grace!
> Such solemnity too! One could see he was wise,
> The moment one looked in his face![23]

If the whole carol has, in fact, been transposed to "An Agony," it must be—as the very title suggests—Carroll's agony, containing locked within it his whole self-contradiction of bowsprit and rudder, east and west, Jerusalem and Jabberwock, in numbed indirection.

Both share the same ballad meter, as if the "cross" of the one had been transformed to the riddling acrostic of the other; "fair Jerusalem" to "chasms and crags"; green fields to that "dismal and desolate valley." As if the "green pastures" of the twenty-third psalm, pervading the carol, had been reduced by Lewis Carroll to "the valley of the shadow of death"—glum with foreboding—where:

> . . . The valley grew narrow and narrower still,
>   And the evening got darker and colder,
> Till (merely from nervousness, not from goodwill)
>   They marched along shoulder to shoulder.

Both move to the same bleak vision of the restless transience of life. For, as its popular title makes clear,

> This carol they began that hour—
> With a hey, and a ho, and a hey nonino—
> How that life was but a flower—
> In spring time,[24]

is not a Christmas carol at all. This Bellman is none other than the public announcer of death—to all "for whom the bell tolls," those "creatures of an hour," who "are here to-day, and to-morrow are gone"; or, in the Baker's dying uncle's last words, "will softly and suddenly vanish away,/And never be met with again!" [25]

The Bellman's Song, then, is a Passion carol or Atonement carol. If the Baker, like Christ, "sublime" on that crag must die, the Butcher, transcending the "perpetual passion" of the Jubjub, is restored, like Christ, to perfect harmony, which is perpetual love. But here, as at every other point of *The Hunting of the Snark,* paradoxes multiply. For should it not have been the Butcher who is "cut down" with his own slaughtering hatchet? Should it not have been the Baker, like his own confectioner's dough, who is "risen indeed"? One thing at least was obvious even to its earliest readers, that the names of all ten crew members began with the initial "B." But then

[117]

so did "Bandersnatch" and "Boojum." "To B or not to B," was that the universal fit? Snarkophilus Snobbs, with tongue-in-cheek profundity, not only pointed to this "most ultimate of all questions," but argued that it was "answered in the universal affirmative—B at any cost!" [26] "An existential poem, a poem of existential agony," Martin Gardner more recently called it, indicating that great Chain of Being from Bellman to Boots.[27]

Carroll's Bellman is certainly "grand"; he is also "musical" as well as "thoughtful and grave." But his most marked characteristic is that of triple repetition, a belief in the sacred power of three. As if speaking in all three persons of the Trinity in succession, he asserts in his most celebrated assertion:

> What I tell you three times is true.

Such threefold verbal concentrations alone seem to carry the full weight of his authority; and his triune presence is suitably greeted at one point by "three cheers." Yet the "Ocean chart" he brings proves a cartographical fraud—"A perfect and absolute blank!"—an uncontaminated square of whiteness, framed with chaos. Compare the pedantic German Professor of *Sylvie and Bruno Concluded.* He describes how his country's cartographers experimented with larger and larger maps until they finally made one with a scale of a mile to the mile:

> "It has never been spread out, yet," said Mein Herr: "the farmers objected: they said it would cover the whole country, and shut out the sunlight! So now we use the country itself, as its own map, and I assure you it does nearly as well." [28]

For Carroll it appeared there was no guide, no chart or clue, between *everything* and *nothing,* between all-pervasive physical reality and a self-devouring inner emptiness.

> Or is it, that in essence whiteness is not so much a color as the visible absence of color, and at the same time the concrete of all colors; is it for these reasons that there is such a dumb blankness, full of meaning, in a wide landscape of snows—a colorless, all-color of atheism from which we shrink?[29]

That blank map, like the Banker's "blank cheque (which he crossed)"—or even the circular blank reasoning of Butcher to Beaver—leads inevitably to an undermining and perverting of meaningful order, a stalemate of self-contradiction and self-confusion, a *reductio ad absurdum* where words too are deliberately emptied of content, blended (portmanteau-style), and tipped to their abstract, incantatory quality of blank, ecstatic *sound.*

What is propped at the Butcher's feet (in Holiday's illustration to "The Beaver's Lesson") but Colenso's *Arithmetic* and a book *On the Reductio ad Absurdum?* Whether at the artist's or poet's prompting we do not know. But Bishop Colenso too had once been a mathematical tutor and author of mathematical textbooks; he too had reduced some of the deepest biblical beliefs, by means of arithmetical arguments or models, to absurdity or literal nonsense, while claiming to remain a devoted member of the Church of England. The Deacon of Christ Church, Oxford, and the Bishop of Natal had much in common. As the Bishop's arithmetical logic could dissolve the haphazard battle figures of Israelites vs. Midianites, the Deacon's far more devastating logic of absurdity could dissolve the *Song of Solomon*—or Isaac Watts' *Divine Songs for Children,* at the very least—to "the voice of the Lobster" (in *Alice in Wonderland)* or to "the voice of the Jubjub" in the *Snark.*[30] An Essex vicar apparently did complain, writing a letter to *The St. James Gazette;* but while the notorious bishop was hounded by his Victorian contemporaries, socially ostracized and excommunicated, the demure Oxford don continued to be quietly feted. One was a heretic; the other, a children's favorite. One refuted Holy Scripture; the other merely parodied it.

As with Melville, such parody was never easy to diagnose; and nonsense, especially, seemed to resist such diagnosis. Only the Butcher and the Baker, with their linked but diverging fates, could conceivably offer a key to the conundrum: both tradesmen, both reckoned dunces, both in their various ways heroic. That stout, ungainly, bewhiskered Baker, above all, is a mysterious character, and the most complex of all that heterogeneous crew. Had he "wholly forgotten his name" perhaps because that name was none other than C. L. Dodgson, alias Lewis Carroll? The merest hint of his fame is immediately undercut. "There was one who was famed for the number of things/He forgot when he entered the ship...." For the Baker is not only anally possessive (with his forty-two inscrutable boxes, neatly packed and stacked), but incurably detached. He manages to leave all his possessions (umbrella, watch, jewelry) behind on the beach; he has wholly forgotten his name; he has even lost the use of his native English, vainly signaling in Hebrew, German, Greek, Dutch—that is, gabbling in double-Dutch. He answers to "Hi!" and he answers to "Ho!" (with a hey, and a ho, and a hey nonino). But it is only to "Thing-um-a-jig!"—or "Thingumbob," to quote the Bellman's parting words—that he utterly responds, as if reduced to some irredeemable, undifferentiated, neutral blank.

Compared to Melville's Ishmael even, it seems a desolating self-portrait of self-alienation. Ishmael also enters the brotherhood of whaling, stripped of all possessions, with nothing but his carpetbag:

> For all men who say *yes,* lie; and all men who say *no,*—why, they are in the happy condition of judicious, unincumbered travellers in Europe; they cross the frontiers into Eternity with nothing but a carpet-bag,—that is to say, the Ego.[31]

Yet at least he was still self-possessed, still able to issue his own terse challenge of anonymity. Charles Dodgson's ultimate alter ego behind screen on masking screen (hot and overdressed in seven coats and three pairs of boots) is already spiritually stripped, that is to say, nameless. Only a pathetic trust in various bourgeois securities, such as bulletproof vests or life insurance, still lingers. And he eagerly promotes those securities:

> The Beaver's best course was, no doubt, to procure
> > A second-hand dagger-proof coat—
> So the Baker advised it—and next, to insure
> > Its life in some Office of note.

"Evidently he dreaded the loss of his body heat as much as he dreaded the loss of his existence," Martin Gardner observes. "The name Candle-ends may imply that the Baker is about to burn himself out." [32] Thus "that mildest of men" is a potentially burnt-out case—though mostly humdrum enough in outward appearance, resolutely candid (so he claims) and straightforward. His courage is "perfect" only because it is the courage of perfect despair:

> "It is this, it is this that oppresses my soul,
> > When I think of my uncle's last words:
> And my heart is like nothing so much as a bowl
> > Brimming over with quivering curds!
>
> "It is this, it is this—" "We have had that before!"
> > The Bellman indignantly said.
> And the Baker replied, "Let me say it once more.
> > It is this, it is this that I dread!" [33]

We only meet the Baker's uncle—that elderly double after whom he was named and who foretells his doom—at the vanishing point of death. Similarly, we meet the Baker already entranced by the infinite; trapped by the evasive, all-embracing vanishing point of mathematical perspective; engaged "with the Snark—every night after dark—/In a dreamy delirious fight." For the inner man, far from sturdy and stout, is a quivering, disintegrating, frothy mass, consumed in an ever-repeated round of nightmares.

Yet it is this very dread that binds the "stupid" Baker and "unlettered Ishmael" (an ex-country schoolmaster) to one another. Boojum or White Whale—the same portents, the same doom threatened both. The tormented Baker faints at the mere sound of that dreaded word; "one grand hooded phantom, like a snow hill in the air" haunts Ishmael's tormented soul.

> I, Ishmael, was one of that crew; my shouts had gone up with the rest; my oath had been welded with theirs; and stronger I shouted, and more did I hammer and clinch my oath, because of the dread in my soul. A wild, mystical, sympathetical feeling was in me. . . .[34]

Yet the Baker succumbs; Ishmael, exalted and magnetized by the hunt, escapes. Not only does a love pact, like the Butcher's, soothe his "splintered heart," but in the terror of the whale chase he transcends death itself. Like Lazarus, like Christ "after his resurrection," Ishmael can say: "A stone was rolled away from my heart . . . I survived myself; my death and burial were locked up in my chest." [35] Only then, after that "ceremony" of self-transcendence, can he confront the teasing horror of the absurd. Only then can he confront that laughing HYENA with a bantering air as a suicidal farce. The Baker's banter with hyenas, however, is a sure sign of self-deception:

> He would joke with hyaenas, returning their stare
>   With an impudent wag of the head:
> And he once went a walk, paw-in-paw, with a bear,
>   "Just to keep up its spirits," he said.

Neither cool nor self-contained, the Baker is far from displaying Ishmael's "free and easy sort of genial, desperado philosophy." Such impudent head-wagging and eye-winking is visible proof merely of a suicidal bravado; the "torrent of laughter and cheers" at his vanishing, merely the audible aspect of that same hysterically pulsing throb, or nervous "spasm," that plunges him over the edge at last—to be released in silence.

But there are three "stupid" hunters, three overt nonintellectuals on board: the Baker, the Butcher, and the shy, lacemaking Beaver. It is these three alone who undergo the decisive, indeed overwhelming spiritual adventures. The impudent absentminded Baker succumbs; the shy single-minded Butcher paradoxically escapes his doom. While natural antagonists (the Beaver and the Butcher) alone are brought to converge, potential soulmates (the Butcher and the Baker) [36] are most widely shown to diverge. So, by the antilogic of this excursion into disorder, natural buddies are parted, unnatural buddies bonded and paired. "Two added to one—if that could be done!" Only Melville's Ishmael, it appears, can complete the sum: part monomaniac hunter (like the Butcher), part desperado and wag (like the Baker); the bosom friend of Queequeg and devotee or acolyte of Ahab; a resolution of each and compound beyond all.

The Butcher, too, presents an insoluble logjam of paradoxes. Fanatically obsessed, so he claims, with "Snark," he turns out to be more single-minded than a Canadian trapper in exterminating Beavers! An even more "incredible dunce" to look at than the Baker, he nevertheless hits on his own independent and "ingenious plan" for a solo foray! No wonder the Butcher turned nervous. But his ornate overdressing for the big occasion, "with yellow kid gloves and a ruff," seems to spring from some deeper-fixed feeling of social insecurity—or, rather, social inferiority.

> "Introduce me, now there's a good fellow," he said,
>   "If we happen to meet it together!"
> And the Bellman, sagaciously nodding his head,
>   Said, "That must depend on the weather."

This mixture of personal trepidation (which makes him cling so anxiously to the Bellman) with murderous monomania (for Beavers) produces restless friction, threatening a total breakdown.

> "Be a man!" said the Bellman in wrath, as he heard
>   The Butcher beginning to sob.
> "Should we meet with a Jubjub, that desperate bird,
>   We shall need all our strength for the job!"

"Be a man!" That terse reprimand—and "that desperate bird" suddenly swooping into the poem—mark the peripeteia or turning point. The Butcher's shy dependence is converted to resolution and independence; his dumb obsession changes to intellectual resourcefulness; his nervous blubbering (having survived the Jubjub) becomes tears of "delight." Even a confrontation with pastoral, in this context, must be inverted to a dismally shadowed valley, a desolate nightmare-haunted country, invaded by a scream. Pitched higher and higher to a "shrill," "shuddering" spasm, that "nervousness" is at last dissolved in an echo of lost childhood.

> He thought of his childhood, left far far behind—
>   That blissful and innocent state—
> The sound so exactly recalled to his mind
>   A pencil that squeaks on a slate!

So the peripeteia is confirmed almost simultaneously by the anagnorisis, or recognition:

> " 'Tis the voice of the Jubjub!" he suddenly cried.
>   (This man, that they used to call "Dunce.")
> "As the Bellman would tell you," he added with pride,
>   "I have uttered that sentiment once.
>
> " 'Tis the note of the Jubjub! Keep count, I entreat;
>   You will find I have told it you twice.
> 'Tis the song of the Jubjub! The proof is complete,
>   If only I've stated it thrice."

It is a recognition not only of the Jubjub but the Bellman's grand triadic repetitions. Now the Butcher's role is proudly patterned after the Bellman's role, perhaps even after his "musical tone" in that rapturous ascent from " 'Tis the voice" to " 'Tis the note" to the exalted height of his great argument, " 'Tis the song. . ."

At that word his monomania for Beavers is transformed from a killer's passion to a lover's. Kindred souls marching shoulder to shoulder in that narrow valley, their bond is celebrated with that holiest of bridal rites from the *Song of Songs* or *Song of Solomon*. For cementing the friendship, however, another ritual is required:

"The thing can be done," said the Butcher, "I think,
   The thing must be done, I am sure.
The thing shall be done!"

Merely to contain that erotic *frisson* (by a childhood trauma) cannot be foolproof; the charged, pent-up emotion must still be abstracted (by the contemplation of pure number). As W. H. Auden put it:

> The Beaver and the Butcher, romantic explorers though they are, who have chosen to enter a desolate valley, where the Jubjub bird screams in passion overhead, and the creatures from *The Temptation of St. Anthony* surround them, escape from the destructive power of sex sublimating it into arithmetical calculations based on the number 3.[37]

Only now does the Butcher turn "genial." Only now, ensconced in that Platonic haven, can he shrug off "all laws of propriety." Only now that he has grasped the mystic import of the Bellman's repeated trinities can he also reject the whole confining semeiology of social etiquette:

> "What's the good of Mercator's North Poles and Equators,
>   Tropics, Zones, and Meridian Lines?"
> So the Bellman would cry: and the crew would reply,
>   "They are merely conventional signs!"

Having transcended those intimidating conventions, those self-devouring inhibitions of "Society," the Butcher, it seems, is free. But that impudent wag of a Baker, who can only bake "Bridecake" unhappily, is trapped. No wedding bells, no *Song of Solomon* for him! Only a jangle of contraries! For in Baker and Boojum, as in Butcher and Beaver, natural opposites again fuse. Not for salvation this time but for an unholy rape. Bedridden, ponderous, grave, what else is the Snark but a prude? Why else "its slowness in taking a jest"? Why else "its fondness for bathing-machines,/ Which it constantly carries about"? What else is "Snark" but the converse of "wag" with whom the Baker (for all his protective anonymity, seven coats and three boots) will collapse by a kind of reciprocal, almost algebraic, cross-cancellation of terms?

All Carroll's descriptions of the Boojum, on Henry Holiday's evidence, "were quite unimaginable, and he wanted the creature to remain so." [38] For a Snark, as "The Barrister's Dream" suggests, is a confused mass of self-contradiction: part counsel, part judge, part jury; now acting for the defense, now ruthlessly condemning that selfsame client—who had, in any case, "been dead for some years." Is the "Dream," then, a premonition of "The Vanishing"? Is the pig's fate, yet another deserter, a shadow image of the Baker's? For he plunges to his annihilation through a looking-glass, as it were, whose mirrored reversal merely seems to reflect his own inner turmoil of self-obliteration. The Baker's very heroic posture, "erect and sublime" on that neighboring crag, was prefigured by the Snark, sublimely erect, on passing sentence: "When it rose to its feet, there was silence like night,/And the fall of a pin might be heard." Such a vanishing—like Kafka's fable of the man before the law, as Robert Martin Adams observed—implies:

> that only he could discover the Snark for whom it was bound to prove a Boojum. The conditions of the problem were such as to lead inevitably to the destruction of its solver, while those who were immune to the consequences could not solve it in the first place.[39]

But the Butcher, in his newfound wizardry, could surely have confronted the problem. If he was immune to the consequences, it was only because he had moved into a realm beyond those paradoxical terrors of the infinite that engulf the Baker:

> "In one moment I've seen what has hitherto been
> Enveloped in absolute mystery,
> And without extra charge I will give you at large
> A lesson in Natural History."

The same insight that reveals the *name* of the Jubjub, in fact, provides a simultaneous and deeper insight into the *nature* of the Jubjub, striking through the enveloping mystery—the *perpetuum mobile* or creative pulse of Nature itself.[40]

> "As to temper the Jubjub's a desperate bird,
> Since it lives in perpetual passion:"

But that "absurd" never-ending sexual trauma of desperate passion has far wider connotations, it turns out, than a mere fascination with fashion and the aphrodisiac flavor of oysters and egg white. Such sexual knowledge, once gained (as Adam and Eve discovered), is absolute: "But it knows any friend it has met once before." There is no going back on that recognition, no evading the Jubjub. Sexual drives, on the other hand, cannot be roused at will or at random: "It never will look at a bribe." Nor must sexual lust be confused with true love, or charity. "And in charity-meetings it stands at the door," though it is an aspect of true love and, if distinct, closely linked to it. The Jubjub itself contributes nothing to that spiritual element of true love, called charity: "And collects—though it does not subscribe." But to survive at all in its human context, true love must pay the Jubjub its dues—pay homage, that is, to the pressures of sex in all its passionate, disturbing forms.

Yet even that seething power is based on mathematical laws—on an infrastructure of equations and symmetrical proportion, which is the very matrix of matter.

[124]

"You boil it in sawdust: you salt it in glue.
You condense it with locusts and tape:
Still keeping one principal object in view—
To preserve its symmetrical shape."

Interpreted in gospel language, this might run: For verily I say unto you, that with *locuses* (or *loci)* and *tape measures* for sawing and glueing together the wooden rods to construct the framework of a regular polyhedron you discover the skeletal or X-ray image that shapes and controls the whole flighty enigma of the Jubjub.[41] Wrapped in this playful doubletalk is the same tremendous question at which Blake pounded:

And what shoulder, & what art,
Could twist the sinews of thy heart?
And when thy heart began to beat,
What dread hand? & what dread feet?

What the hammer? what the chain,
In what furnace was thy brain?
What the anvil? what dread grasp,
Dare its deadly terrors clasp?

Tyger, Tyger burning bright,
In the forests of the night:
What immortal hand or eye,
Dare frame thy fearful symmetry?[42]

This "perpetual passion" is no longer Christ's of "The Bellman's Song" ("for the saving of our souls") but the Jubjub's (for our bewilderment). The Jubjub's symmetry, not Christ's cross, now seems to align on a single intersection "charity" and "passion," those two key concepts of all hymns of atonement.

Sobs of "delight," after that *rite de passage,* are answered by "affectionate looks." For lovers' tears and lovers' songs without words confirm this intense, unorthodox companionship—or at-*one*-ment. Thus cannibal Butcher and his prey, like Ishmael and his South Sea cannibal at the Spouter-Inn, are mated:

How it is I know not; but there is no place like
a bed for confidential disclosures between friends.
Man and wife, they say, there open the very bottom
of their souls to each other; and some old couples
often lie and chat over old times till nearly morning.
Thus, then, in our heart's honeymoon, lay I and
Queequeq—a cosy, loving pair.[43]

And when quarrels arose—as one frequently finds
    Quarrels will, spite of every endeavour—
The song of the Jubjub recurred to their minds,
    And cemented their friendship for ever! [44]

"Be a man!" the Bellman had warned. But their return "hand-in-hand" confounded even him. Now *all* roles were reversed. Now he himself was "unmanned": only momentarily, of course, and not with nervous dread—not the Butcher's inferiority complex at all. With "noble emotion" he speaks the peroration in a formal thanksgiving: "This amply repays all the wearisome days/We have spent on the billowy ocean!"

But it is the Butcher who has the last word. His is the final recognition at their final appearance in that craggy landscape.

"There is Thingumbob shouting!" the Bellman said.
    "He is shouting like mad, only hark!
He is waving his hands, he is wagging his head,
    He has certainly found a Snark!"

They gazed in delight, while the Butcher exclaimed,
    "He was always a desperate wag!"
They beheld him—their Baker—their hero unnamed—
    On the top of a neighbouring crag. . . .

Now the Butcher is the unacknowledged hero. The dunce has passed his initiation with a new and heightened awareness,[45] while the Baker (their so-called hero) is reduced in ironic contrast, on his high-raised perch as melodramatic clown, to antihero. That jovial pun not only unsettles the Boojum in the gathering dusk (it may only just have had breakfast!), and so insures the rest of the crew,[46] but in delivering the peroration over the Baker pronounces his epitaph. For "Fry me!" or "Fritter my wig!" or "Toasted-cheese" (call him what you will) is "desperate" in the same sense as the Butcher had declared the Jubjub "a desperate bird." Perpetually overstewed like the Jubjub, overheated in his seven coats, he too lives "in perpetual passion." What the Butcher alone seems to recognize is that such boisterous impudence cries out for nervous dissipation; that the Baker's sexual heat—without mathematical insight, uncontrolled to affection—is doomed.

Of the Bellman's crew only the Butcher (with his ruff and yellow gloves) and the Baker (with his multiple coats and boots) could conceivably be ranged among the Jubjub's disciples, whose "taste in costume is entirely absurd—/It is ages ahead of the fashion." [47] With his mountain of lost luggage and lost identity, in fact, this desperate Baker seems as victimized by the Jubjub as the Butcher. As Baker of "Bridecake" exclusively, who was more exposed to its heart-piercing screech? The Butcher, with his "blissful" childhood memories, could overcome that awful shudder, but one must assume the Baker had an unhappy childhood. The Bellman unfortunately cut off the Freudian preliminaries:

"My father and mother were honest, though poor—"
"Skip all that!" cried the Bellman in haste.

Without a lost Eden of childhood memory, without his "forty-two boxes" even (of harmonious numbers), what could the Baker assert against that shrill assault? How could he mathematically tune that "scream" to a "voice," a "note," a "song"? The Butcher's algebraic formula

$$\frac{(x + 7 + 10)\ (1000 - 8)}{992} - 17 = x$$

is a triumphant, if irrelevant, proof of identity, that $X = X$; something of which the Baker, who had identified himself in terms of names and chattels (to his loss), was quite incapable. Harmony equals Number equals Identity equals Love. Each is related to each; and whoever attains one, attains all.

But the Baker attains none. Like the Beaver at its crisis, he "fairly lost heart, and outgrabe in despair," until quivering, quaking, desperately confused, his Snark becomes that ultimate dread, the all-encompassing mirror image, or expunging Boojum. The crew gaze their last at his sublime erection, at a pitch of shuddering passion that had originally set him off so courageously on his quest. Lacking is the symmetrical balance—that "musical tone" of the Bellman's cajoling presence, that hold on the ultimate woof and warp of existence. His terrible *disintegration* must be read in contrast to the Butcher's and the Beaver's idyll, reinaugurated forever in memory of the Jubjub's song, forever *cemented.* Thus the obvious Freudian significance of the Baker's final release with the disintegrating effect of a pent-up orgasm, as he collapses toward the Boojum in "a torrent of laughter and cheers": one moment "erect and sublime" on that neighboring crag; the next, "(as if stung by a spasm) plunge into a chasm." [48] As the Butcher's and the Beaver's inseparable friendship at the Jubjub's evening appearance proved sexual, so does the Baker's wild twilight collapse toward the Boojum. The creative and destructive forces of sex at root are one.

But that terrible disintegration must also be read in conjunction with the Banker's fate: whose "fit" precedes the Baker's; whose name is distinguishable by only a single letter. Compared to the Butcher, the Baker is antihero; compared to the Banker, the Baker is truly heroic. Both are "inspired with a courage." The Baker's is "perfect," however; the Banker's, mad. The oppressive "dread" of the one becomes "that fear-stricken yell" of the other. Terrorized by the Bandersnatch, the Banker offers cash—with a skip and a hop and a flop—till at last he faints, as the Baker had earlier fainted at the mere mention of the Boojum. "It is just as I feared!" declares the Bellman, solemnly mocking such fear. The nightmare visions of the one introduce the groveling terror of the other, as this snatch-and-grab raid on a Banker plays farcical prelude to the Baker's vanishing. His mad shouting, hand waving, and head wagging across that distance among those mountainous crags seems almost a parody at first, an exhilarating burlesque of the other's "senseless grimaces," word chants, and restless hands. Certainly the crew, which had viewed the Banker's transports with "horror," views the Baker's mysterious signaling "in delight"—until that awesome, sublimely mock-heroic disappearance.

Far from vanishing, the Banker (a Bandersnatch is no Boojum), merely turns blank, a sort of photographic negative, a black-and-white print in reverse: with black face (for white) and white waistcoat (for black) in perpetual "full evening dress" jibbering *con imbecillità*.[49]

> Down he sank in a chair—ran his hands through his hair
> And chanted in mimsiest tones
> Words whose utter inanity proved his insanity,
> While he rattled a couple of bones.

So white turns black; a rich man, poor man; and the Banker, on that pivotal B, to Mr. Bones playing his black-and-white minstrel castanets whose hollow rattle picks up from his prattle clickety-click, clickety-click *ad infinitum*.

Such is the range and complexity of this great poem that seems at times almost a meditation on some of those earlier heroic voyages by Carroll's American contemporaries—Herman Melville and Edgar Allan Poe. The Baker, in the end, seems not so much like another Ishmael or Ahab as another Arthur Gordon Pym swept across that mysterious polar vanishing point of white light; the Banker with his castanets seems like nothing so much as a wittily revised version of Melville's poor demented Negro, the *Pequod*'s bellboy, little Pip![50] Wholly explicable nevertheless on its own portmanteau terms, as Carroll's "Preface" makes clear, *The Hunting of the Snark* needs no external clues nor allegorical key, but like *Moby-Dick* (its closest analogue) is symbolically self-contained, concealing its own best and sufficient commentary.

NOTES

1. W. H. Auden, *The Enchafèd Flood* (New York: Random House, 1950).

2. Robert Martin Adams, *Nil, Episodes in the Literary Conquest of Void during the Nineteenth Century* (New York: Oxford Univ. Press, 1966), Chs. 4 and 6.

3. "Parodie rageuse ou seulement réminiscences lointaines, ordonnées (cela va de soi) sans souci de parallélisme strict, dans la sérénité d'un divertissement détaché?" Marcel Marnat, "Du serquin au cachalot blanc," in *Lewis Carroll*, ed. Henri Parisot (Paris: Cahier de L'Herne, 1971), p. 132.

4. "Symbole pour symbole, il double le sien et le Boujeum est d'autant plus terrible qu'on ne l'a jamais vu." Marnat, p. 131.

5. "Il n'a pu le faire qu'avec vertige, avec passion. Mais aussi un terrible malaise. . . ." Marnat, p. 130.

6. To Nathaniel Hawthorne, 17 November 1851, *The Letters of Herman Melville,* ed. M. R. Davis and W. H. Gilman (New Haven: Yale Univ. Press, 1960), p. 142.

7. Lewis Carroll, *Pillow Problems, and other Mathematical Trifles* (London, 1893).

8. Carroll, "Alice on the Stage," *The Theatre,* April 1887.

9. *The Diaries of Lewis Carroll,* ed. Roger Lancelyn Green (London: Cassell, 1953), II, p. 345.

10. "The last level of metaphor in the ALICE books," Martin Gardner concludes, "is this: that life, viewed rationally and without illusion, appears to be a nonsense tale told by an idiot mathematician." *The Annotated Alice* (New York: Clarkson N. Potter, 1960), p. 15.

11. As Beatrice Hatch claims on the authority of Lewis Carroll himself: *Strand Magazine,* April 1898, pp. 413–23.

12. By Stephen Barr in *The Annotated Snark,* ed. Martin Gardner (New York: Simon and Schuster, 1962), p. 45. All recent readers owe a special debt to Martin Gardner's edition, reprinted by Penguin Books in 1967. Future references to *The Hunting of the Snark* are to this edition.

13. To Florence Balfour, 6 April 1876, *A Selection from the Letters of Lewis Carroll to his Child-Friends,* ed. Evelyn M. Hatch (London: Macmillan, 1933), p. 98.

14. To Mary Brown, 2 March 1880, Hatch, p. 165.

15. *Moby-Dick,* Ch. 45. All references to *Moby-Dick* are quoted from *Moby-Dick,* ed. Harold Beaver (London: Penguin Books, 1972). In deference to the large number of editions in use, I cite chapter number only, not page.

16. 8 January 1852, *Letters,* p. 146.

17. Carroll, "Alice on the Stage," *The Theatre,* April 1887.

18. To "The Lowrie Children," 1896, Hatch, p. 243.

19. *Moby-Dick,* Ch. 42, "The Whiteness of the Whale." Most of the preceding paragraph is quoted from my introduction to the Penguin edition of *Moby-Dick.*

20. *The Works of Lewis Carroll,* ed. Roger Lancelyn Green (London: Paul Hamlyn, 1965), p. 854.

21. Alexander L. Taylor, *The White Knight* (Edinburgh: Oliver and Boyd, 1952), p. 159.

22. *The Oxford Book of Carols* (London: Oxford Univ. Press, 1928, rpt. 1964), No. 46. "The Bellman's Song," a popular favorite, was frequently reprinted in broadside form during the eighteenth and nineteenth centuries.

23. Snarkophilus Snobbs, alias F. C. S. Schiller, in the parody issue, *Mind!,* 1901, though absurdly identifying the Butcher with Mohammedanism and the Banker with Judaism, more or less lighted on this key: "In the leading figure, that of the *Bellman* we easily recognize *Christianity,* the bell being the characteristically Christian implement, and the hegemony of humanity being equally obvious." In this context, I also like Snobbs's comment on the opening stanza:

> "Just the place for a Snark!" the Bellman cried,
>   As he landed his crew with care;
> Supporting each man on the top of the tide
>   By a finger entwined in his hair.

"The meaning evidently is that Christianity 'touches the highest part of man and supports us from above.' "

24. Shakespeare, *As You Like It,* V, iii, 27 ff.

25. Since Lewis Carroll so carefully vetted–and vetoed–the illustrations, I assume, with Henry Holiday, that the uncle's "last words" were literally pronounced on his death bed.

26. F. C. S. Schiller in the parody issue *Mind!*

27. *The Annotated Snark,* p. 28.

28. *Sylvie and Bruno Concluded* (1893), Ch. 11. The passage is quoted by Martin Gardner in *The Annotated Snark,* p. 57.

29. *Moby-Dick,* Ch. 42.

30. "The voice of the turtle" (*Song of Solomon* ii, 12) becoming Watts's "the voice of the sluggard" (1715), which Lewis Carroll first parodied in "The Lobster Quadrille" (*Alice in Wonderland,* Ch. 10). See Martin Gardner, *The Annotated Alice,* pp. 139–40.

31. Letter to Nathaniel Hawthorne, 1851 April 16, *Letters,* p. 125.

32. *The Annotated Snark,* p. 51.

33. Unlike the Butcher, who will triumphantly master the Bellman's triple repetition, the Baker wildly overshoots that score (to the Bellman's alarm) first by a fourfold, then desperately raised to a sixfold, repeated stake.

34. *Moby-Dick,* Ch. 41.

35. *Moby-Dick,* Ch. 49, "The Hyena." See my Commentary, pp. 798–99.

36. For their common origin in another macabre voyage of the nursery, cf.

> Rub-a-dub-dub,
>
> Three men in a tub,
>
> And how do you think they got there?
>
> The Butcher, the Baker, the Candlestick-maker,
>
> They all jumped out of a rotten potato.
>
> 'Twas enough to make a man stare!

37. *The Enchafèd Flood,* pp. 86–87.

38. Henry Holiday, "The Snark's Significance," *The Academy,* 29 January 1898. Lewis Carroll, that is, rejected Holiday's fine illustration of the Boojum as some kind of monstrous, bloated, maniacal walrus.

39. *Nil,* p. 98.

40. Succeeding where Ahab, the Baker's analogue, so dismally and suicidally fails: "All visible objects, man, are but as pasteboard masks. But in each event–in the living act, the undoubted deed–there, some unknown but still reasoning thing puts forth the mouldings of its features from behind the unreasoning mask. If man will strike, strike through the mask!" *Moby-Dick,* Ch. 36.

41. I accept and follow the geometrical interpretation given to this concluding stanza by John Leech. See *The Annotated Snark,* p. 81.

42. William Blake, "The Tyger," *Songs of Experience,* 1794.

43. *Moby-Dick,* Ch. 10, "A Bosom Friend."

44. I am assuming, of course, that the Butcher and the Beaver, in Martin Gardner's phrase, "became a pair of ship buddies." In an otherwise masculine crew, the Beaver is certainly odd man out–always neutrally referred to by Carroll as "it." The idea that

the Beaver might actually be feminine must have been influenced by the illustrations. For it was Henry Holiday who first added those whimsical touches of elevating "care" and "hope" to the status of female allegories. (Carroll at first demurred, but was completely won over. See "The Snark's Significance.") It was a small leap, then, for a reviewer like Andrew Lang to conclude that Holiday's "drawing of the Beaver sitting at her bobbins is very satisfactory, the natural shyness of the Beaver in the presence of the Butcher being admirably rendered." (*The Academy,* 8 April 1876.)

But Lang was peculiarly unresponsive to the poem. For the Butcher and the Beaver, though natural antagonists, from the start showed affinities: both "shy," both easily moved to tears, both stupid looking, both independently hitting on the same ingenious, foolhardy plan. Despite the blood-curdling image that he projects, it is the Butcher who starts nervously fussing and dressing up at the Bellman's signal for action, while "the Beaver went simply galumphing about"–galloping triumphantly, that is, portmanteau-style. The Beaver too, in the Bellman's judgment, had often "saved them from wreck." In fact, after the Butcher's epiphany into the nature of number (and number of nature), their mutual discrepancies became more rather than less acute than that obvious antagonism of the opening. Thus their occasional quarrels. At the climax the Beaver is still as physically restless as ever, "bounding along on the tip of its tail," while the Butcher is enrolled as ship's wag. An intellectual now, he can patronize the Beaver's "poor brains" and worse schooling with an affectionate bid at popularization. Though the Beaver's disarming confession that "It had learnt in ten minutes far more than all books/Would have taught it in seventy years," suggests its own sudden surge of mathematical virtuosity in converting the biblical "three score and ten," or lifetime, to exactly seventy.

45. The Butcher may even have been meant to spoof that other illiterate butcher–from Wagga Wagga, New South Wales–the Tichborne claimant. A bit of farcical icing, at any rate, was provided by Henry Holiday, who clearly caricatured Edward Kenealy, the claimant's counsel, in the role of the Barrister.

46. As Martin Gardner proposed: *The Annotated Snark,* p. 94.

47. The maker of Bonnets and Hoods, though a man of fashion, is himself most soberly dressed in Holiday's illustration.

48. Cf. Ahab's heroic pose: "when, with body arched back, and both arms lengthwise high-lifted to the poise, he darted his fierce iron..." *Moby-Dick,* Ch. 135.

49. Printed on the sheet music lying upside down at the Banker's feet in Holiday's design.

50.   "Leave him here to his fate–it is getting so late!"
                       The Bellman exclaimed in a fright.

Cf. black Pip, that "timorous wight," so "gloomy-jolly" deserted by Stubb: another Mr. Tambo with his tambourine singing snatches of *Old King Crow;* another fearful coward crazed in a confusion of black and white; another "castaway."

The *Sylvie and Bruno* Books as Victorian Novel

BY EDMUND MILLER

THE *Sylvie and Bruno* BOOKS TOGETHER FORM LEWIS CARROLL'S MOST AMBITIOUS literary work. Yet the general public is hardly aware of its existence. This is a great shame, for the work is more interesting and rewarding than it is generally given credit for being. While perhaps not a great work or an ideally conceived one, it contains many delightful examples of Carroll's brand of nonsense and is unique in the Carroll canon in that that consistently attempts to address an adult audience. The antiutopia of Outland, the charming escapism of Elfland (Fairyland), and the witty and significant talk of Elveston (England) are separately interesting.[1] However, full appreciation and understanding of the *Sylvie and Bruno* books depends on seeing that they are based on a carefully articulated plan.

The volume titled *Sylvie and Bruno* was published in 1889, and *Sylvie and Bruno Concluded* was published in 1893. This publication history perhaps gives the impression that Carroll first wrote *Sylvie and Bruno,* that is, Volume I of the full work, as a self-contained work and then produced a sequel four years later. But his own story of the writing is of a general assembling between 1885 and 1889 of substantially the whole of the two volumes. He had been gathering material with a book in view for many years; he claims to have done very little new writing when he came to put these pieces together. It was the great length of the completed manuscript that dictated the two-part publication. We know certainly that some of the illustrations that go with Volume II were among the first illustrator Harry Furniss worked up in consultation with Carroll.[2] The narrative (the plot is summarized in note 1) is continuous between the two volumes, and many incidents of Volume I find their natural resolution in Volume II. Carroll has also developed an elaborate pattern of character parallels that unifies the work stylistically.[3]

But I think it is worthwhile to make the point that Volume I is not complete as it stands. Carroll describes it as having a "*sort* of conclusion," which he supposed had fooled all but one of his little girl friends when the volume was originally published by itself. But surely readers of ordinary sensibility would not think a work complete that ended without an overturning of the misrule of the Sub-Warden. And Arthur's sort of conclusion in deciding to set out for India is acceptable only in his personal history. The narrative needs a resolution of Lady Muriel's feelings as well. Yet at the end of Volume I we feel very strongly that Lady Muriel cannot bear to hear Eric talk to her of love despite his official status as her fiancé: "But Lady Muriel heard him not: something had gone wrong with her glove, which entirely engrossed her attention." (I.xxii.467)

Carroll clearly intended us to have a single work in two volumes called *Sylvie and Bruno*. The diverse materials of this book are all rather neatly interwoven. There *are* minor discrepancies. Bruno, the son of the Elf king, should probably not report himself the servant of Oberon or say that he can sneak somebody into that king's hall because he knows one of the waiters, as he does in "Bruno's Revenge." (I.xv.398, 402) And the Narrator should certainly not condescendingly address the reader as a Child, as he does suddenly in "Fairy-Sylvie."[4] (I.xiv.389) But such discrepancies chiefly involve details in a number of self-contained early stories Carroll has incorporated, stories that inspired the longer work but are not always perfectly consistent with it. Discrepancies do not typically involve details of the English and Outlandish plot or the transition from Volume I to Volume II.

II

The whole *Sylvie and Bruno* deserves special critical study of a structural sort. There are thematic implications to the elaborate method of storytelling Carroll has adopted. The great technical skill with which he manages the constant movement between dream and reality is generally acknowledged.[5] But I think many readers are unhappy that Carroll chose so often to drift away from the nonsense of Outland and the antiutopia of Mein Herr's other world, and I do not think such readers have typically considered what is illustrated thematically by the very process of this constant movement from one kind of reality to another.

In the *Alice* books we may say that nonsense exists for its own sake. Perhaps one reason for the lesser popularity of *Sylvie and Bruno* is that Carroll was not content simply to copy himself in this genre, a point he makes in the Preface to Volume I. The *Alice* books have a structure of dream and a texture of nonsense. *Sylvie and Bruno* has the texture of dream itself. It presents dreaming, the various states of eeriness Carroll tabulates in the Preface to Volume II, much the way the *Alice* books present nonsense. Nonsense may be said to have a higher order of logical consistency than ordinary reality. At least, the way nonsense works is by assuming a higher order of logical consistency than the complexities of our everyday language commonly allow.[6] There *are* many and wonderful nonsense details in *Sylvie and Bruno,* but these have a different feel than the nonsense details of the *Alice* books. There often seems to be an insistent moral purpose to the *Sylvie and Bruno* nonsense. The *Alice* books are about another reality. In them dream has taken us outside normal reality to a place where we agree to suspend normal expectations. A new logic confronts us with its rigorous but alien consistencies. And we know we are dreaming. The plot is in fact resolved only by a waking up.

Sylvie and Bruno makes no such simple leap to another reality. It concerns the borderline between dreaming and waking, but there is no confrontation. The first line of the dedicatory poem suggests a theme: "Is all our Life, then, but a dream. . . ?" We learn in the course of the work that the rigorous logic of nonsense is not so unreal after all. Of course, we also learn that the events of life work themselves out with unreal rightness in the end even in the "real" world. Normal expectations are shown to be underestimations of the power of love to influence events. A character such as Arthur Forester could not enter the world of either *Alice* without destroying the dream. The problem is that he is too logical. He operates in the same way that nonsense characters do, by taking problems to their logical extreme. But the problems are themselves real problems under real rules in his case. That is, the problems are real *moral* problems. And neither he nor Carroll questions the rules of Victorian Christianity under which moral decisions are to be made. In fact, Arthur often makes us go back and reexamine the full meaning of the rule. Through him we see the assumptions behind the normal expectations of our moral universe. He lectures us wittily on everything—and usually knows what he is talking about.

In a sense Carroll even finally chips away at our expectations of what nonsense itself should amount to. Bruno functions as a normal nonsense character. He is also logically consistent. But through him we see the assumptions behind the most normal things in our natural world, rather than as with Arthur in our moral universe. Bruno talks "real" nonsense. He is the one who can see "about a thousand and four" pigs in a field because, though he cannot be sure about the thousand, it is just the four he can be sure about. (II.v.565) He is the one who can see *"nuffin!"* in the box of Black Light ("It were too dark!") because, as the Professor explains, that is exactly what the untrained eye would see. (II.xxi.713)

Mein Herr, the Professor as he appears in the real-world scenes at Elveston, to some extent fuses nonsense and moral purpose. He might even be seen as returning the absolute consistencies of logic to the real world when he inevitably enters that world. On his planet they do everything the English way—but they go all the way. They try the two-party system, for example, not only in politics but in life, dividing their farmers and soldiers into teams of those who try to get the work done and those who try to prevent the others from doing it. Coming from the nonsense world of extreme logic and logical extremes, Mein Herr sometimes seems absurd to the characters of the real world who are incompletely educated to the moral purposes of the universe, as when Lady Muriel asks him to explain the curious experiments he participated in to try to improve dinner-party conversation. She, of course, thinks he is merely talking about "small-talk," but the whole point of the bizarre series of experiments is that people do not talk to each other enough about serious things. The real world needs the higher logic of Mein Herr just as it needs the invisible matchmaking of Sylvie and Bruno and the circle ruled by Sylvie's Jewel.

The logical nonsense of Mein Herr skirts the arbitrary abandon so appropriate to the two worlds of the *Alice* books by requiring us to think about the meaning of things in the real world. This is nicely shown in the incident of Fortunatus's Purse, an imaginative literary use by Carroll of the mathematical conception of the Klein bottle. We are familiar with the Möbius strip, a closed band with a half-twist in it that has the peculiar property of being a single continuous surface with only one side. The Klein bottle is the extension of this conception to an additional dimension. It is a single continuous surface without inside or outside. Mein Herr suggests that Lady Muriel construct Fortunatus's Purse, a purse with all the world's riches in it, by sewing handkerchiefs together in a particular way. The first step is to make two handkerchiefs into a Möbius strip with a slit for the mouth of the purse. When Lady Muriel has done this, Mein Herr tells her that now all she has to do is sew a third handkerchief to the four exposed sides and she will have a purse of which the inside is continuous with the outside. Lady Muriel, having grasped the principle, puts the purse aside for final sewing up after tea. (II.vii.577–79) She is wise to do so, for the two-dimensional curiosity of the Möbius strip can assume a tangible physicality in our world, but the Klein bottle exists only in the fantasies of non-Euclidian geometers.[7]

Mein Herr presents Lady Muriel and us with the conception of inside as outside. But Lady Muriel's discretion avoids a confrontation between logic and reality. Fortunatus's Purse both exists in the real world and does not. All the riches of the world are available to those who love. The task Carroll set for himself in *Sylvie and Bruno* was to sensitize his readers to this sort of hyper-reality. Fortunatus's Purse may be taken as an emblem of the theme of the work, that love is teachable and its power is boundless. We must learn to reach the depths of love contained in Fortunatus's Purse. And this love is all around us if we know how to look for it aright.

In the *Alice* books dream may be seen as an escape from our normal reality. Dream has a more psychologically sophisticated (or adult) function in *Sylvie and Bruno*. The Red God dreams a new game of creation, but the reader is quite awake through it all—or at least confident that he *can* awake to reality. But *Sylvie and Bruno* is contrived to make it much more difficult for the reader to maintain this sort of psychical distance from the material.[8] He drifts in and out of Fairyland with the Narrator. Thus he is gradually taught to understand that the limits of reality are blurred, that it is not so easy to say that this is the world of reality while that is the world of nonsense and fantasy. Ruth Berman has plausibly suggested that what she calls the dullness of the English scenes ("earnestness" would perhaps be more relevant and charitable) has a structural significance at least for the modern reader of the novel in making the Fairyland and particularly the Outland scenes seem more lively, more free, and finally more "real" in contrast.[9]

Dreaming functions in *Sylvie and Bruno* as problem solving—as it often does in life. Dreams can restructure reality by omitting, changing, and adding details so that we can work out at least partial solutions to the continuing problems we have in the real world. This can sometimes be materially helpful, and it can often be psychologically helpful. In *Sylvie and Bruno* the characters of dream are vitally necessary to the solving of problems in the real world. Because they are, the work becomes a flux of reality and dream. It is no accident that here we find Carroll inventing the Time Machine (he is several years before Wells[10]). An Outlandish Watch would be pointless in Wonderland because there we have lost all sense of what time it "really" is; the Mad Hatter's watch "doesn't tell what o'clock it is." But real time and eerie time exist simultaneously in the world of *Sylvie and Bruno,* and Carroll means for us to discover that neither is all there is. Reality is not enough; we need nonsense too. Drifting into a world of fantasy is not an escape from reality but a significant education about the nature of life. And reality is not an escape from nonsense. Our education goes on everywhere. Arthur teaches us most directly, but there are professors everywhere in this work (and college officers, the Warden and Sub-Warden). And it is only natural that the Narrator's dreams discover Bruno at his lessons, twiddling his eyes to see what letters do not spell, for example, and then seeing in EVIL only LIVE backwards. (II.i.529) Eric Lindon learns the greatest lesson, that God answers prayer. This too is a lesson of love. And if we do not learn the lesson of love ... why, we turn into porcupines.

III

That *Sylvie and Bruno* attempts to show the playful underside of a rather prim moral and religious view of reality, that it illustrates what we might call a leavening of reality with nonsense, has probably been understood by everyone who has read it. But the complementary point seems to have been equally important to Carroll, and perhaps too many readers come to the book from the *Alice*'s with fixed expectations. Do we want to hear that nonsense sometimes has to give place to reality, to a Carrollian reality of moral platitudes and sentimentality? And Carroll's moral view of reality does seem to be the source of our trouble. Side by side with his nonsense, Carroll presents an ostensibly real world whose values are sentimental and where events fall out according to the artifices of romance. The plot that animates and coordinates the two worlds is certainly a romance.

The genuine weaknesses of the novel for modern tastes all have to do with its nature as Victorian romance. There is, of course, a kind of general sentimentality to the whole treatment of love and religion. But there are also, admittedly, occasions when Carroll is rather more insistent than he should be even on his own terms if the book is to stand alone and actually demonstrate its theme of love and not simply proclaim it. An instance occurs when the Narrator has described Lady Muriel as "all that is good":

> "—and sweet," Arthur went on, "and pure, and self-denying, and true-hearted, and—" he broke off hastily, as if he could not trust himself to say more on a subject so sacred and so precious. Silence followed: and I leaned back drowsily in my easy-chair, filled with bright and beautiful imaginings of Arthur and his lady-love, and of all the peace and happiness in store for them. (I.vi.330)

Most such sentimental excursions occur, however, in the fairy material. Somehow when Sylvie and Bruno pass through the Garden Door of Outland into the larger Fairyland beyond, Carroll seems to lose his sense of proportions and to give over his novelist's task of evoking emotional response. This is a common enough lapse for a Victorian novelist; Dickens lapses this way all too often. What is interesting is that in *Sylvie and Bruno* Carroll also on occasion manages to satirize what is conventionally sentimentalized. At one point Arthur is asked if he will not allow that someone is a sweet girl. He answers, "Oh, certainly. As sweet as *eau sucrée*, if you choose—and nearly as interesting!" (II.x.611) While there is much in Dickens that is not sentimental, I do not recall any incident that actually questions the sentimental system of values.

While we may not enjoy Carroll's Victorian sentimentality in this book, we can at least see that it is there for a definite purpose. This is a heavily moral book. It is a perennially difficult task for the writer to make his good characters interesting; Carroll has at least attempted to give some substantive life to his world of good. There is even a kind of narrative plausibility to his sentimentalizing of Sylvie. I find Sylvie the least rounded and least satisfactory of the main characters.[11] The ending of the book could serve nicely as a *locus classicus* of Victorian sentimentality about feminine sweetness. The Narrator listens for a word from "Sylvie's sweet lips" but thinks that he hears instead "not Sylvie's but an angel's voice . . . whispering." (II.xxv.749) Yet is not such a characterization of Sylvie as angel better justified by the plot and theme of this book than, for example, the similar characterization of Agnes Wickfield in *David Copperfield?* Sylvie is in fact a supernatural being who exists to do good. The whole order of fairies exists in the book to show us in outline the workings of love. Sylvie's Jewel is merely the physical embodiment of a psychological truth for Carroll: "For I'm sure it is nothing but Love!" (II.xix.693) The legend of the Jewel is both Sylvie will love all and all will love Sylvie (we cannot tell which) because to love is to be loved. The plot should be seen as a real attempt to demonstrate this point.

The sophisticated modern reader is almost bound to be unhappy with such a qualitative resolution of plot. He has nothing against love, but he would rather see it growing out of plot than magically justifying the most agreeable but unlikely developments. The resurrection of Arthur is like something out of Mrs. Radcliffe. But Carroll obviously did not see it that way. There is certainly a moral purpose behind his vision. And this sort of moral plot manipulation was a common feature of the Victorian novel. Carroll's contrivance is really rather clean and direct compared to the long-missing heirs and mistaken identities of Dickens.

But of course we do not usually come to *Sylvie and Bruno* from *Our Mutual Friend*. We come from the *Alice* books with the expectation of nonsense. And there is enough to reward our expectation so that we do not reshape it but rather find the book interesting in parts and not quite right. If we saw *Sylvie and Bruno* in its proper context as a Victorian novel, it would not be *Bleak House* or *Vanity Fair* or *The Egoist* because it is obviously not in the mainstream of novelistic development. But it does bear comparison, structurally, with *Wuthering Heights*. It is even more daring structurally. Both works are infused with the sentiments of the age and yet combine traditional materials in completely original ways.

And like the plot of *Wuthering Heights,* the plot of *Sylvie and Bruno* is pure romance. *Wuthering Heights* is a psychological study of the power of passion. But the conclusion of the plot, when it comes, is still a happy marriage that incidentally resolves the inheritance of two estates. *Sylvie and Bruno* ends with the conversion of the godless, the metamorphosis of the loveless, the resurrection of the good, and the reuniting of lovers. The complications that delay the righting of the universe in each novel also owe a lot to the tradition of romance. Romance multiplies improbabilities and coincidences to show the underlying neatness of a cosmic plan—exactly the way David Goldknopf has so astutely shown to be typical of the Victorian novel.[12] Emily Brontë's young Cathy must symmetrically marry her cousins on both sides to resolve the passions of the senior generation, something the girl can only have the power to do because she was born into a family with such a neat genealogy. Carroll's Arthur must die to live—to live happily ever after with Lady Muriel in the knowledge that Eric has found God.

To say that *Sylvie and Bruno* is a romance in this sense means that it is a proof through narrative that reality has the moral purpose we wish it did. Such books exist to tell us what life cannot. To put the matter in the sharpest perspective, we may quote Miss Prism in *The Importance of Being Earnest:* "The good ended happily, and the bad unhappily. That is what Fiction means." Such a view of reality is implied by *Sylvie and Bruno,* implied structurally as well as thematically. The good do end happily, but the plot of the book exists almost exclusively for the morality. The characters are less important for themselves than because they illustrate the moral. Of course, the texture of the book, the texture of dream movement between Fairyland

and the world of reality, often diverts us, sugarcoats the pill. But events are being manipulated to make a point about the way things should work out in the real world. That is the whole reason why things do happen in the book. And the fact that things do work out as they do is explicitly attributed to the power of a higher Providence than the Narrator's art. "I *know* that God answers prayer!" (I.xxv.501)

The test here is surely the supposed death and miraculous salvation of Arthur. We get to see Lady Muriel's faith bring her through the loss of her lover on their very wedding day. But then the high-comedy lovers get a second chance, and we know that when Arthur recovers they will have a perfect marriage of love.[13] Of course the grave objection may be made to such a plot that reality seldom illustrates either perfect grief or happy marriage. This is, in substance, exactly the objection always made to romance (but it isn't true!). If we consider this manipulation of plot for moral purpose against the background of Victorian fiction, we see that Carroll is not only well within the limits of good form but also exercising considerable literary skill to keep the sentimentality in bounds. Arthur's death is handled with a good deal more restraint than the death of Barkis or of Paul Dombey, to pick places where Dickens succeeds beautifully in his gamble for our emotional commitment. The death of Mr. Dorrit's brother is such a muddle of sentimentality and abstraction that one is not even sure it is a death scene. The interminable death of Little Nell is, of course, the classic excess. In contrast, the supposed death of Carroll's Arthur is only inferred by the reader from a newspaper clipping. When it is presented to us, the clipping makes the event seem the properly cold and arbitrary work of fate. But in retrospect the newspaper format serves the more important function of justifying the misleading information. The Narrator did not commit himself to the death. Mistakes themselves are a kind of reality. The reader is tempted to complain that he has been cheated, but his complaints ring hollow in his own mind. We are tricked but not exactly lied to. Both the seeming death and the discovery are plausibly presented. The plan is out of fashion, but it is worked expertly. Even the Narrator's disgust when he believes that Lady Muriel has too hastily agreed to marry Eric after Arthur's death is worked expertly as narrative. We may cringe when he quotes *Hamlet* to himself, "The funeral baked meats did coldly furnish forth the marriage-tables." (II.xxv.744) But we also feel that the quotation as well as the sentiment is appropriate to the Narrator. His opinion *would be* both passionate and literary—and he would keep it to himself.

The whole romance structure of the work builds toward this religious validation of Arthur's supposed death. It is thus interesting that, in his notes on the drawings for *Sylvie and Bruno,* Carroll suggested Furniss draw Arthur as he would "King Arthur when he first met Guinevere."[14] That the *event* is arbitrary is not a flaw but a consequence of the moral point proved by it, that love can work miracles. By the standards of moral contrivance in the Victorian novel it works very well. It is a good deal less surprising than Oliver Twist's genealogy or the blinding of Mr. Rochester or the ability of Tess of the d'Urbervilles to sleep through a sexual assault. The magic of Sylvie's Jewel simply works to tie the resurrection of Arthur to the various changes we have made and can make between eeriness and reality; it is one more transmigration from one world to another coexistent world. In this way Sylvie's Jewel performs its magic to make *Sylvie and Bruno* a single work structurally and a Victorian novel. This is in contrast to the *Alice* books, which share many elements of point of view with each other and some of these at times with *Sylvie and Bruno* but are contained by their separate dreams. The antiutopia of *Through the Looking-Glass* is very obviously structured within its dream of a chess problem. This chess problem is completely arbitrary and so does a wonderful job of organizing everything else in the nonsense book. In contrast, the incident of Arthur's resurrection is structurally arbitrary but demonstrates miraculously the morality expounded by its book. And so it is, in a higher sense, the inevitable culmination of the plot.

IV

We might also profitably consider the sensibleness of *Sylvie and Bruno* as part of the Victorian character of moral earnestness. Of course nonsense is a variety of logic. But *Sylvie and Bruno* also contains a lot of serious talk well expressed, serious talk that might be called socially aware. Arthur is, for example, presenting a serious and worthwhile analysis when he argues that the introduction of small stakes in card games raises the whole moral tone of the enterprise by discouraging cheating (because we take all money matters seriously) and by consequently making what cheating does occur seem repugnant rather than amusing. He recommends the introduction of betting as a cure for the silliness of croquet matches. (II.ix.597) On a number of occasions Arthur calls our attention to the difficulties of making conventional moral judgments. Victories over equal temptations, he argues, can have very different effects for the world because of irrelevant differences in environment. (II.viii.590) "If we once begin to go back beyond the fact that the *present* owner of certain property came by it honestly, and to ask whether any previous owner, in past ages, got it by fraud, would any property be secure?" (II.iii.545) Arthur is clearly Carroll's *raisonneur* despite the tentative disclaimer in the Preface to Volume II, "I do *not* hold myself responsible for *any* of the opinions expressed by the characters in my book." Nevertheless, he cannot help remarking that he sometimes feels a great sympathy for one of Arthur's arguments. Carroll does not go so far with the aesthetic principle as more modern authors. And other characters sometimes speak with Arthur's voice of earnestness. It is the Earl, for example, who argues that we should take our pleasures quickly so that we can get more of them into life—though his suggestion of listening to music played at seven times its normal speed is perhaps not the most convincing conceivable. (I.xxii.471) But Carroll's personality and thinking are clearly more a part of the personality of Arthur than they are of even the Narrator, the "Mister Sir" of Bruno, who is learning about the structure of life and so needs labels for everything.

It sometimes seems quite clear that Carroll's social conscience guided him in selecting many of the incidents for this work—a work Carroll says "... had to grow out of the incidents, not the incidents out of the story." Carroll's concern with social causes is parallel to Dickens's. He is not against people who adopt causes. But he is very much against simple moral equations. This we see very clearly in the incident of the Anti-Teetotal Card, which says *That's where all the money comes from!* in answer to the Teetotal Card's *That's where all the money goes to!* Arthur's analogy of giving up sleeping to set an example for people who oversleep (II.ix.599–601) shows us the importance of analyzing the problem of drinking to excess as a problem not of drink but of excess.

If anything, Carroll is too much in earnest. The particular suggestions made along the way in the work are often nonsense—betting on croquet matches, high-speed music appreciation, discontinuing overpricing at charity bazaars to cut down on moral self-satisfaction—are often nonsense or at least of no abiding importance. But the principles these suggestions force us to consider are always terribly in earnest and useful in helping us make ethical or moral discriminations. It is ironic that Carroll, who refused to play chess with bishops in nonsense books, should have felt it necessary in the preface to Volume II of *Sylvie and Bruno* to answer the charge of having in the person of Arthur condemned most sermons as foolish. (I.xix.436) It is precisely because he was one of the few people wishing to take sermons seriously that he was able to have Arthur voice the complaint. Many preachers *do* misuse their privilege from interruption to talk twaddle. Again we may doubt that Carroll's solution—less frequent sermons—would answer to the problem now or would have answered to it in his own day. Unless we become, like the seventeenth century, an age that wants to learn from sermons and is perhaps even willing to pay lecturers for extra series in the evening, we are not likely to get good sermons no matter how infrequent.

Carroll's earnestness is one of the defining characteristics of *Sylvie and Bruno*. The fairy material may, in fact, even be seen as existing in the work only because of his earnest religious orientation. We have remarked Carroll's use of Victorian romance but we may go perhaps a step further and say that his specifically religious explanation of the workings of fate marks this work, despite its late date, as of the spirit of the *early* Victorian novel. Goldknopf has pointed out how a gradual reluctance develops in Dickens to attribute the fortuitous determinism of plot to God. By the time we reach Hardy, there is no God—or rather Hardy has taken over the work of God.[15] And the direction of the modern novel has been to eliminate improbability and coincidence from plot because it no longer wants to give them the necessary moral justification. In *Sylvie and Bruno* Carroll has all the faith in coincidence of Charlotte Brontë. He knows that God orders our lives with love, and he humbly draws back from presuming to speak for God. Because he is a gentleman in religion, he creates the middle world of Fairyland to express the workings of fate. But we know his real characters are finally in the hands of God.

NOTES

1. Since the substance of these books is certainly nowhere near so familiar to the general reader as the stories of Carroll's other major works, a plot summary may be helpful:

The Outland country of Fairyland, we discover as the story begins, is in political flux. The Warden of Outland (who is also King of Elfland), though a saintly man with great power for good, is nonresident. His brother the Sub-Warden arranges through subterfuge and a false report of the Warden's death to have himself elected Emperor, setting aside also the hereditary rights of the Warden's cute young son Bruno in favor of Uggug, his own selfish son. Bruno is being taught goodness by his sister Sylvie. He rebels against the formalities of lessons, but his logical thinking is wonderfully advanced for a boy so young and his heart is full of love, especially for Sylvie. Having ascertained the really great extent of love in the hearts of these two children, a Beggar reveals himself to them as their father and gives Sylvie a magic Jewel to help them grow even further in love. All this history of Fairyland is revealed to the Narrator, an unnamed London lawyer or businessman, in various eerie trances during a country visit to his old friend Dr. Arthur Forester at Elveston. The Narrator meets the charming Lady Muriel Orme, Arthur's beloved. Arthur has just come into money, but he will not speak to Lady Muriel of marriage because he thinks she is in love with her cousin, Captain Eric Lindon. It is obvious Lady Muriel cannot love Eric because he has no religious convictions, yet she is worried about his soul and feels herself promised to him. Soon after Sylvie and Bruno have materialized as children in order to do works of love, the dashing Eric shows his mettle by rescuing Bruno as he is about to be hit by a train. When Eric receives a long-awaited military promotion, he claims his bride. Arthur thinks this is for the best, perhaps, since Eric will have the religious model he needs. Arthur has decided to go to India as Volume I ends.

Volume II *(Sylvie and Bruno Concluded)* begins several months later with the Narrator's discovery that Eric, in deference to Lady Muriel's religious scruples, has released her unconditionally from any obligation to him. However, she is fearful that he has released her under duress until she talks the point over with the Narrator. Arthur has hesitated to press his own suit in the circumstances. But, with the fairy help of Sylvie and Bruno and the collusion of the Narrator, the lovers quickly come together. The fairies also bring about the reformation of a drunkard and do other good works in the neighborhood. When plague breaks out in the harbor town, Arthur hurriedly marries Lady Muriel and then goes off the same morning to help. When it is all over, a newspaper clipping reports his heroic death. On his next visit to Elveston, the Narrator finds that Lady Muriel's faith has remained unshaken by the tragedy and that she also can experience the eerie state. Together they overhear Sylvie and Bruno singing about the secret of love. In Outland events reach a climax at a banquet to celebrate Uggug's birthday. The Warden-Beggar-Elfking returns and seems to cast a spell of remorse over his brother, who is left as Emperor of the place. But Prince Uggug, because he has lived without love, turns into a porcupine. In Elveston Arthur is suddenly and miraculously discovered among the survivors of the plague. He was, in fact, rescued by Eric, who now knows that there is a God who answers prayers. The work ends as the Elfking helps his children understand the magic Jewel better and thus see that to love is to be loved.

2. Carroll has a substantial discussion of the process of writing the book in the Preface to Volume II. My references will be to volume (I, *Sylvie and Bruno* proper; II, *Sylvie and Bruno Concluded*) and chapter, and also include page numbers from the most easily accessible edition, the Modern Library (New York: Random House, n.d.). Confirmation of Carroll's story of the writing is provided by the Diaries and by Stuart Dodgson Collingwood, *The Life and Letters of Lewis Carroll* (1898; rpt. Detroit: Gale Research, 1967), p. 259.

3. The character parallels are among the most commented-on features of the work: Ruth Berman, *Patterns of Unification in Sylvie & Bruno* (Baltimore: [T. & K. Graphics], 1974), pp. 4–10; Alexander L. Taylor, *The White Knight* (London: Oliver & Boyd, 1952), p. 191; Phyllis Greenacre, *Swift and Carroll* (New York: International Universities Press, 1955), p. 199.

4. In a letter to a Mrs. Ritchie dated 24 October 1887, reprinted in Derek Hudson, *Lewis Carroll* (London: Constable, 1954), p. 285, Carroll refers to his work in progress as "one single book (a story, but for rather older readers than 'Alice')." I think Carroll was, in fact, writing a novel and not a children's book at all. A work in which the characters make jokes involving Latin tags and casually use words like *oscillations, zoöphytic, adiposity, isochronous, fallible, bonhommie,* and *rumination* is for older children indeed. Whether the fairy material is necessarily for children or not, it is certainly inconsistent with the point of view maintained by the rest of the work for the Narrator to take any notice of the reader at all.

5. See especially Greenacre, p. 194. Hudson has some interesting notes on the possible influence of the work's point of view, pp. 288–89.

6. The reader will recognize my theoretical debt to Elizabeth Sewell in this passage, *The Structure of Poetry* (London: Routledge & Kegan Paul, 1951), especially Ch. 7, "Order and Disorder," pp. 44–58.

7. Carroll's use of the Klein bottle here has been called to our attention by Martin Gardner in his "Mathematical Games" column, "The Games and Puzzles of Lewis Carroll, and the Answers to February's Problems," *Scientific American,* 202, 4 (March 1960), p. 172.

8. The classical study of psychical distance in literature is Edward Bullough, "Psychical Distance as a Factor in Art and an Aesthetic Principle," *British Journal of Psychology,* 5 (1912–1913), pp. 87–118.

9. Berman, p. 15.

10. Lin Carter, "Have Time, Will Travel!" *Fantastic Universe,* 7 (January 1960), p. 99.

11. Critics often assert that the fairy characters in the book are well rounded and the English characters are dull. Even Ruth Berman, who has been so careful to show us that "the line between excellence and failure in *Sylvie and Bruno* by no means coincides with the line between fantasy and realism," p. 4, sometimes seems to make this mistake. To me the contrast between Lady Muriel and Sylvie shows a striking exception to the usual generalization. Lady Muriel is charming and intelligent, and in her religious scruples about her engagement she has a real depth of character. But Sylvie does comparatively little to evoke all the sweet verbiage lavished on her. Of course, the fairies *are* generally more interesting. And Bruno is the most lively character in the book.

12. *The Life of the Novel* (Chicago and London: University of Chicago Press, 1972), pp. 100–124, 159–76.

13. I cannot agree with Phyllis Greenacre that we feel Arthur's bout with the plague has rendered him sexless, pp. 196, 219. Unlike Mr. Rochester, who is too overwhelming to make a satisfactory husband without some degree of emasculation, Arthur is all along Carroll's ideal husband. The function of the plague episode is not to change Arthur but to change Eric–and incidentally to bring out certain qualities in Lady Muriel. I think that in her concentration on the implication of the book for a study of Carroll's own psychology Dr. Greenacre has sometimes misrepresented its subtlety as a literary work. There is, for example, nothing villainous about Eric from the beginning–he is simply without faith. His heroism in saving Bruno from the train suggests that Carroll tried to make him as good a man as it is possible to be without faith. And his conversion is in the quality of his life, not in its outward direction; he is not making any plans as the book ends to convert the heathens in emulation of Carroll's brother Edwin. Cf. Greenacre, p. 196.

14. Letter quoted by Collingwood, p. 260.

15. Goldknopf, pp. 167–73.

Lewis Carroll as Artist:
Fifteen Unpublished Sketches
for the *Sylvie and Bruno* Books

Introduction
BY EDWARD GUILIANO

SKETCHING WAS A CONSTANT LOVE IN LEWIS CARROLL'S LIFE. HE ENJOYED TURNING out clever little humorous sketches, often adorned them to letters to his child friends, and treasured afternoons spent sketching a live model at a fellow artist's studio or in his own rooms. His drawings have survived from as early as 1841, when he was nine, right through to the last few years of his life in the 1890s. The duration of his interest in drawing, though not the quantity or overall quality of his output, rivals that of his interest in writing and greatly exceeds that of his other form of artistic expression, photography.

Most of Carroll's extant drawings are rough and lack technical expertise; nevertheless, some are clearly outstanding artistic achievements. Carroll had little formal training in drawing. Only late in life did he regularly submit his sketches for constructive criticism to an artist, Miss E. Gertrude Thomson, a friend and subsequent illustrator of his *Three Sunsets* (1898). He made do with enthusiasm and an awesome imagination. When he let his fanciful imagination reign, as in the early pen and ink sketches to *Mischmash* and *The Rectory Umbrella*—and also in many of the sketches published here for the first time—the results are fresh and delightful. His illustrations to *Alice's Adventures Under Ground,* many of which are reprinted and discussed in this volume, are his best-known drawings. They are among his finest works, and a few are superior to all other illustrations of *Alice.* However, when he sought to achieve realism, to accurately mirror nature, as apparent in Figure 7 and in the portraits he produced late in life, the results lack distinguishing qualities.

Carroll's best drawings, like his best literary efforts, tapped deep springs of imagination that seem inconsistent with the outward appearance and manners of the Reverend Charles Lutwidge Dodgson. We do not expect expressions of violence and nastiness from him, but they are there in the *Alice* books and in his illustrations, although not in his photographs. His photographic achievements derive from a different artistic impulse: a quest for purity and beauty. This drive, rather at odds with the impulse toward the grotesque evident in his drawings and writing, is more in harmony with the personality of Dodgson and with Victorian standards. It is not surprising that Carroll's contemporaries admired his photographs while his talent for drawing was not so much appreciated. According to Stuart Dodgson Collingwood, John Ruskin, the most influential art critic of the age (from whom Carroll regularly sought advice), advised him that his talent was not sufficient to merit devoting much time to sketching. Today, however, with our widened artistic outlook, we are not bothered by anatomical abnormalities in drawings. On the contrary, we are often attracted to the grotesque and so are free to admire Carroll's special talent.

In his middle and late years, Carroll turned more actively and consciously to the pursuit of beauty, first through portrait photography, including nude studies, and then through figure drawing. During this period he came to place an exceptionally high premium on drawing from life. While his quest for beauty and his faith in working from the visually concrete produced superior photographs, it regularly denied the freely flowing imagination that was the source of his best drawings. His insistence upon drawing from models led not only to a deterioration in the quality of many of his drawings but to awkward if not strained relationships with his illustrators. He repeatedly pressed his collaborators to draw from life; he suggested models, sent scores of photographs and letters filled with suggestions and criticisms. It is curious that among his many excellent illustrators only the preeminent Tenniel declared, as reported in a letter from Carroll to Gertrude Thomson, that he no more needed a model than Carroll should need a multiplication table to work a mathematics problem.

Carroll's relationships with his illustrators were complex, and the accounts of their histories are both engaging and entertaining. Tenniel found Carroll overly fastidious, and as many readers will recall, he declined initial offers to illustrate *Through the Looking-Glass.* Only after months of persuasion did he reluctantly consent.

Harry Furniss, looking back after seven years of successful collaboration with Carroll, enjoyed repeating that Tenniel was among the artists who declared that Furniss would not work with Carroll for seven weeks. Tenniel had warned Furniss that Carroll was "impossible." Carroll and Furniss, both eccentrics, got on well. Furniss put up with a great deal. Although he once quit the job he had undertaken for Carroll after a drawing was rejected, only to revoke his decision a few days later, he ultimately termed their relationship splendid.

While Carroll was exacting and hard to please, he was also exceptionally sensitive to many of the needs of his illustrators. He was extremely understanding about delays and generously remunerated them for their work. Perhaps the most telling example of Carroll's concern is the famous story of the first printing of *Alice in Wonderland*. Tenniel was dissatisfied with the printing of the pictures when the book was initially published, and Carroll recalled the edition and at considerable personal expense had the entire book reset.

Harry Furniss's long collaboration on the *Sylvie and Bruno* books began in 1885. On March 9, Carroll wrote to Furniss, whom he described in his diary as "a very clever illustrator in *Punch*." Carroll asked if he would be open to proposals to do drawings for him. Furniss accepted immediately. When the *Sylvie and Bruno* books were published after more than twenty years of sporadic work on Carroll's part, the forty-four illustrations in each volume were the result of painstaking, intense collaboration between author and artist. Carroll literally had his hand in every stage of every drawing. "He subjected every illustration, when finished, to a minute examination under a magnifying glass," wrote Furniss (*Some Victorian Men*, [1924], p. 78). "His practice was to take a square inch of drawing, count the lines I had made in that space, and compare their number with those on a square inch of an illustration made for *Alice* by Tenniel! And in due course I would receive a long essay on the subject from Dodgson the mathematician."

Carroll visited Furniss regularly to discuss the illustrations, particularly in the early going when they certainly shared ideas and made many decisions. They supplemented their meetings with piles of letters, sometimes corresponding for months about the face of just one character. Carroll's letters, as always most exacting, convey a good number of criticisms, corrections, and sketches showing Furniss what he had in mind. Furniss took Carroll's suggestions seriously. According to Morton Cohen, editor of Carroll's letters, chunks of the letters to Furniss are missing apparently because Furniss cut out the parts he wanted to use in making a new picture or correction and brought them with him to his worktable.

The fifteen pen-and-ink sketches by Lewis Carroll that follow are taken from the Carroll-Furniss correspondence. They are exact reproductions made from manuscripts now owned by the Lilly Library, Indiana University. All but two are preliminary to a published version by Furniss. I have identified the position intended for each sketch by citing the appropriate page in the first editions of *Sylvie and Bruno* (Macmillan, 1889) and *Sylvie and Bruno Concluded* (Macmillan, 1893).

Carroll was well pleased with Furniss's final illustrations, calling them "wonderful" in the preface to *Sylvie and Bruno Concluded*. They are definitely good, well-drafted drawings. The illustrations to the realistic portions of the story are highly creditable renderings in the Victorian society-novel tradition. The lively, clever drawings for the fairy-world portions, poems, and songs are equally fine. However, putting Carroll's rough sketches alongside Furniss's polished drawings, one cannot help but think there is an extra spark in Carroll's art and that his sketches have lost nothing to time.

Certainly the accomplished drawings of Carroll's professional illustrators did more to promote his books in the late nineteenth century than his own awkward sketches could; still, one wishes after seeing these *Sylvie and Bruno* sketches and after his promising illustrations for *Alice* that he had done more of his own illustration.

Discarded preliminary sketch of Uggug "blubbering loudly," S&B, *p. 39*

Preliminary sketch of "How Cheerfully the Bond He Signed!" S&B, *p. 144*

Preliminary sketch of "Poor Peter Shuddered in Despair," S&B, *p. 147*

p. 51. [Ch. XVI.] Crocodile walking *along* fourd its own
forehead along its own back

It is a difficult subject!

yours very sincerely
C. L. Dodgson.

Preliminary sketches of "A Changed Crocodile," S&B, p. 229 (*This one reproduction is a slight reduction of Carroll's manuscript.*)

Each in his mouth a living

Preliminary sketches of "Those Aged Ones Waxed Gay," S&B, *p. 252*

Lerring bone

26/11/86

Preliminary sketch of "Three Badgers on a Mossy Stone," S&B, p. 247

19/8/90

[T.O.]

Preliminary sketch of "Mein Herr's Fairy-Friends," S&BC, *p. 248*

"NEVER!" yelled Tottles. And he meant it.

31/8/89.

Preliminary sketch of " 'Never!' Yelled Tottles," S&BC, *p. 248*

Preliminary sketch of "Long Ceremonious Calls," S&BC, *p. 266*

Preliminary sketch of "The Voices," S&BC, *p. 248*

"That so tenderly sat down beside her."

3.

Discarded preliminary sketch of "Tenderly sat down beside her," S&BC, *p. 268*

Preliminary sketch of "Horrid Was That Pig's Despair!" S&BC, *p. 268*

Oh, horrid was that Pig's despair!

Preliminary sketch of "The Fatal Jump," S&BC, *p. 362*

3.

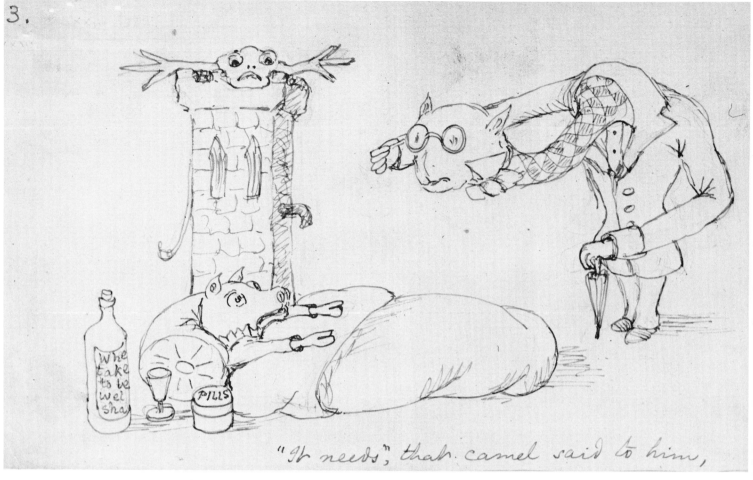

Preliminary sketch of "That Pig Lay Still As Any Stone," S&BC, *p. 362*

Preliminary sketch of "Still He Sits in Miserie," S&BC, *p. 373*

Lewis Carroll the Pre-Raphaelite "Fainting in Coils"

BY JEFFREY STERN

Our image of the Pre-Raphaelites is that of a group of young revolution-ary painters, determinedly archaic at times, often libertine, immoral, and dangerously explorative. Our image of C. L. Dodgson is that of a retiring, stammering, celibate cleric, a stalwart of the English Establishment. How can these images superimpose, even if we admit exaggeration? How can Carroll be considered a Pre-Raphaelite?

One primary error in forming our image of Carroll and in attempting to understand his creativity is neglecting to focus on C. L. Dodgson's most creative years—c. 1860–76. And even when we do so we must still be selective. The diaries are a catalogue of boredom if taken as a whole, and yet they give glimpses of extraordinary days, showing Carroll's involvement with his contemporaries, especially poets and painters.[1] Indeed, he was as enthusiastic about the visual arts as was his heroine: " 'And what is the use of a book,' thought Alice, 'without pictures.' " Alice adds, of course, "or conversations"—and Carroll here too was eager, especially when the conversations were with eminent Victorians. He spoke with and watched painters, bought reproductions of their work, photographed original pictures, gave pictures their titles, made suggestions and criticisms, and visited art schools.[2] He knew, among others, Tenniel, Furniss, Crane, Watts, Holman Hunt, Woolner, Collins, Leighton, Paton, Hughes, Prinsep, Munro, Doyle, Millais, Rossetti, and Ruskin. He owned prints and books about paintings as well as original drawings and paintings.[3]

Among the latter was an original oil by Arthur Hughes, "The Lady with the Lilacs," which was purchased in 1863 and will be discussed later in this article. It is not, after all, enough to say that Carroll knew this or that person, painting, or idea; the important question is "what was the effect?" In order to show this we will look at just two of the artists Carroll knew—D. G. Rossetti and Arthur Hughes—and a few pictures.

II

It has been recognized for some time that Rossetti was obsessed by a particular image, a particular female face (see Figs. 1–5; *cf.* 6), this coming from a Spenserian belief that "soule is forme and doth the bodie make." J. D. Hunt argues this case:

> Pre-Raphaelite ideal beauty has often been described as 'soulful'. But the gibe contains an important truth: for Rossetti, a beautiful woman *was* an image of his soul. This ideal beauty dominates his poems and paintings because much of his work, introspective at its best, seeks in her features an adequate mode of articulation.[4]

Fig. 1. Dante Gabriel Rossetti, "Ecce Ancilla Domini!" Oil, 28⅝ x 16½ inches, 1850 (Tate Gallery, London)

Fig. 2. Dante Gabriel Rossetti, "Joan of Arc," Oil, 28½ x 26 inches, 1863 (Mrs. C. B. Scully, U.S.A.)

Fig. 3. Dante Gabriel Rossetti, "Lady Lilith," Oil, 1868 (version of painting in Bancroft Collection, Wilmington Society of Fine Arts, Delaware, U.S.A.)

Fig. 4. Dante Gabriel Rossetti, "Fair Rosamund," Oil, 20½ x 16½ inches, 1861 (National Museum of Wales, Cardiff)

Fig. 5. Dante Gabriel Rossetti, "Bocca Baciata," Oil, 13¼ x 12 inches, 1859 (Mrs. Suzette M. Zarcher)

Fig. 6. Tenniel, Alice Infringes Rule Forty-Two, "All persons more than a mile high to leave the court" (Alice's Adventures in Wonderland, *Ch. 12)*

As early as 1856 his sister Christina Rossetti had arrived at a similar conclusion in her poem "In an Artist's Studio":

> One face looks out from all his canvases,
> One selfsame figure sits or walks or leans:
> We found her hidden just behind those screens,
> That mirror gave back all her loveliness.
> A queen in opal or in ruby dress,
> A nameless girl in freshest summer-greens,
> A saint, an angel—every canvas means
> The same one meaning, neither more nor less.
> He feeds upon her face by day and night,
> And she with true kind eyes looks back on him,
> Fair as the moon and joyful as the light:
> Not wan with waiting, not with sorrow dim;
> Not as she is, but was when hope shone bright;
> Not as she is, but as she fills his dream.[5]

And we find that Carroll at certain frankly nostalgic moments, as here in the terminal poem to *Through the Looking-Glass,* confessed to the same kind of obsession with an image and a type: "Still she haunts me, phantomwise,/Alice moving under skies/Never seen by waking eyes . . ."[6]

Perhaps, despite the anguish that will now flicker across my reader's face, one of the most productive ways in which to understand such a phenomenon is to attempt an explanation from a basic Jungian viewpoint. Even in simplest psychoanalytical terms, such obsessions with a person or personality resembling no one living individual is, for the Jungian school at least, usually categorized as the appearance of the "anima"– the eternal feminine, the ideal woman, or (most significantly for Carroll) the "woman of one's dreams." Any actual discrepancy between the real and ideal would not be noticed by the dreamer or obsessed person, so that Alice is seen as an angel instead of a child who doubtless had the real imperfections that all children do. The vital point is that Carroll's manuscript drawings of Alice for *Alice's Adventures Under Ground* look nothing like Alice Liddell.

Similarly, according to Holman Hunt, Rossetti significantly converted the truth about *his* model to his own needs:

> Rossetti's tendency ... in sketching a face was to convert the features of his sitter to his favourite ideal type, and if he finished on these lines, the drawing was extremely charming, but you had to make-believe a good deal to see the likeness, while if the sitter's features would not lend themselves to the preordained form, he, when time allowed, went through a stage of reluctant twisting of lines and quantities to make the drawing satisfactory.[7]

Jungians trace the anima to the great female figures in history, literature, mythology, and the Bible: to Helen of Troy, Venus, Lilith, Beatrice, Joan of Arc, Ophelia, the Virgin Mary (all of these, incidentally, are subjects of Rossetti paintings; see Figs. 2 and 3, for example) and so on. Each is a personification or deification–or both–of an exclusively feminine quality as seen by the men who created them. As such, so the Jungian theory goes, they are expressions of the suppressed feminine part of the male voiced in these myths and stories, and they often occur in dreams in order to maintain a personal psychological equilibrium. Certainly one might suppose that some process of this kind was observed by the acute Christina Rossetti in her brother, and is what she meant by the lines: "A saint, an angel–every canvas means/ The same one meaning, neither more nor less/ He feeds upon her face by day and night/ And she ... looks back on him/ ... Not as she is, but as she fills his dream."

To Jungians the anima (along with much else in our dreams) represents a quality in *ourselves*. We do not necessarily create the anima image because we are threatened by or attracted to the female; we sometimes dream of the female in order to explain the femininity we feel. Thus we can dream, if male, of the feminine qualities that exert an influence upon our personal lives and behavior and are in everyday life repressed and made subordinate to the overt role and position. The anima personifies feminine psychological states such as prophetic power, the irrational urge, the relation to the unconscious world. If female, then the anim*us* is a feature of our dreams, and for similar reasons.[8]

What light does this kind of theory throw on Rossetti and, more importantly here, on Carroll? Certainly Rossetti spent much of his time painting portraits of the anima in many obvious manifestations that mostly looked alike (although none the less impressive for that). Certainly it also would seem that Carroll's friendship with those countless little girls did allow legitimate expression of an often female tenderness on his part toward them, and a chance to enter into the world of (female) childhood unreason, and to escape from his severely guarded male world of strict logical sense. But is there any connection between Rossetti and Carroll in this respect—and are their images of the ideal feminine soul related?

We know from Carroll's diaries that in 1863 he spent some time in Rossetti's studio:

> Oct: 6. (Tu). Went over to Mr. Rossetti's, and began unpacking the camera, etc. . . . [After taking portrait photographs of the Rossetti family] I looked through a huge volume of drawings some of which I am to photograph—a great treat, as I had never seen such exquisite drawings before. I dined with Mr. Rossetti, and spent some of the evening there. . . . A memorable day.
>
> Oct: 7. (W). Spent the day at Mr. Rossetti's photographing. . . .
>
> Oct: 8. (Th). Was at work most of the day photographing drawings of Mr. Rossetti's.

Some of the photographs evidently came out well, for Carroll received a letter shortly afterward from Christina Rossetti asking for fifty photographs (many of them duplicates), including five of her brother's sketches.[9] It is difficult to know just what of Rossetti's work Carroll did photograph as Christina's description is unclear, and presumably in any case Carroll took many more shots than just the five since on October 8 he spent most of the day photographing Rossetti's drawings. The Gernsheim Collection of Lewis Carroll's photograph albums at the Humanities Research Center at the University of Texas does have one photograph identified by Carroll (in his hand in the index of the album) as a drawing by Rossetti (see Fig. 7). There is also a print of a Rossetti drawing in another album. We shall consider their significance shortly, but with this imprecision about which particular sketches (apart from the two in the Gernsheim Collection) Carroll did photograph, it may be more illuminating to look at the general effect of his contact with Rossetti at this time, and then look for a possible influence from particular paintings.

As a major piece of circumstantial evidence, we find the following details about the composition and execution of the manuscript *Alice's Adventures Under Ground* entered in Carroll's hand on a blank page in the ninth volume of the manuscript diaries:

Fig. 7. Photograph by Carroll of a drawing by D. G. Rossetti in Album III *(picture 7), Courtesy of the Gernsheim Collection, The Humanities Research Center, The University of Texas at Austin. The original drawing is 2¾ x 3¼ inches and is identified as Rossetti's in Carroll's own hand in the index of the album.*

It was first told July 4 (F.) 1862.
Headings written out (on my way to London) July 5, 1862.
MS copy begun Nov. 13 (Th.) 1862.
Text (of *Alice's Adventures Under Ground)* finished before Feb. 10, 1863.
Pictures in MS finished Sept. 13 (Tu.) 1864.
MS finally sent to Alice, Nov. 26, 1864.

Effectively this means that Carroll had been in Rossetti's studio and photographed some of his work *before* he illustrated (though after he wrote) the embryonic *Alice in Wonderland.* Crucially this fact perhaps explains why Alice in Carroll's manuscript looks absolutely nothing like Alice Liddell. How else can we account for the fact that Alice in the manuscript has long, waved, luxurious hair, large sad eyes, and a pursed melancholic mouth (see Fig. 9) when, in fact, Alice Liddell had short straight hair and a rather impish face? Carroll's image is, it seems, unmistakably less like Alice Liddell and more like Rossetti's image of, for example, "Helen of Troy" (a painting still in his studio in 1863—see Fig. 8). It is even more certainly like Rossetti's drawing "Miss Miller," a print of which he owned (see Fig. 10)—i.e., the visualization of the anima. The Gernsheim Collection photograph and print also might have been taken/ collected by Carroll because they corresponded with both his and Rossetti's ideas about the perfect image of the female soul.

Fig. 8. Dante Gabriel Rossetti, "Helen of Troy," Oil, 12¼ x 10½ inches, 1863 (Kunsthalle, Hamburg)

Fig. 9. Lewis Carroll's own illustration of Alice in White Rabbit's house for Alice's Adventures Under Ground

Fig. 10. Print of a Rossetti drawing initialed "DGR" and dated 1860 from Carroll's photograph album "(A.) III" in the Gernsheim Collection, Humanities Research Center, The University of Texas at Austin. The print is titled "Miss Miller."

This resemblance between images may be more than merely coincidental in another important way if the face of Alice/Helen is considered in the light of what is known about the original model who sat for both "Helen of Troy" and the Rossetti drawing in Carroll's album—Annie Miller. She epitomized much of what the Pre-Raphaelites and their followers thought about (and expected from) women. Rosalie Glynn Grylls writes:

> It all began with Holman Hunt who had used [Annie Miller] as a model for "The Awakened Conscience" and then decided that she was an innocent in danger of corruption whom it was his duty to save. To this end he undertook to pay for her education and to improve her health under a good doctor. . . . When she had been cured and educated, she was to be rewarded with a wedding ring.
>
> The Pre-Raphaelite group were particularly addicted to this form of matrimony; there was Maddox Brown and his Emma; Stephens and Clara (whom he later taught to write in school copybooks); Frederick Shields, a later friend, who was about as unsuccessful in his marriage with the sixteen-year-old Matilda Booth, as the better known "classic" cases of Watts and Ellen Terry, Ruskin and Effie Gray.
>
> It was part of the Victorian ethos, a passion for improvement that went with faith in progress. If a woman were succoured she would be grateful and become good and devoted to the man responsible.[10]

To say that the male desire to be Pygmalion is "part of the Victorian ethos" overstates the case, but there does seem to have been a good number of men who cast themselves in this role—particularly among the Pre-Raphaelite Brotherhood. Unlike the good fortune of the original Pygmalion and his sculpture, Annie was corrupted by her contact with artists and she never collected her wedding-ring reward from Hunt. During the years he left her so that she might become educated while he traveled to Palestine to paint "The Scapegoat," she used her increasingly eloquent charms to help herself to the enjoyment of a gay social life. She almost certainly had an affair with Rossetti and thereby caused the rift between him and Hunt, and she sat as a model (an infamous profession) for more artists than Hunt stipulated she could. Eventually she became Lord Ranelagh's mistress and was consequently loathed and scorned by Hunt on his return. Curiously enough, despite the soap opera, Annie's name is actually less well known than the other Pre-Raphaelite models (Lizzie Siddal, Effie Ruskin/Millais, and Jane Burden/Morris).

It seems somehow inadmissible that Carroll's innocent heroine should look so like such a notorious woman. Yet, as we have seen, it seems possible nevertheless to conclude that there are certain factors that they have in common. Though physically Annie meant more to Hunt and Rossetti than Alice meant to Carroll, it was above all the ideal and almost spiritual light in which both were viewed (so that Annie could hardly help cast a shadow) that makes their similar visual identity seem appropriate.

The vital similarity was that they were both seen as an intellectualized visualization of an emotional and psychological need. To men captivated by an image, it may also have been important for Annie and Alice to have been intellectually inferior to their admirers (as were Effie Gray, Ellen Terry, Emma Brown, Clara Shields, and Lizzie Siddal–as Rosalie Grylls has noted). For this idealization, moreover, the image rather than the actual person had to be submissive and as diametrically opposite in every possible way to the dreamer. The consequent gap between the loved image and the "lover" could then become an occasion for melancholy joy–at least as far as Carroll was concerned. He was wiser than his fellow idealists and never made the mistake of trying to marry his dreams,[11] as he makes clear in the introductory poem to *Through the Looking-Glass:*

> Child of the pure unclouded brow
> And dreaming eyes of wonder!
> Though time be fleet, and I and thou
> Are half a life asunder,
> Thy loving smile will surely hail
> The love-gift of a fairy-tale.

Carroll was wiser than his artist friends, for to have the love object always beyond grasp effectively meant that it became even more a symbol than a reality, and the idealist could be constantly gratified by the righteousness born of impeccable abstention mixed with chaste desire. It is perhaps irrelevant to note that Carroll's diaries are full of self-chastising prayers, and it is probably our corruptness that draws harmful conclusions from his pleas for purification of "this sinful heart ... this corrupt affection."[12] Such guilt was an inevitable reaction to the love that is central to his best work, but to assume that his love was not disinterested, or that it did not inform Carroll's creation at this time is as erroneous–and for very similar reasons–as to suppose that Rossetti's soulful women had nothing to do with his idealized sexual tastes as well as corresponding to his vision of the spiritual female. Just as Carroll must have detected the ambiguity of Rossetti's pictures where both divine and human passions are interlocked, so his contact with them might be said to have stirred his human love for Alice, or rather what she stood for, *and* stimulated his idealism to find an adequate expression for it. Their solution in any case was identical–they selected the female face that epitomized their preferred and adored image of heavenly and human beauty, and it turned out to be an almost identical image; "Not as she is, but was when hope shone bright;/Not as she is, but as she fills his dream."

III

In addition to Rossetti there was another artist in particular, Arthur Hughes, whom Carroll knew, admired, and was probably influenced by. Hughes's influence was very similar to Rossetti's in determining the way in which Alice is visualized.

Carroll first met Hughes on July 21, 1863, through the introduction of Alexander Munro, the sculptor. Carroll's interest in Hughes and his work had been aroused a year earlier when he saw some illustrations that had been done for George MacDonald. He noted in his diary (July 9, 1862) that he accompanied MacDonald "to a publisher with the MS of his fairy tale 'The Light Princess' in which he showed me some exquisite drawings by Hughes." (Hughes also illustrated a large number of other books by MacDonald, including *At the Back of the North Wind* and *Phantastes.)*

Fig. 11. Arthur Hughes, illustration for George MacDonald's At the Back of the North Wind *(1871), Ch. 36*

Fig. 12. Arthur Hughes, "Fancy," a drawing that first appeared in Good Words *in 1870*

Fig. 13. Arthur Hughes, illustration for George MacDonald's At the Back of the North Wind *(1871), Ch. 6*

Fig. 15. Arthur Hughes, "The Long Engagement," Oil, 41½ x 20½ inches (1859), Birmingham City Museum and Art Gallery, Birmingham, England

Fig. 14. Arthur Hughes, "April Love," Oil, 35 x 19½ inches (1855–56), Tate Gallery, London

These drawings are best described as uneven in quality, largely because they are often anatomically strange despite being imaginatively composed (see Figs. 11, 12, and 13). Percy Muir observes of these drawings: "There can be no doubt that . . . there was a very close and very special kind of sympathy between MacDonald and Hughes, especially in the fairy tales." (p. 144) Muir cites MacDonald's son Grenville's introduction to the 1905 edition of *Phantastes:*

I know of no other living artist who is capable of portraying the spirit of *Phantastes;* and every reader of this edition will, I believe, feel that the illustrations are a part of the romance, and will gain through them some perception of the brotherhood between George MacDonald and Arthur Hughes. . . .

In the same vein Forrest Reid in his standard *Illustrators of the Sixties* cites the occasional naïveté on Hughes's part as the laudable result of his entering into the childlike imagination celebrated by MacDonald's stories—a subtlety doubted by Muir, but which is certainly the very effect of Carroll's own illustrations to *Alice's Adventures Under Ground.* In these, for example, Derek Hudson in his biography of Carroll goes as far as discerning a "Blake-like intensity." Notwithstanding the hyperbole, Carroll's drawings do have an immediacy that Tenniel's hypercontrolled drawings lack; undoubtedly they also look at times distinctly Hughesian in their energies.

Perhaps most significant of all is the fact that the only important original painting that Carroll actually owned was Hughes's "The Lady with the Lilacs" [later renamed "Girl with Lilacs"] [13] (see Fig. 16). Relevant diary entries make clear that this was painted by Hughes in 1863 and bought by Carroll in the same year:

> Oct: 10 (Sat). Was at . . . Mr. Rossetti's . . . Mr. Munro and Mr. Arthur Hughes came in afterwards, and Mr. Hughes told me that the picture I bought of his is finished, and we arranged that he should bring it (as well as his children to be photographed) to the MacDonalds' on Monday.

> Oct: 12. (M). Mr. Hughes came over to be photographed with his children, and brought the picture I bought of him some time ago—"The Lady with the Lilacs." Got a splendid picture of him with Agnes [his daughter].

In the famous photograph taken by Carroll of his own study (it is reproduced in Collingwood's *Life and Letters* on p. 134 and elsewhere) this painting can be seen as being on the wall over the fireplace. Effectively this means that Hughes's painting (just like Rossetti's drawings and paintings) was freshly in Carroll's mind as he illustrated *Alice's Adventures Under Ground* for Alice Liddell. It therefore does not seem coincidental that there are certain obvious similarities between Alice and Hughes's lady with her lilacs in pose, dress, and especially in facial characteristics (see Figs. 16 and 17).

But, good though it is, Carroll was not merely following Hughes under the influence of this one picture alone. Rather, as before with Rossetti, Carroll was sympathetic to the point of imitation because Hughes's paintings were mostly variations on a single constant theme: the celebration of feminine innocence and fragility. This theme had an obvious and direct appeal to Carroll. In many paintings

Fig. 16. Arthur Hughes, "Girl with Lilacs," Oil, 44.5 cm. x 22.5 cm., 1863. Courtesy of the Art Gallery of Toronto. Painted for and once owned by Lewis Carroll

against the ceiling, and she stooped to
her neck from being broken, and
put down the bottle, saying to herself

quite
I hope
grow a
I wish
drunk

Ala
was to
she w
growin
growing
soon h
kneel
another minute there was not room ev
this, and she tried the effect of
down, with one elbow against the

Fig. 17. Lewis Carroll's own illustration of Alice for Alice's Adventures Under Ground

Hughes's preoccupation is with the essential fragile virginity; for example, see, "Ophelia" (1852); "The Long Engagement" (1859); "Madeleine" (c. 1860); "Mariana with Lute" (c. 1855); "Silver and Gold" (c. 1860); "Girl with Swans" (c. 1870); "Girl with Calf" (c. 1870); and "The Dangerous Path" (c. 1870). Despite obvious influence from his master Rossetti,[14] there is great distinction between their work. Rossetti's women are monumental and eternal; Hughes's are perfect, one feels, just for the moments in which they posed for him to paint them. This sense of imminent decay because of the inherent transience of the beautiful is conveyed by Hughes at his best—as in "April Love" (see Fig. 14) and "The Long Engagement" (see Fig. 15)—partly by the often overpowering colors. These were usually vivid greens and violet, serving to emphasize the subtle coloring of the faces of the people in the picture. Emblematically, therefore, the delicate portraits of the young women are often threatened like virginity itself by an encircling environment that can readily engulf and destroy them. It does not seem coincidental that Ruskin with his penchant for virgin beauty fixed on "April Love" in his *Academy Notes* for 1856, saying that it was: "Exquisite in every way; lovely in colour, most subtle in the quivering expression of the lips, and sweetness of the tender face, shaken, like a leaf by winds upon its dew, and hesitating back to peace."

Such quivering at the precise moment of change from innocence to commitment, from childhood to adulthood, is seen as the first step to decay, which once taken is irreversible. This is then surely also the quality of the saddest passage in *Through the Looking-Glass:*

> "Oh, please! There are some scented rushes!" Alice cried in a sudden transport of delight. "There really are—and *such* beauties! . . . may we wait and pick some?" Alice pleaded.
>
> . . . So the boat was left to drift down the stream as it would, till it glided gently in among the waving rushes. And then the little sleeves were carefully rolled up, and the little arms were plunged in elbow-deep, to get hold of the rushes a good long way down before breaking them off.
>
> "I only hope the boat won't tipple over!" she said to herself. "Oh, *what* a lovely one! Only I couldn't quite reach it." And it certainly *did* seem a little provoking ("almost as if it happened on purpose," she thought) that, though she managed to pick plenty of beautiful rushes as the boat glided by, there was always a more lovely one that she couldn't reach.
>
> "The prettiest are always further!" she said at last, with a sigh at the obstinacy of the rushes in growing so far off, as, with flushed cheeks and dripping hair and hands, she scrambled back into her place, and began to arrange her new-found treasures.
>
> What mattered it to her just then that the rushes had begun to fade, and to lose all their scent and beauty, from the very moment that she picked them? Even real scented rushes, you know, last only a very little

while—and these, being dream-rushes, melted away almost like snow, as they lay in heaps at her feet—but Alice hardly noticed this, there were so many other curious things to think about.... (pp. 256-57)

Though this passage stops short of the full implication of its gloomy conclusion, it remains the most explicit expression in the whole of Carroll's work of what was essentially both a dread of death *and* a delight in the contemplation of it, which is an attitude found, of course, not only in his writing but also in much else Victorian. Most importantly, it was Hughes's specialty.

More than simply being about the transience of life, such moments in Carroll's *Alice* books, and in many of the paintings that he saw and admired, are also vitally concerned with the proposition that growing up is itself a kind of death. Thus in one sense they celebrate the death of the chrysalis at the moment of birth of the butterfly. This certainly seems to be the dominant theme not only behind many of Hughes's best paintings but also of Rossetti's, such as "Ecce Ancilla Domini" (1849-50), (see Fig. 1); "The Girlhood of Mary Virgin" (1848-49); and even his simultaneous homage to Dante and tribute to his dead wife Elizabeth Siddal, "Beata Beatrix" (1863-65), which also looks beyond that death toward reincarnation. This theme can also be traced most explicitly in Millais's "Christ in the House of His Parents," where the blood and pain of the future crucifixion is already rehearsed in childhood—which is itself already saddened by the inevitable event. Millais manages to evoke this even more in his painting "Autumn Leaves," which brilliantly conveys the intuitively felt sadness that overshadows the four girls who sweep up autumn's debris. The unconsciousness, or at least only partial awareness, of the children in these pictures is the origin of their poignance. With a similar degree of sadness, Carroll recognized in his heroine just such a death of childhood, foreshadowing the difficulties of impending adulthood, as, for example, when she destroys her belief in the world behind the looking-glass:

> "I can't stand this any longer!" Alice cried as she jumped up and seized the table-cloth with both hands: one good pull, and plates, dishes, guests, and candles came crashing down together in a heap on the floor.
>
> "And as for *you*," she went on, turning fiercely on the Red Queen, whom she considered as the cause of all the mischief—but the Queen was no longer at her side—she had suddenly dwindled to the size of a little doll [...]
>
> "... As for *you*," she repeated, catching hold of the little creature in the very act of jumping over a bottle which had just lighted upon the table, "I'll shake you into a kitten, that I will!"

She took her off the table as she spoke, and shook her backwards and forwards with all her might.

The Red Queen made no resistance whatever; only her face grew very small, and her eyes got large and green: and still, as Alice went on shaking her, she kept growing shorter—and fatter—and softer—and rounder—and—

—and it really *was* a kitten, after all.

(*Looking-Glass,* pp. 336–39)

It is not so much that the world behind the glass is really so pleasant, for the frustrations of childhood are all there too. But because it cannot be reached again (just as Millais's young Christ will no longer be ignorant of pain after the event in the painting), this moment is one of anguish rather than liberation. In this context it does not seem mere coincidence that Shakespeare's Ophelia, the archetypal doomed virgin-heroine, was painted by no less than three of the artists whom Carroll knew and admired. It certainly seems probable that in so doing, Hughes, Rossetti, and Millais were all fired by a vision of threatened virgin beauty (literally on the brink of death in Hughes's picture) akin to Carroll's in his more intense moments of melancholia. These moments intrude only occasionally in the *Alice* books, as in the "scented rushes" sequence, but they do so repeatedly in *Sylvie and Bruno;* that is, they increased naturally enough as Carroll aged and are a sad testimony to his mounting disquiet about the fact of mortality. The death of Ophelia, or the metamorphosis of Alice from childhood to adulthood, are ways in which such a personal inevitability can be entertained in its most pleasing—because controlled—form, and is in a sense preparatory rather than anything else:

> . . . She waited for a few minutes to see if she was going to shrink any further: she felt a little nervous about this; "for it might end, you know," said Alice to herself, "in my going out altogether like a candle. I wonder what I should be like then?" And she tried to fancy what the flame of a candle looks like after the candle is blown out, for she could not remember ever having seen such a thing. . . .
>
> (*Wonderland,* p. 32)

What essentially is happening here is that Carroll (and the reader if he takes the point) is entertaining an otherwise difficult problem more easily because it is in abstracted symbolic form. If the symbolic event can be faced, then the reality is brought under some kind of control.

Such a mimetic purpose has, of course, always been one of art's functions, and yet it is perhaps significant to note that in a sense it reached its apotheosis with the Victorians and their so-called "narrative pictures." Raymond Lister points out that these pictures, often a vulgarization of the Hogarthian principles of narration, did speak "particularly to the condition of that age [since they] provided the bourgeois with his parables; he could look comfortably at the sad moral tales told by "The Last Day in the Old Home" and feel secure. . . ." [15] Alternatively, and more importantly, such a painting by its skillful emotional manipulation would tell the onlooker what it felt like to be in such a situation and either prepare him for it or warn him to keep away. That said, it can readily be seen that famous *memento mori* paintings such as Hughes's celebrated "Home from the Sea" (1863), where a young sailor boy lies by his mother's grave and weeps, or Landseer's "The Old Shepherd's Chief Mourner" (1837)—his faithful dog—or Windus's "Too Late" (1859)—among many, many others—prepare the onlooker for his own death, evoking and often exceeding the license of art in order to do so. Such blatant instruction is both the object of Carroll's satire *and* often his own purpose:

> "Crawling at your feet," said the Gnat (Alice drew her feet back in some alarm), "you may observe a Bread-and-Butterfly. Its wings are thin slices of Bread-and-Butter, its body is a crust, and its head is a lump of sugar."
>
> "What does *it* live on?"
>
> "Weak tea with cream in it."
>
> A new difficulty came into Alice's head. "Supposing it couldn't find any?" she suggested.
>
> "Then it would die, of course."
>
> "But that must happen very often," Alice remarked thoughtfully.
>
> "It always happens," said the Gnat.
>
> *(Looking-Glass,* p. 223)

It seems valid to conclude that although Carroll's comedy and delicacy of presentation here contrasts very favorably with the labored efforts of many painters whose work was well known to him and who tried to make the same point, there is an element of morbid delight in the fact that "it always happens." This inevitability, presented comically here by Carroll, was always a wholly serious subject for Arthur Hughes. Nevertheless, it was a mutual preoccupation, and the melancholic bittersweetness that gives Hughes's best work such power is also a quality never far away in Wonderland. It seems therefore predictable that Carroll liked Hughes's canvas of a melancholic maiden at the moment of imminent decay enough to buy it, proudly hang it on a wall of his study, and look admiringly up at it as he illustrated his masterpiece. It seems similarly fitting that Carroll responded to Rossetti's anima image and his world of ultimate beauty (just out of touch and half illusory, like scented rushes). Because portrayal of these emotions was a pressing Pre-Raphaelite concern, Carroll was more than a mere art gallery visitor; he was a Pre-Raphaelite.

NOTES

1. See *The Diaries of Lewis Carroll,* ed. Roger Lancelyn Green (London: Cassell, 1953), July 14, 1864, and April 18, 1865.
2. See *Diary,* September 29, 1856; November 21, 1857; October 6, 1863; April 8, 1865, and

April 9, 1867—which is an unpublished entry from the manuscript now in possession of the British Museum.

3. See *Dodgson Sale Catalogue* (short title for "Catalogue of the Furniture, Personal Effects and the Interesting and Valuable Library of Books . . . the property of the late Rev. C. L. Dodgson) (Oxford: Brooks, 1898), items 128, 271, 407, 417, 123–44, 237–96.

4. *The Pre-Raphaelite Inspiration 1848–1900* (London: Routledge & Paul, 1968), pp. 177–78.

5. *Poetical Works,* ed. W. M. Rossetti (London: MacMillan, 1904), p. 330.

6. All references to the *Alice* books are to the editions contained in Martin Gardner's *The Annotated Alice* (New York: Clarkson N. Potter, 1960).

7. *Pre-Raphaelitism and the Pre-Raphaelite Brotherhood* (London: Chapman and Hall, 1913), I, p. 341.

8. See J. A. Hadfield, *Dreams and Nightmare* (London: Pelican, 1961), p. 60f.

9. The letter is cited by Helmut Gernsheim in *Lewis Carroll—Photographer* (1949; rpt. New York: Dover, 1969), p. 55.

10. *Portrait of Rossetti* (London: MacDonald, 1964), p. 70. Also, though there is little resemblance between Rossetti's "Helen of Troy" and Hunt's "The Awakened Conscience," primarily since Hunt retouched the face and altered its expression (1856–57) for a buyer who found it too painful, it should be noted that Annie Miller was the original model for both.

11. Or can we believe Gernsheim's statement in the 1969 preface to the Dover edition of *Lewis Carroll—Photographer:* "I learned soon after the publication of my book [1949] from Alice's son, Wing Commander Caryl Hargreaves, that Lewis Carroll had wanted to marry his mother but had been rejected by her parents. . . ."

12. MS Diaries, June 5, 1866; many of the self-chastising prayers that appear in the original Diaries do not appear in Green's edited version.

13. Owned now by the Art Gallery of Toronto; oil on wood; 44.5 by 22.5 cm. and called by them "Girl with Lilacs." Collingwood notes, "Poetry, music, the drama, all delighted [Carroll], but pictures more than all put together. I remember his once showing me 'The Lady with the Lilacs,' which Arthur Hughes had painted for him, and how he dwelt with intense pleasure on the exquisite constrasts of colour which it contained—the gold hair of the girl standing out against the purple of lilac blossom." *(Life and Letters of Lewis Carroll,* London: Fisher Unwin, 1898), p. 362.

14. "Mariana with Lute," for example, is described by Leslie Cowan in the notes to his *Catalogue of the National Museum of Wales exhibition of Hughes' paintings* (October 1971) as being "so close to Rossetti's style that it can only be explained by his having painted it beside Rossetti and having shared the services of one of his models. It is known that in 1855 Hughes was painting in Rossetti's studio. . . ." One of the models used by Hughes was, incidentally, Annie Miller. There is also an obvious similarity between Rossetti's "anima" figure and that of Hughes.

15. *Victorian Narrative Paintings* (London: Museum Press, 1966), p. 10.

The Game of Logic:
A Game of Universes

BY ERNEST COUMET

Translated by Peter Heath

IT IS NO MYSTERY THAT LOGIC WAS ABLE TO SEDUCE AND ENTHRALL LEWIS CARROLL. He sought it only because he had already found it. The author of *Alice* was *already* a logician. But in construing these facts, agreement vanishes. Did the gray shadow of logic grow in the twilight of inspiration? Or conversely, was the motive for recourse to a hallowed discipline that of elucidating in full scientific clarity the questions confusedly asked in the literary works?

Since the end of the nineteenth century, logic has had so many faces that it is an elementary precaution of method to ask what logic we are talking about. As to the two works by Lewis Carroll, *The Game of Logic* and *Symbolic Logic,* I have already attempted to determine their sense and significance at the precise moment in the history of logic at which they appeared.[1] But a more insidious question arises about them: In what respect do they authenticate the pseudonymous signature that C. L. Dodgson adopts for the second of them? The answer, as I seek here to show, must be looked for more deeply than the in simple persistence of a tone and humor brought in from outside to enliven a forbidding subject matter and render it entertaining to young minds. The answer must be sought in symbolic logic itself.

Let me hand over the key to my reading at once: a term, namely, *"universe of discourse."* This term seems itself to propose its own commentary, so extraordinary has been the fortune of the word "universe" in the most varied fields, and especially in literary criticism, which speaks so readily of the universe of this creator or that. But I am actually thinking of a far more limited use of this expression, which arose and spread in the narrow field of the symbolic logic evolved by English logicians in the first half of the nineteenth century. Unlike such authors as John Venn and J. N. Keynes, by whom he was directly inspired, Lewis Carroll, whenever he deals with an elementary logical problem of syllogism or sorites, meticulously delimits its "universe of discourse." It is this apparently harmless mania whose implications I shall try to unravel.

When logicians "are putting the final touches to the grouping of their proposition, just before the curtain goes up, the copula—always a rather fussy 'heavy father'—asks them: 'Am *I* to have the "not," or will you tack it on to the predicate?' " [2]

Is logic a dramatized version of language? To all appearances, Lewis Carroll was adapting for the use of a juvenile public the know-how of the new stage directors. But was he, for all that, convinced by their *performance?*

II

The notion of a universe of discourse is due to Augustus De Morgan;[3] in order to designate it he coins a new expression ("inventing a new technical name") in connection with a critique directed at Aristotle on the subject of predicates of the type *not-man:* "The expression 'not-man,' " says Aristotle, "is not a noun. There is indeed no recognized term by which we may denote such an expression, for it is not a sentence or a denial. Let it then be called an indefinite noun . . . since [it applies] equally well to that which exists and to that which does not." [4] "I stated that the expression 'not-man' was not a noun, in the proper sense of the word, but an indefinite noun, denoting as it does in a sense a single thing." [5] De Morgan rejects such a distinction between names, appealing, remarkably enough, to the usage of everyday language, against the practice of the logicians, paradoxically restricted, in spite of appearances; whereas they feel they have elbowroom only in the entire universe of possible conceptions, they could and even should take more limited "universes" as their field of activity:

> It is not true that the aorist or indefinite character of the mere contrary actually exists in the use which we make of language. Writers on logic, it is true, do not find elbow-room enough in anything less than the whole universe of possible conceptions: but the universe of a particular assertion or argument may be limited in any matter expressed or understood. And this without limitation or alteration of any one rule of logic . . . By not dwelling upon this power of making what we may properly (inventing a new technical name) call the *universe* of a proposition, or of a name, matter of express definition, all rules remaining the same, writers on logic deprive themselves of much useful illustration. And more than this, they give an indefinite negative character to the *contrary,* as Aristotle did when he said that not-man was not the name of anything. Let the universe in question

be 'man': then *Briton* and *alien* are simple contraries; alien has no meaning of definition except not-Briton. But we cannot say that either term is positive or negative, except correlatively. As to a claim of right to be considered a prisoner of war, for instance, alien is the positive term, and Briton the negative one. We separate formal logic from language, if we refuse to admit this.[6]

A conversation is in progress; an intruder arrives, who wishes to contradict what he has just heard. "But we were talking of . . . ," he is promptly told.[7] Nothing could reveal more effectively than this reply the existence of a more or less extended sphere of thought and presupposition, in which every conversation is enclosed. Here is another counter-example, showing the necessity of not confusing distinct universes—one Lewis Carroll could have slipped into *Euclid and his Modern Rivals:*

> A proposition, false in the whole universe of thought, is true in the universe of the speaker's argument. The first sentence in Euclid is a marked instance: a point is that which has no part. My firm conviction that Euclid was a man and not a myth *has no part:* I cannot dichotomize it; is it then a point? Anyone can answer that Euclid was talking of space, not of historical beliefs and convictions: space and its laws are the universe of his book.[8]

It is in everyday conversation, "ordinary discourse," that the notion of a "universe of discourse" taps a power of suggestion that secures it admission as a natural condition of all use of language. This condition can just as plainly be discovered at the root of more elaborate forms of discourse, and is equally obeyed by the internal discourse whereby the thinking subject organizes his thoughts.

George Boole in his first work, *The Mathematical Analysis of Logic,* made an abrupt start to the enunciation of his principles by using the symbol 1 to represent the Universe: "Let us employ the symbol 1, or unity, to represent the Universe, and let us understand it as comprehending every conceivable class of objects whether actually existing or not. . . ."[9] But in *The Laws of Thought* he adopts the views of De Morgan, emphasizing that all discourse operates in a field whose limits are implicit or explicit: "In every discourse, whether of the mind conversing with its own thoughts, or of the individual in his intercourse with others, there is an assumed or expressed limit within which the subjects of its operation are confined. . . . Now, whatever may be the extent of the field within which all the objects of our discourse are found, that field may properly be termed the universe of discourse."[10]

W. S. Jevons takes as his example the barrister who, however general his statements, is understood to speak only of persons and things under the English Law; he introduces the notion of limited identities to take account of such propositions as: "Within the sphere of the class A, all the B's are all the C's," denoted symbolically by

AB = AC, and even asks "whether all identities are not really limited to an implied sphere of meaning." [11] Finally, John Venn, in *Symbolic Logic,* devotes an entire chapter to the notion of a universe of discourse, laying vigorous stress on its "varieties of form." We may retain from his analysis both the unlimited plasticity of such "universes," depending on the associations of the speaker, and the *indefinite latitude of arbitrary choices* otherwise offered to the logician. In ordinary language, the usage of negative terms very often implies extremely narrow limits in regard to the subject we think ourselves to be talking about:

"... What does 'not-black' include? Does it apply to all things without exception to which the colour black cannot be applied; including, say, the Geological Glacial Period, the sources of the Nile, the claims of the Papacy, the last letter of Clarissa Harlowe, and the wishes of our remote posterity? Clearly not: some kind of limit, more or less restricted, is generally understood to be drawn; but where exactly it may be traced must depend upon the nature of the subject and the associations of the speaker." [12]

Though the use of terms of the non-X type may be artificial and infrequent in ordinary conversation, such use is necessarily imposed on symbolic logic; and from the purely formal point of view, nothing specifies the extension of the class non-X, which depends entirely on what is "given"; the conception of a "universe," strictly speaking, is extralogical and depends on the application of the symbolic formulae:

"When thus regarded, the conception of a universe is seen to be strictly speaking extra-logical; it is entirely a question of the *application* of our formulae, not of their symbolic statement." [13] "Between them, X and not-X must fill up the whole field of our logical enquiry; they can leave nothing unaccounted for there. But when the question is asked, How wide is that field? the only answer that can be given is, just as wide as we choose in any case to make it." [14]

Among the Prolegomena of logic must be listed the necessity for speakers to specify the conventional limitations they impose on the realm of objects to which their words apply:

To this narrow conventional denotation of our terms the name of Universe of Discourse has been given. Its consideration does not strictly belong to the province of Formal Logic, and but for the convenience of explaining the distinction here in connection with Denotation, the topic might more appropriately have found its place amongst the Prolegomena of our science. We might, for instance, have inserted, amongst the assumptions of Logic, the claim that the speaker and hearer should be in agreement, not only as to the meaning of the words they use, but also as to the conventional limitations under which they apply them in the circumstances of the case. [15]

As a result, the respective extent of the different possible "universes" can be exceedingly variable. According to the usage to which, in De Morgan's view, the logicians have improperly restricted themselves, this extent may perfectly well be, quite simply, that of the Universe itself: "The most unfettered discourse is that in which the words we use are understood in the widest possible application, and for them the limits of discourse are co-extensive with those of the universe itself." [16] "Two such terms as S and not-S must between them exhaust the *universe of discourse,* whatever that may be; and we must not be precluded from making this, if we care to do so, the entire universe of existence." [17]

The Universe [18] is thus found paradoxically enlisted, by way of *example,* among universes of discourse: "Let, for instance, the universe of discourse be the actual Universe." [19] To be sure, in what is in some sense the reverse direction, there is nothing to prevent consideration of universes "restricted" in the extreme.

Thus Lewis Carroll (who puts the Universe at the head of his treatise) considers "boys in this school" or "ducks in this village" to be universes. It is possible to confine oneself to the corners of a square,[20] or, like Venn, to restrict one's discourse to two individuals:

> Of course, if our universe were very wide, the selection out of it of one individual would leave a miscellaneous host behind, but there is no necessity that the universe should be this wide. Look, for instance, at the expression $x\bar{y} + \bar{x}y$. There is nothing to hinder us from restricting our universe here to Mr. Gladstone and Lord Beaconsfield, and to the fact of their being in or out of office. Whichever then of the two statesmen we mark by x, the other will be marked by $\bar{x}$; and if we indicate the fact of being in office by y, then that of being out of office will be indicated by $\bar{y}$. Hence the formula $1 = x\bar{y} + \bar{x}y$ simply asserts the fact that one of them must be in office and the other out of it.[21]

As for the objects belonging to such universes of discourse, the moment we make their assembly depend solely on a *selection,* of which nothing is required except that it be a selection of *objects*—this notion of object being left vague—we thereupon open the way to selections of the most fantastical kind. (A right unrenounced to this day, I may add in passing, by textbooks of so-called "group theory"). We shall thus come to set up *incongruous collections,* where Aristotle is called upon only for one of his birthday parties, and whose elements will have no feature in common save that of having been brought together by an arbitrary act:

> Some may be disposed to think that *selections* exist—they will not say *classes*—the individuals of which really have no common difference, nothing which distinguishes them, and them alone, from all other things. I challenge such a selection. While awaiting an answer I imagine an acceptor; and I think I do nearly as well for him as he could do for himself, if I suppose him to select from the universe 'material object, past or present,' as a lot which he defies me to difference from all other things, the

following miscellany:—all men who have killed their brothers, the hundred largest ink-stands that ever were made, and Aristotle's dinner on his twenty-first birthday. What is the class-mark of these objects? I answer that to them alone belongs the epithet—'Selected by the fancy of *(here insert name and date)* in unsuccessful impeachment of the unlimited right of logical division.' [22]

Finally, the limitations of "universes" can be of different types, and can depend on differences of time, place, and circumstances.[23] Just as Venn admits very tolerant criteria when dealing with denotation (depending on the context, Rosinante may or may not form part of the denotation of the word "horse"),[24] so he also allows that certain "universes" may include "imaginary" beings, provided we merely insist that the criteria of "existence" be specified in each case: "If we are talking of ordinary phenomena we must know whether we refer to them without limit of time and space; and if not, within what limits, broadly speaking. If we include the realms of fiction and imagination we must know what boundaries we mean to put upon them." [25]

Such, in broad outline, is the notion of a universe of discourse. Was it ever limned in anything other than broad outline by those who upheld it? The age of Frege and his critical requirements had not yet arrived. One might see in it only a confused sketch of the concept of a group. But let us rather stick at this point to its declared source, namely, ordinary language, and to everything that binds it to a perfectly everyday practice. It was owing to this slant, indeed, that it had such power to seduce Lewis Carroll.

III

What about the notion of a "universe" in *Symbolic Logic?* There can be no doubt it comes straight from the works we have just been recalling, and which might be drawn upon, in the first place, to defend Lewis Carroll against the reproach made against him of indulging in a monotonous litany of examples, redundant to anyone who sees in them a uselessly iterated repetition of the same formal schema.[26] If, from this viewpoint, it can be no "universe" that finds letters sufficient to name the objects it contains, it will be granted that the above-mentioned authors felt obliged to test the as yet unmastered powers of a logic only recently become symbolic, by exploring a multitude of concrete cases and there discovering by experience the virtue of illustrations of the most elementary kind. If there is something simplistic in the litany of examples, the reason for it is the simplicity of a logic still without any intention of providing a foundation for mathematics, accepting almost without question the notion of a "universe," solely on the strength of evidence drawn from its natural origin. But it is no part of our purpose to excuse one set of naïvetés by another, nor to enumerate the influences to which Mr. Dodgson may have been subjected. For in our view it was Lewis Carroll himself, his subtle sensitivity to the resonances of words, his refined ear for natural language, that laid hold of the notion of a "universe" as an instrument adapted to modulate, under cover of rather stiff pedagogical motives, original language games of a delicately subversive kind.

An argument, for the logician, was enclosed within a very limited domain of objects, rather in the manner of talkers preoccupied with a single topic of conversation: an inducement for the storyteller to discourse on fanciful subjects—since the logician was prepared to admit stories and fairy tales as universes of discourse. Speaking of the criteria of "existence" appropriate to such universes, he was even ready to allude to *Alice in Wonderland:* "Or if we were concerned with Wonderland and its occupants we need not go deeper down than they do who tell us that March hares exist there." [27] How could one fail to be tempted into making the regions of Wonderland figure as logical universes? At least in terms of possibility, the logician gave his endorsement to "absurd" universes, absurd in creating collisions between objects assembled seemingly at random: "All applications of our logic are, as remarked, at our free choice; we might limit our application of the terms 'good' and 'not-good' to the London cabs with odd numbers, and every logical rule will hold valid as well as if we had selected a less absurd sort of universe." [28] How could one fail to be seduced by the license thus offered to the most preposterous associations?

These liberties, seemingly taken by the author of *Alice* when he frames assertions fraught with nonsense, were thus unreservedly offered to him. Congenial to his playful temper, they also legitimized the application of a personal style to a domain apparently refractory to literary effects. It is from them, we may say, that the "problems" of *Symbolic Logic* derive whatever is specifically "Carrollian" about them.

Every logician, indeed, will think himself able at first blush to account without trouble for the humor and the antics of these "problems." Lewis Carroll, with all the talent he possessed, was simply putting into practice the following shrewd pedagogical maxim: In order to make clearer that the formal schema of the syllogism is independent of the "content" of the premises, we should choose statements as remote as possible from current usages. But this does not explain why these problems—as is shown by those who enjoy them without having any interest in solving them—can *also* be read as Lewis Carroll *texts*. Their unity of tone derives, in effect, from the fact that he continues his tale-telling by way of the choice and elaboration of such-and-such universes of discourse. Witness a mildly lunatic bestiary bearing quite visible marks of its origin; witness the outcropping of personal passions even in the name of some universes (riddles, photographs); witness, finally, the recurrence of certain major themes (food, races).

It is not, however, my purpose to pursue such an account into detail. It is from those respects in which treatment of the notion of a universe appears to be at its most formal that I wish to bring out more unquestionable correspondences with the Carrollian point of view.

Let us return, indeed, to the very point at which De Morgan began his analysis: the regulations governing "negative" terms. What response do "The Logicians" give to the copula, when, as we heard at the outset, it asks them: "Am *I* to have the 'not,' or will you tack it on to the predicate? . . . The result seems to be that the grasping Copula constantly gets a 'not' that had better have been merged in the Predicate, and that Propositions are differentiated which had better have been recognized as precisely similar. Surely it is simpler to treat 'Some men are Jews' and 'Some men are Gentiles' as being, both of them, *affirmative* Propositions, instead of translating the latter into 'Some men are-not Jews,' and regarding it as a *negative* Proposition?" [29] This attitude, apparently relating to a very limited point of theory, means far more to Lewis Carroll, in my view, than a mere academic dispute. Does he not even confess this indirectly when he asserts: "This is no question of Logical Right and Wrong: it is merely a matter of *taste.*" [30]

Quite clearly, he was not fighting alone: De Morgan, from his first article onward, had declared that terms cannot be called positive or negative except in correlation with one another. The following paradox and anecdote, drawn from his subsequent discussions, furnish an amusing demonstration of this thesis. First, a profound logico-geographical question, which we may file along with the *Pillow Problems* of Lewis Carroll:

> As to the aorist character, I should like to know, supposing a name to include just half the universe, which is the aorist, that name or its privative? This is the most nicely balanced question in logic, just as the following, which even *Notes and Queries* cannot answer, is the most nicely balanced question in geography. If all the northern hemisphere were land, and all the southern hemisphere water, which should we have to say, that the northern hemisphere is an island, or the southern hemisphere a lake? I am Buridan's ass in respect to both questions.[31]

And here is the anecdote, showing how, in a "limited universe," names that are "contrary" cease to be pure negations of one another and even become separate positive names on their own:

> The most amusing instance which ever came within my own knowledge is as follows. A friend of mine, in the days of the Irish Church Bill, used to discuss politics with his butcher: one day he alluded to the possible fate of the Establishment. "Do you mean do away with the church?" asked the butcher. "Yes," said my friend, "that is what they say." "Why, sir, how can that be?" was the answer; "don't you see, sir, that if they destroy the church, we shall all have to be *dissenters!*"[32]

From the quarrel that divided the British logicians, and often drifted into other problems (the relation of such terms as "black" and "white," the nature of "privative" terms, the possibility of distinguishing between "relatively negative" and "absolutely negative" terms), let us retain a few assertions tending to erase all essential distinctions whereby negative and positive terms might be opposed. In accordance with what he calls the Law of Duality, there exists, according to Jevons, a perfect equilibrium between affirmation and negation. "Every affirmative proposition implies a negative one, and vice versa. It is even a matter of indifference, in a logical point of view, whether a positive or negative term be used to denote a given quality and the class of things possessing it. If the ordinary state of a man's body be called *good health,* then in other circumstances he is said *not to be in good health;* but we might equally describe him in the latter state as *sickly,* and in his normal condition he would be *not sickly.*" [33] According to Venn, the common idea among logicians that the class not-X is "infinite," or ought in some way to be more extensive than the class X, is a prejudice that symbolic logic tramples under foot: There is nothing to hinder us—and the remark is echoed by Lewis Carroll—from putting not-X to stand for the members of some "narrow" class, and X for the innumerable individuals that do not belong to it.[34]

In attaching the "not" to the predicate, we are at least adopting, in Lewis Carroll's opinion, a useful convention; the symbolism liberates the syllogism from illusory constraints which afflict "The Logicians" with that "morbid dread" they feel when confronted with negative attributes, so that they "shut their eyes, like frightened children, when they come across such terrible Propositions as 'all not-x are y.' " [35]

But if symbolic logic gains in power by overcoming this dread, may we not suspect another, a left-handed child, of finding in her a willing ally to combat another dread, that of a world where all the weight of positivity bears only on one side? To put on a level the two subdivisions resulting from the operation of dichotomy is to proclaim *the right to symmetry,* a symmetry which Lewis Carroll makes even more clearly evident by the transformation he imposes on Venn's diagrams. In the latter the opposition of positive and negative terms still remained visible; Carroll, in assigning a *square* to each universe of discourse, erases this opposition, and by the same token stresses the act whereby he closes such a universe upon itself, and writes the purely formal function of the "not" into the symmetrical distributions. These establish the diagram as a mirror held up to language; and now how do things fare with the diagram-universe?

With each copy of *The Game of Logic* one could purchase two diagrams, intended to represent propositions or resolve syllogisms, and in this work the notion of a universe is quite intimately bound up with these cardboard squares, designed to represent this or that "class of things." The first universe considered is a "universe of cakes," playing on the words *board* and *cupboard.* Lewis Carroll employs the most realistic of metaphors in order to convey that the universe is a *closed* area, where his "things" are shut in: "Now please to look at the smaller Diagram on the Board, and suppose it to be a cupboard, intended for all the Cakes in the world (it would have to be a good large one, of course)." [36] Question to the pupil: "In what sense do we use the word 'Universe' in this Game?"

Answer: "As a name of the class of Things to which the whole Diagram is assigned." [37]

In *Symbolic Logic,* on the other hand, where a weighty introduction reiterates the fundamental concepts of the traditional logic, the notion of a universe laboriously seeks its place within a framework but little adapted to receive it: "If the Name of each Term is *completely expressed* (i.e., if it contains a Substantive), there is no need to determine the 'Universe'; but, if either Name is *incompletely expressed,* and contains *Attributes* only, it is then necessary to determine a 'Universe,' in order to insert its Name as the Substantive." [38] Lewis Carroll is interested here in "Propositions of Relation," which have, for their terms, "two Specieses of the same Genus, such that each of the two Names conveys the idea of some Attribute *not* conveyed by the other." [39] "The Genus, of which the two Terms are Specieses, is called the 'Universe of Discourse,' or (more briefly) the 'Universe.' " [40] It may be doubted, indeed, if these theoretical considerations are to be taken quite literally, seeing how Carroll himself makes light of traditional distinctions, when—as Alonzo Church has noted—he gives definitions of "men" or "London." [41]

The textbook writer, respectful of customary instruction and the academic syllabus, an innovator only in his methods, might have thought it necessary to uphold and lay stress on such considerations. But why should they not have been an alibi for the tale teller, discreetly hesitating to flaunt from the very outset the strange liberty that the logicians had granted him? If, like De Morgan and Venn, he had proclaimed in his opening lines the right to be arbitrary, would there not have been exception taken to his too fantastic imagination?

Be that as it may, and more clearly than the "method of subscripts"—a transcription procedure too clumsy to form the basis of a true calculus—the diagrammatic method remains at the heart of *Symbolic Logic*. This method turns logic into a game, a game played with checkerboards and counters. A game, too, that even children can understand, and one expressly devised for them in any case. We may therefore be inclined to reduce the motives of this amusing mode of presentation to pure pedagogical artifice; the teacher, uneasy in his didactic role, is anxious by "interesting" his pupils, to have them forget that he teaches.

But the true bond of interest perhaps lies elsewhere. Logic a game? If so, a superficial logic, is the immediate reply. But what if the virtue of the diagrammatic method, secretly explored and patiently cultivated, were precisely that of *making discourse superficial? "A plane surface gives the character of a discourse...."* This proposition of Lewis Carroll's, which has been subtly employed by Gilles Deleuze as a key to the reading of his fantasy writings,[42] brings out with equal clarity the function, in logic, of the diagram-universe: a language-trap that flattens out words and propositions on a plane, squared-off, closed surface. Though there is no point in reiterating here the details of this motif of the surface—a subject analyzed elsewhere [43]—we may insist on one aspect, which is appropriate to *Symbolic Logic:* In passing from one example to the next in the list of exercises, we are leaping each time from one universe to another, and these leaps are just like the breaks so frequent in the fantasy writings. Taken as a whole, the tour of universes will thus be a *simulacrum of the Carrollian narrative.*

IV

A simulacrum of narrative: Does this mean a monochrome sketch? Colorless, in being a formal schema where a smoothed-out language achieves univocal meaning

[190]

and is nothing more than a transparent medium. A hushed affair, too, where the continual disputes of the Carrollian narratives are extinguished, the verbal violence is calmed, the imperious tones softened; with all noise eliminated, communication proceeds without a hitch in cushioned "universes" and everyone understands everyone else. On the one hand the fictional writings, bristling with puzzles and paradoxes, ruffled by linguistic squalls; on the other, one book and the promise of another, in logical guise, where the aim is to establish a perfect language.

For those who divide the works of Carroll into questions and answers, the contrast is a seductive one. But in my view it needs to be challenged. The questions are still there in *Symbolic Logic,* and the author directs them to "teachers"; and what are we to make of those paradoxes whereby the logic of the day is to be punctured at chosen points? It is, however, at the very heart of the examples enumerated in *Symbolic Logic,* and thus in the portions intended to illustrate the logic, that we wish to uncover a mining operation which shatters the coherence of the notion of a universe by a play of arguments deployed within the universes of discourse themselves.

Undoubtedly revealing are the moves of withdrawal in the fourth edition of *Symbolic Logic,* whereby Carroll, anxious to smooth the reader's path, causes "difficulties" to disappear, and so sets in broad daylight the risks that logic may run in its most elementary enterprises.

In the Appendix to this edition he provides a new version of the "Five Liars" problem, shorn of its "metaphysical puzzles"; this he does by translating "telling 2 Truths" into "taking *both* of 2 condiments (salt and mustard)." "Telling 2 Lies" becomes "taking *neither* of them," and "telling a Truth and a Lie . . ." becomes "taking only *one* condiment. . . ." [44] In this new form the premises turn out to be incompatible. A switch of the problem as instructive as it is ingenious, says A. N. Prior. But though such a solution may satisfy us in regard to the second version, it is not appropriate to the first, which is nothing else but a variant of the Paradox of the Liar: "For it is quite patently not inconsistent to suppose five people to *say* the things attributed to them in this version of the problem." [45]

There remains, then, the mystery that arises as soon as we attempt to consider a proposition as being its own subject, or a set of propositions as being subjects for one another: a "shadowy host," a "procession of phantoms," says Lewis Carroll ironically; it is impossible to pounce in passing on a single proposition of which we can say with confidence that it is necessarily true or false! [46] It is by a similar torment of Tantalus that the Tortoise will put Achilles on the rack—condemned indefinitely to entering propositions in his notebook, without ever being able to assert the truth of the statement for which the Tortoise has demanded proof.[47]

Now, in regard to this same notion of *assertion,* which compelled Russell to face up to the Paradox of the Tortoise in *The Principles of Mathematics,*[48] John Venn, in a passage that seems hitherto to have gone unnoticed, had made use of a superlatively Carrollian metaphor to exorcise a perilous contingency, of which philosophical logic was due ultimately to accept all the consequences: "Again if the assertion of the truth of X is different from its bare assertion, and is yet a proposition, does not *its* truth give rise to a new proposition, and so on? If so, we are like a man trying to determine the last image of a light between two parallel mirrors." [49]

Every proposition would thus become a phantom, endlessly reflected in that space between two mirrors where all human speech would be confined.

The second correction introduced by Lewis Carroll in his fourth edition concerns soriteses presenting the following difficulty: in one example the *given universe* was "ducks in this village" and the third premise was "Mrs Bond has no gray ducks"; the terms here are specieses, not of the universe of discourse, but of the larger class "ducks," of which that universe is only a portion. The reader was supposed to perceive that the premise should be treated as if it were "Mrs Bond has no gray ducks in this village"; and was required to ignore, as superfluous, what it asserts as to the *other* portion of the class "ducks," namely that "Mrs Bond has no gray ducks *out of* this village." [50] A trap, therefore, for the reader, in the obligation laid on him to step out of the prescribed universe of discourse, in the hope that he will forget to *return* once more into that universe at the moment of stating his conclusion. But a trap, above all, where the notion of a universe of discourse itself becomes entangled: To posit a universe amounts to defining limits that must not be overstepped. Now, in the example just cited, Carroll is tracing limits *in order that* they may be violated. John Venn had stated the ban in a particularly telling manner: "The outside of our Universe itself is of course simply disregarded. . . . We simply do not suffer our minds to dwell upon it. The outside of any particular universe may in fact be considered to stand in much the same relation to all possible logical predication that the field of 'view' at the *back* of our heads stands to all possible colours." [51] A ban on turning one's head: Carroll, no doubt, did not expressly formulate any such defense; in reviving, on his own account, the ancient trio of Genus, Species, and Difference, he appears to give himself every means of framing it. He puts the notion of a universe into practice after the manner of the exponents of symbolic logic, but in order to legitimize it he couples it to the traditional system. Is it again so as to "evade a difficulty" for the reader? A formidable difficulty: The notion of a universe shatters the distinction between subject and predicate. The true "subject" is the universe of discourse; [52] that is what we are speaking of, though we cannot ourselves say so. Is Carroll avoiding the obstacle in conceding the right to repair, whenever necessary, to the class of *things*, or of *existing things?* He has laid out his whole treatise so as to lead his pupil to think so. If, in *The Game of Logic,* the Thing without Attributes encounters a contemptuous silence, [53] in the fourth edition of *Symbolic Logic* it is revealed to us that in reverting to things themselves, we retreat the better to get lost: ". . . the difficulties of the '5 Liars' problem . . . are 'trifles, light as air,' compared with the bewildering question 'What is a Thing?' " [54]

The puzzle lies at the outset. From then on, all the instructions that follow are clouded with suspicion and can no longer be accepted simply for what they provide; in particular, the "arguments" that evolve within each "universe," placed there in principle to be dispersed in the lattices of a diagram, regain their weight and opacity. Perhaps it will be in order to examine some of them in the same light as the episodes in the fantasy writings. Let us rouse none other than logical anxieties: Their very designation draws certain universes to the attention of the least distrustful—"names," "stories," "my ideas," and "riddles," not to mention "Logic-examples worked by me," a universe of which one might wonder, since it is itself the topic of a logic-example, what relations it bears to itself. Let us pick out from these utterances only the image there reflected of logic, as such. A reassuring, traditional, and reasonable image, sufficient to content the philosopher and encourage the well-disposed adult: "Babies are illogical," "Illogical persons are despised," "All philosophers are logical," "Everyone who is sane can do Logic." But here are one or two that evoke some truly dismal prospects for logicians: No doubt "A lively logician, who is really in earnest, is in no danger of losing money," but "A logician who eats pork-chops for supper will probably lose money," "A logician who is in danger of losing money had better take to cab-driving." And then a threat: "None of *your* sons can do Logic." Nor is that all. Let us listen to some confidences: "Every idea of mine, that cannot be expressed as a Syllogism, is really ridiculous." Logicism run mad? In an instant the claim will be reduced to dust: The Syllogism will syllogistically expose its own vanity. The admission is there, tucked away among the examples of syllogisms:

> Nothing intelligible puzzles me;
> Logic puzzles me;
> Logic is unintelligible.

May it not be that, behind its facade of intelligibility, logic, through a hidden destiny, has the tendency to manufacture puzzles? Alongside the meticulous professor of *Symbolic Logic,* there stands revealed a disturbing Humpty Dumpty, no longer a master of words only, but the overlord of "universes." The surveyor of diagram-universes has subverted, by successive slides, those "universes of discourse," of which the "logicians" had claimed mastery in all innocence, with no suspicion of the paradoxes that only the multiple resources of mathematical logic will one day be able to neutralize.

But puzzles remain—one of them told to us at the theater, where we now return to conclude, in the company of a new logician:

> There is, however, a difficulty, which is illustrated by Hamlet's mother when he asks if she does not see the ghost:
> Hamlet: Do you see nothing there?
> Queen: Nothing at all; yet all that is I see.

I have always wondered how she knew she saw "all that is." [55]

NOTES

"Jeu de logique, Jeux d'univers" appeared in *Lewis Carroll,* ed. Henri Parisot (Paris: Éditions de l'Herne, 1971), pp. 17–29. It is translated with the permission of the publisher.

1. "Lewis Carroll, Logicien," in *Lewis Carroll: Logique sans peine* (Paris: Hermann, 1966), pp. 255–88. [French translation of *Symbolic Logic* and *The Game of Logic;* references to Carroll's text are given in the paging of the original, retained in the Dover reprint of 1958. –Tr.]

2. *Symbolic Logic,* 4th ed., p. 172.

3. De Morgan's main articles on logic have lately been collected by Peter Heath in *On the Syllogism and other Logical Writings* (London: Routledge & Kegan Paul, 1966). Referred to, in the notes that follow, as *On the Syllogism* . . . .

4. Aristotle, *De Interpretatione,* 16a [Oxford translation].

5. *Ibid.,* 19b.

6. De Morgan, *On the Syllogism* . . . , p. 2f.

7. "But not only is common thought conducted in a limited universe, but this so palpably that express mention is seldom needed. A person strikes into a conversation to deny the first he has heard of it, and is instantly put down by, We were talking of . . . ." *On the Syllogism* . . . , p. 95f.

8. *Ibid.,* p. 95.

9. George Boole, *The Mathematical Analysis of Logic* (1847; rpt. Oxford, 1951), p. 15.

10. George Boole, *An Investigation of the Laws of Thought* (1854; rpt. Dover Publications, n.d.), p. 42.

11. W. S. Jevons, *The Principles of Science* (London: Macmillan, 1892), p. 43.

12. John Venn, *Symbolic Logic* (London: Macmillan, 1881), p. 181.

13. *Ibid.,* p. 184.

14. *Ibid.,* p. 185.

15. John Venn, *The Principles of Empirical or Inductive Logic* (London: Macmillan, 1889), pp. 180f.

16. Boole, *An Investigation of the Laws of Thought,* p. 42.

17. J. N. Keynes, *Studies and Exercises in Formal Logic* (London: Macmillan, 1884), p. 29.

18. Cannot this effort at totalization be carried further still? "This universe is sometimes all that exists objectively, and sometimes all that can exist in thought. If there be anyone who demands yet more, and wants room for that which cannot be in thought, whether as possible or impossible, he invades the universe of a higher power, and will perhaps square the circle: a problem which a speculator of the last century reduced to the following –*Construere mundum divinae menti analogum*" (De Morgan, *On the Syllogism* . . . , p. 304, n. 1).

19. Boole, *An Investigation of the Laws of Thought,* p. 42.

20. De Morgan, *On the Syllogism* . . . , p. 2.

21. Venn, *Symbolic Logic,* p. 364.

22. De Morgan, *On the Syllogism* . . . , p. 313.

23. Venn, *The Principles of Empirical or Inductive Logic,* p. 180.

24. *Ibid.,* p. 179.

25. Venn, *Symbolic Logic,* p. 128.

26. Cf. the judgment of T. B. Strong, quoted by F. B. Lennon, *The Life of Lewis Carroll* (London: Cassell, 1947), pp. 275f.

27. Venn, *Symbolic Logic;* pp. 127f.

28. *Ibid.,* p. 186.

29. Carroll, *Symbolic Logic,* p. 172.

30. *Ibid.*

31. De Morgan, *On the Syllogism . . .* , p. 305, n. 1.
32. *Ibid.,* p. 180.
33. Jevons, *Principles of Science,* p. 44.
34. Venn, *Symbolic Logic,* p. 184.
35. Carroll, *Symbolic Logic,* p. 172.
36. Carroll, *The Game of Logic,* p. 4.
37. *Ibid.,* pp. 38, 56.
38. Carroll, *Symbolic Logic,* p. 13.
39. *Ibid.,* p. 12.
40. *Ibid.*
41. Review of the reprint of *Symbolic Logic* and *The Game of Logic: The Journal of Symbolic Logic,* 25 (September 1960), pp. 264f.
42. Gilles Deleuze, *Logique du sens* (Paris: Editions de Minuit, 1969), p. 21.
43. *Ibid.,* pp. 20f., 34, 37, 275.
44. Carroll, *Symbolic Logic,* pp. xiiif. It will be observed that the solution, or rather substitute, for the problem is oddly based on the duality of speaking and eating, which occupies such an important place in Carroll's writings (Cf. G. Deleuze, *Logique du Sens,* pp. 105f.).

   We may perhaps draw attention here to an ancient paradox, that of the Crocodile, as much for its Carrollian echoes as for the intertwining it achieves between the impossibility of speaking the truth and the danger of being eaten; here it is, extracted from a logic textbook of Carroll's own day: "A Crocodile is supposed to have taken a child, and then tells the mother that if she will *truly* inform him whether he will determine to eat it or not, he will give it up to her. On her giving either answer, an argument arises similar to that which has just been considered. If she says you will resolve to eat it, the crocodile replies that, to make this answer true, he must eat the child: if she says you will resolve not to eat he replies that the answer is not true, and therefore, he will eat it." (W. H. S. Monck, *An Introduction to Logic,* Dublin, 1880, p. 241). Was Carroll thinking of this paradox when he proposed a sorites beginning "Babies are illogical" and having as its conclusion: "Babies cannot manage crocodiles"?
45. Review of the reprint of Carroll's *Symbolic Logic: Journal of Symbolic Logic,* 22, No. 3 (September 1957), pp. 309f.
46. Carroll, *Symbolic Logic,* p. xiii.
47. Carroll, "What the Tortoise Said to Achilles," *Mind,* N.S. 4 (1895), pp. 278-80; *Logique sans Peine,* pp. 281-88.
48. Cf. J. Vuillemin, *Leçons sur la première philosophie de Russell* (Paris: Armand Colin, 1968), p. 18.
49. Venn, *Symbolic Logic,* p. 347.
50. Carroll, *Symbolic Logic,* p. xiii.
51. Venn, *op. cit.,* pp. 188–89.
52. Boole, *Laws of Thought,* p. 42.
53. "People have asked the question 'Can a Thing exist without any Attributes belonging to it?' It is a very puzzling question, and I'm not going to try to answer it: let us turn up our noses, and treat it with contemptuous silence, as if it really wasn't worth noticing" *(The Game of Logic,* p. 2).
54. Carroll, *Symbolic Logic,* p. xii.
55. Bertrand Russell, *An Inquiry into Meaning and Truth* (London: 1940), p. 91.

The
Film Collector's Alice:
An Essay and Checklist

BY DAVID H. SCHAEFER

To many, the words "Alice in Wonderland" conjure up only one set of images—Disney's animated characters. Indeed, it is possible that more people know of the *Alice* stories through motion pictures than through reading the actual books. In 1903, only five years after Carroll's death, the first *Alice in Wonderland* film appeared. More than fifteen motion picture versions of the Alice stories have been produced since then. There have been shorts, full-length features, silent films, musical versions, television versions, animated adaptations, and a drug education version. Even the real-life Alice, Mrs. Alice Liddell Hargreaves, has been captured on newsreel film.

Part I of this article chronicles the major *Alice* films, with special attention to the silent versions. Part II lists all motion picture films known to the author that relate to Lewis Carroll.

I

It is interesting to speculate about Lewis Carroll's knowledge of motion pictures, and to wonder if he ever went to see this new invention. As a highly accomplished amateur photographer, he must have had an interest in the development of this offshoot of his hobby. As early as February 1896, the Lumière Cinematograph was being shown as part of the entertainment at the Polytechnic in London. In the late

1890s, Brighton, one of Lewis Carroll's favorite resorts, was a major film production area. At the time of Carroll's death in 1898, motion pictures were widely shown in vaudeville houses as "chasers" at the end of the stage presentation.[1]

By 1903 theaters exclusively devoted to motion pictures had arrived. These small theaters, known as "nickelodeons" in the United States, were generally converted stores with chairs rented from a nearby caterer or funeral parlor. Here a nickel bought a variety of film presentations that were repeated every fifteen minutes or so. Similar theaters in England were called "electric palaces" or "bioscope theaters."

Among the subjects available in 1903 was the first motion picture version of *Alice in Wonderland.* This ten-minute film was produced by Cecil Hepworth, one of the major producers of films in England. In the early 1900s the Hepworth organization produced more than one hundred motion pictures a year at its primitive studio at Walton-on-Thames. In spite of the apparent mass production, the operation was a family affair. In the *Alice* film, for example, Mrs. Hepworth is the Queen. Miraculously, fourteen out of sixteen scenes of the Hepworth *Alice* have been preserved by the British Film Institute. Even though the film is faded in parts and large amounts of emulsion are missing, it is technically excellent and is enjoyable to watch.

The most interesting scenes show Alice growing and shrinking (Figs. 1 & 2). It appears that these shots were made by the superposition of two films, although they are so well done that it is difficult to tell. Trick photography had become common by 1903, with the Frenchman Méliès producing fantastic films on such subjects as trips to the moon. His films, however, used stage settings, and many of his special effects were those of the live stage. In contrast, in the Hepworth *Alice* the shrinking and growing scenes are completely photographic, and appear to be a step beyond the technique of Méliès. A more common type of special effect occurs in the rabbit's house where a very overgrown Alice escapes by fanning herself and slowly fading away. Other sequences involving trick shots include the metamorphosis of the Duchess's baby into a very lively little black pig, and the abrupt comings and goings of an actual cat. Toward the end of the film pleasant outdoor shots of children in the royal procession marching to the croquet ground contrast sharply with the photographic trickery of earlier scenes.[2]

Silent films knew no bounds due to language, and these films circulated freely through Europe and America. The Hepworth *Alice* was released in the United States by the Edison Manufacturing Company, appearing in their January 1904 catalogue. Six years later in 1910, the Edison Company filmed its own *Alice In Wonderland* in the Bronx. This first American *Alice,* like its British predecessor, is just ten minutes long. It consists of fourteen scenes all relating to *Alice's Adventures.* Scene Twelve (Fig. 4) is a surprise. The Edison Company advertising describes it as showing "a banquet at which the dastardly Knave steals the tarts and gets away with them, as told in the familiar rhyme. Although Alice is the only one to see him, she refuses to tell even when summoned to the trial, which takes place in the next scene."[3]

Figs. 1 and 2 —1903 Alice changing size in the hall of doors

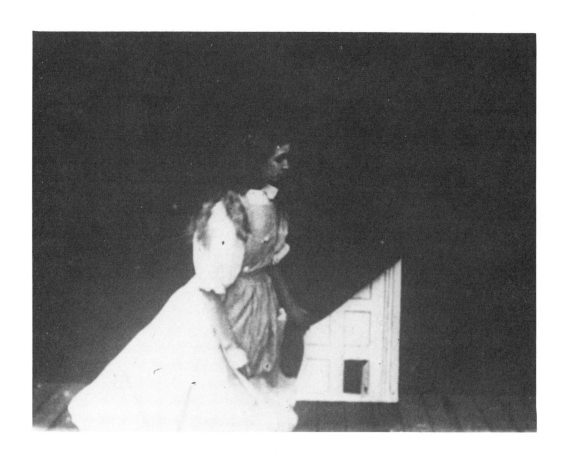

The motion picture film critic had come into existence in time for us to have the following review of the 1910 film, which appeared in the *New York Dramatic Mirror* on September 14, 1910:

> *Alice in Wonderland* (Edison Sep 9) – This is the most original and most interesting film that has appeared in many a day, although its charms may not be quite evident to one who has never accompanied the heroine on her journey down the rabbit burrow. From first to last Alice's work was delightful: facial expressions can never say more than hers did in the very first scene. The shrinkage in her size was skillfully managed in the early part of her adventures. The duchess with the baby that turned into a pig, the diminutive hatter, the sleepy dormouse, the mad March Hare who put butter in his watch to make it go – all parade through the film until Alice defies the laws of Wonderland. Then they disappear in a whirling pack of cards. Although the making of such a film must have necessitated much time, labor and expense, the result has justified the outlay – at least artistically. It reflects credit upon all connected with it.[4]

A less positive view of the movie was taken in 1918 by an unknown person who scribbled on an index card in the Library of Congress: "Grainy, very crudely produced, but will always interest children." This is probably the last word on the merits of the production, as no copies of this film are known to exist today. Figures 3 and 4 are, however, actual frames from the film. They were deposited in the Library of Congress for copyright purposes.

After 1912 motion pictures began to have greater mass appeal, and comfortable neighborhood theaters began to appear throughout the country. In New York the movement away from primitive nickelodeons took a giant step in April 1914 when the Strand Theatre opened with gilt, marble, deep pile rugs, crystal chandeliers, original works of art, luxurious lounges, a mighty Wurlitzer to accompany the shorts, and a thirty-piece symphony orchestra to accompany the feature. The price of a ticket skyrocketed from the nickelodeon nickel all the way to a full quarter.[5]

Before members of the press and invited guests, and to the accompaniment of the thirty-piece orchestra, a delightful *Alice* had its "initial showing" at the Strand Theatre on January 19, 1915.[6] This film, unlike its ten-minute predecessors, ran a complete hour. Various versions of this film are commercially available today. The print in my collection commences with Alice and her sister meandering through pastoral farm scenes, filmed on an estate outside New York City.[7] After falling asleep on her sister's lap, a shadowy Alice leaves the body of the sleeping Alice and follows the rabbit (Fig. 5). Most of the sequences and characters of *Alice's Adventures* are incorporated, including a Father William who actually performs a back somersault and balances an eel on the end of his nose. The lobster quadrille scene was filmed on a rocky beach at Cape Ann on the Massachusetts coast. In this scene two tremendous

Fig. 3–1910 Edison Alice, *The Mad Tea-Party*

lobsters (with striped pants) come out of the pounding surf. On shore they meet a very sad Mock Turtle (Fig. 6).

This film is charming from beginning to end, with elaborate, as well as delightful, costuming. Actors who were midgets portrayed the animals so that Alice would always be taller than her friends. The use of natural surroundings throughout the film sets a tone totally missing in later productions. There is no attempt to have Alice change size, which is somewhat surprising considering the earlier films did include such changes. Interestingly, this highly successful film was directed by a newspaper editor whose only motion picture experience outside of *Alice* appears to have been as editor of British Government official war films.[8] *Alice* was apparently exhibited in many different versions. The original contains both *Wonderland* and *Looking-Glass* sequences. Reviews at the time were most favorable, and as late as 1921 the film had a New York screening at Town Hall.

The silent film era ended with surprising suddenness in 1927 when the sound motion picture *The Jazz Singer* was exhibited amid much excitement. The first *Alice* portrayed with a sound track is a six-minute dance sequence from the 1930 film *Putting on the Ritz*. Joan Bennett is a beautiful Alice who goes through the looking glass and dances with characters from both *Alice* books, including a glamorous chorus

Fig. 4—1910 Edison Alice *party*

line of playing cards. The music was composed by Irving Berlin. Reviewers singled out the *Alice* sequence for special praise.

The first full-length "articulate" *Alice in Wonderland* was filmed in Fort Lee, New Jersey (the former capital of silent films) in 1931. The actors are not well known, and the sound techniques are abysmal. Added to these troubles, the rabbit proclaims his love for the Duchess and confesses that he stole the tarts for her!

A full-blown Hollywood production of *Alice* arrived in 1933. Paramount proudly proclaimed that the film had forty-six speaking parts, each played by "a well-known actor." Stars from Cary Grant to Baby LeRoy appeared in the film. Charlotte Henry, the film's Alice, was selected from seven thousand girls who applied for the part with urging from a national publicity campaign.

This film provides a bonanza for lovers of special effects. The illusion of Alice going through the looking glass is close to perfection. The ability to have a giant Alice pick up and inspect small live chessmen who squeal in frightened horror is remarkable, and a leisurely fall down the rabbit hole is skillfully accomplished. Growing and shrinking occur on four different occasions. Unfortunately, cylindrical lenses were used for three of these shots—a technique that causes Alice to visually undergo wild distortions while being contracted or expanded. In addition to the

[201]

Fig. 5–1915 White Rabbit

major feats called for in the books, the film also presents minor ones such as "drink me" bottles that suddenly appear, a Cheshire Cat that surprisingly leaves not only his grin but also his ears and eyes, a White Queen changing into a sheep, and a leg of mutton that is mobile and articulate. Befitting a Hollywood spectacle, live flamingos are used as croquet mallets.

In 1948 the puppeteer Lou Bunin made an *Alice in Wonderland* in France. The film had puppets for all characters except Alice. The English version arrived in the United States just as the Walt Disney *Alice* was being released. Annoyed, Disney went to court in an unsuccessful attempt to delay the showing of Bunin's film. However, it never offered any real competition to Disney. The Disney film was first distributed in 1951 and again appeared on American screens in 1974.[9] The critical reaction of audiences and reviewers in 1951 was generally negative, and at that time the film was not a financial success. Despite its early troubles, however, the impact of the film has been great. This is evidenced by Disney Enterprises' ability to promote everything from Alice rides at Disneyland and DisneyWorld to Alice bibs for babies. The Big Golden Book of Walt Disney's (mind you) "Alice in Wonderland" went through its twenty-fifth printing in 1974–one example of Disney's imprint on the *Alice* image.

[202]

Fig. 6—1915 Mock Turtle filmed at Cape Ann, Mass.

The latest feature film adaptation of *Alice in Wonderland* was produced by Joseph Shaftel in 1972. The film, in wide screen Technicolor, should have been a success since it is both visually beautiful and is laden with a cast of stars. The sets faithfully followed Tenniel and the dialogue is from the book. The songs, however, are not in the Carroll spirit and tend to ruin the film's continuity. The film was not well received in either England or America. It is now available for 16mm. rental, and is shown frequently on television.

Alice in Wonderland has always been a challenge for film producers. Every time there have been advancements in film techniques, an *Alice* has appeared sporting these improvements. Even though many of the productions have not been considered outstanding examples of film art, they have provided a powerful stimulus to continued interest in the Alice stories.

II

The following checklist shows the many forms taken by motion picture and television productions based on Carroll's stories. Some of the entries are attempts at faithful presentation while others, to varying degrees, are "inspired by" Carroll's art. To those desiring further information, a limited number of reviews and secondary references are provided.

1903   *Alice in Wonderland.* Produced and directed by Cecil Hepworth. Filmed in Great Britain. Alice is played by May Clark. The film has sixteen scenes, all from *Alice's Adventures.* Running time: approximately ten minutes (one reel).

1910   *Alice's Adventures in Wonderland (A Fairy Comedy).* Produced by the Edison Manufacturing Company, Orange, New Jersey. Alice is played by Gladys Hulette. The film has fourteen scenes, all from *Alice's Adventures.* Running time: approximately ten minutes (one reel). Reviewed: *N. Y. Dramatic Mirror,* 14 September 1910, p. 32. Full description with illustrations: *Edison Kinetogram,* 1 September 1910, p. 7. Description also in *Moving Picture World,* 3 September 1910, p. 533. Edwin S. Porter is often listed as the director of this film; however, George Pratt, Associate Curator of Motion Pictures at George Eastman House, says this is impossible since Porter left the Edison Company late in 1909 and the film did not appear until September 9, 1910.

1915   *Alice in Wonderland.* Produced by Nonpareil Feature Film Company, directed by W. W. Young, "picturized" by Dewitt C. Wheeler. Alice is played by Viola Savoy. The film as originally made contained scenes from *Alice's Adventures* and *Through the Looking-Glass.* Running time: approximately fifty minutes (five reels). Reviewed: *The Moving Picture World,* 6 February 1915, p. 841; *Motography,* 20 February 1915, p. 307; *New York Times,* 22 March 1921, p. 15. Book illustrations from film: *Alice in Wonderland* (New York: Grosset & Dunlap, 1918).

1930   *Alice in Wonderland.* Produced by John W. Considine, Jr., directed by Edward H. Sloman. Music and lyrics by Irving Berlin. Joan Bennett is featured in this six-minute dance sequence from the film *Putting on the Ritz.* Eight- and sixteen-millimeter versions released by Nu-Art Films, Inc. *Putting on the Ritz* reviewed: *New York Times,* 15 February 1930, p. 15.

1931   *Alice in Wonderland.* Commonwealth Pictures Corporation. Screen adaptation by John E. Godson and Ashley Miller. Produced at the Metropolitan Studios, Fort Lee, New Jersey. Directed by "Bud" Pollard. Alice played by Ruth Gilbert. The first sound *Alice.* All scenes are from *Alice's Adventures.* Reviewed: *New York Times,* 28 December 1931, p. 22.

1932   *Alice in U.S. Land!* Paramount News. Newsreel of Mrs. Alice Liddell Hargreaves, eighty, arriving for one-hundredth anniversary celebration of Carroll's birth. Talks of trip down the river with "Mr. Dodgson." Her son, Caryl Hargreaves, and her sister, Rhoda Liddell, are identifiable. Filmed aboard the Cunard Lines *Berengeria* in New York harbor, April 29, 1932. Running time: seventy-five seconds.

1933   *Alice in Wonderland.* Paramount Productions. Produced by Louis D. Leighton, directed by Norman McLeod, screenplay by Joseph J. Mankiewicz and

William Cameron Menzies. Music by Dimitri Tiomkin. Alice played by Charlotte Henry. An all-star cast of forty-six includes: W. C. Fields as Humpty Dumpty; Edward Everett Horton as the Mad Hatter; Cary Grant as the Mock Turtle; Gary Cooper as the White Knight; Edna May Oliver as the Red Queen; May Robson as the Queen of Hearts; and Baby LeRoy as the Deuce of Hearts. Scenes from *Alice's Adventures* and *Looking-Glass.* Running time: ninety minutes. Reviewed: *New York Times,* 23 December 1933, p. 19; *Time,* 22, No. 26 (December 25), p. 20; *Newsweek,* 30 December 1933, p. 30; *Nation,* 17 January 1934, p. 84. Book illustrations from film: *Alice's Adventures in Wonderland and Through the Looking-Glass* (New York: Grosset & Dunlap, n.d.); *Alice in Wonderland* (Racine, Wisconsin: Whitman Publishing Company, 1934) – tells the story as it is presented in the motion picture.

1933 *Betty in Blunderland.* Cartoon directed by Dave Fleischer. Animation by Roland Crandall and Thomas Johnson. Betty Boop follows *Wonderland* and *Looking-Glass* characters from a jigsaw puzzle via subway station down the rabbit hole. Running time: ten minutes.

1936 *Thru the Mirror.* Walt Disney Productions. A Mickey Mouse cartoon based on *Through the Looking-Glass.* "A brilliant short cartoon." [10]

1948 *Alice in Wonderland.* Produced in France at Victorine Studios by Lou Bunin. Directed by Marc Maurette and Dallas Bowers; script by Henry Myers, Edward Flisen, and Albert Cervin. Marionette animation by Lou Bunin. Alice played by Carol Marsh. Voices for puppets by Joyce Grenfell, Peter Bull, and Jack Train. The prologue, which shows Lewis Carroll's life at Christ Church, has Pamela Brown as Queen Victoria and Stanley Baker as Prince Albert. Color. Produced in French and English versions. Condensed version distributed by Castle Films. Exclusive of the prologue, all the characters are puppets except Alice, who is a live adult. Reviewed: *New York Times,* 27 July, 1951, p. 15.

1950 *Alice in Wonderland.* Television production shown on the Ford Theater in December 1950. Alice played by Iris Mann and the White Rabbit by Dorothy Jarnac.

1951 *Alice in Wonderland.* Walt Disney Productions. Production Supervisor, Ben Sharpsteen. Alice's voice by Kathryn Beaumont. Animation. Color. Sequences from *Alice's Adventures* and *Looking-Glass.* Running time: seventy-five minutes. (Available 8mm sound sequences are "The Mad Tea Party" and "Alice and the White Rabbit.") Reviewed: *New York Times,* 30 July, 1951, p. 12; *Saturday Review,* 11 August 1951, p. 30; *Time,* 6 August 1951, p. 69.

1955 *Sweapea Thru the Looking Glass.* King Features Syndicate cartoon. Executive Producer, Al Brodax. Directed by Jack Kinney. Color. Sweapea goes through a looking glass and falls down a golf hole into the "Wunnerland Golf Club."

1962 *Mad Gardner's Song.* Animation by Jacques Espagne. Produced in France. "Un delicieux film d'animation." [11]

1966 *Alice of Wonderland in Paris.* Childhood Products Inc. Color. A cartoon about some adventures of Alice in Paris. Running time: fifty-two minutes.

1966 *Alice in Wonderland or What's A Nice Kid Like You Doing in a Place Like This.* Made for television. Hanna-Barbera Productions. Book by Bill Dana. Music and lyrics by Lee Adams and Charles Strauss. Color. Animation. Alice's voice by Janet Waldo; Cheshire Cat by Sammy Davis, Jr.; White Knight by Bill Dana; Queen by Zsa Zsa Gabor. Running time: fifty minutes. Alice follows her dog through a television tube.

1966 *Alice Through the Looking Glass.* Television production shown November 6, 1966, and rebroadcast November 22, 1974. Script by Albert Simmons, lyrics by Elsie Simmons, music by Moose Charlap. Judi Rolin as Alice; Jimmy Durante as Humpty Dumpty; Nanette Fabray as the White Queen; Agnes Moorehead as the Red Queen; Jack Palance as the Jabberwock; The Smothers Brothers as Tweedledum and Tweedledee; Ricardo Montalban as the White King. Running time: ninety minutes.

1966 *Alice in Wonderland.* BBC television production. Directed by Jonathan Miller. Relatively serious presentation of Wonderland as a Victorian social commentary. Grand production with a star cast: Sir John Gielgud as the Mock Turtle; Sir Michael Redgrave as the Caterpillar; Peter Sellers as the King; Peter Cook as the Hatter; Sir Malcolm Muggeridge as the Gryphon; Anne-Marie Mallik, a young schoolgirl, as Alice. Reviewed: Malcolm Muggeridge in *New Statesman,* 72 (December 23, 1966), 933; John Coleman, p. 947. Also discussed by Sibley and Benayoun; see notes 10 and 11.

1969 *Alice in Acidland.* Bernhard Films. Shown in adult film houses. Running time: sixty-seven minutes.

1969 *The Three Voices.* Amateur surrealist film produced by Peter Blundell-Jones. Shown at the Lewis Carroll Society, London, May 15, 1969. A film version of Carroll's poem first published in 1856.

1970 *Alice in Wonderland.* O.R.T.F. (French television) production. Directed by Jean-Christophe Averty. Burlesque with stunning visual and auditory overlay. Alice Sapritch and Francis Blanche as the King and Queen. Discussed by Benayoun; see note 11.

1972 *Alice's Adventures in Wonderland.* Executive Producer, Joseph Shaftel. Producer, Derek Horne. Director, William Sterling. Musical Director, John Barry. Lyricist, Don Black. Alice played by Fiona Fullerton. Peter Sellers is the March Hare, Dame Flora Robson is the Queen of Hearts, Dennis Price is the King of Hearts, and Sir Ralph Richardson is the Caterpillar. Color. Wide screen. A lavish production, visually beautiful. The Tenniel illustrations were faithfully followed. Sequences from *Alice's Adventures* and *Looking-Glass.* Running time: ninety minutes. Reviewed: *Washington Post,* 14 February 1973, p. F-1; *The Evening Star* and *Daily News* (Washington, D.C.). 14 February 1973, p. F-11. Book illustrations from film: *Alice's Adventures in Wonderland* (London: Pan Books Ltd., 1973).

1972   *Curious Alice.* Written, designed, and produced by Design Center Inc., Washington, D.C. Made for the National Institute of Mental Health. Color. Part of a drug course for elementary school children. A live Alice has a journey among animated characters. The Caterpillar smokes marijuana, the Mad Hatter takes LSD, the Dormouse uses barbituates, and the March Hare pops amphetamines. The White Rabbit is a leader already into drugs. The Cheshire Cat is Alice's conscience. Running time: approximately fifteen minutes.

c.1972   *Jabberwocky.* Produced by Katky Film, Prague. Screenplay, design, and direction by Jan Svankmajer. This animation begins with a reading of "Jabberwocky." "Sequence of images composed of seemingly nonsense activities." Color. Running time: fourteen minutes.

1973   *Through the Looking-Glass.* BBC television production. Produced by Rosemary Hill; adapted and directed by James MacTaggart. Twelve-year-old Sarah Sutton as Alice; Brenda Bruce as the White Queen; Freddie Jones as Humpty Dumpty; Judy Parfitt as the Red Queen; and Richard Pearson as the White King. Reviewed: *The Sunday Times* (London), 30 December 1973, p. 34.

NOTES

1. See Rachael Low and Robert Manvell, *History of the British Film 1895-1906* (London: George Allen and Unwin, 1948), Ch. 4.

2. I would like to thank Miss Elizabeth Hepworth, Executor of the Hepworth Estate, for her assistance and for permission to publish Figs. 1 & 2.

3. *Edison Kinetogram,* 1 September 1910, p. 9.

4. *The New York Dramatic Mirror,* 14 September 1910, p. 32.

5. Information about the Strand Theatre is contained in Arthur Knight, *The Liveliest Art* (New York: New American Library, 1957), p. 53.

6. *The Moving Picture World,* 6 February 1915, p. 841.

7. W. W. Young, "How Alice Got Into the Wonderland of 'Movies,'" in the program to a benefit performance of the 1915 *Alice in Wonderland* film at Carnegie Hall, 5 April 1920. A copy of the program is in the Theatre Collection of the New York Public Library at Lincoln Center.

8. *Who's Who in America 1928-1929,* p. 2294.

9. Brian Sibley has a complete discussion of the Disney production in his article "A Californian Yankee at the Court of Queen Alice," *Jabberwocky: The Journal of the Lewis Carroll Society,* 2, No. 2 (1973), 5-14.

10. Brian Sibley, *Microscopes and Megaloscopes* (Kent, England: privately printed, 1974), p. 4.

11. Robert Benayoun, "Tout ce que peint mon imagination," *Lewis Carroll,* ed. Henri Parisot (Paris: Éditions de l'Herne, 1971), p. 98.

A Note on Carroll Bibliography

BIBLIOGRAPHERS HAVE NOT KEPT PACE WITH THE TREMENDOUS RESURGENCE OF interest in Lewis Carroll that has taken place in the past fifteen years. As a result, contemporary commentators are handicapped since many of the new editions, reprints, book-length studies, and articles that are produced yearly are not found in the standard annual bibliographies. It is only in the past few years that Carroll studies has developed an unabashed position in university and scholarly circles, which has resulted in the regular publication of Carroll articles in leading scholarly journals. Many important pieces, however, are still printed in unlikely or obscure publications and regularly go unnoticed and unrecorded. Carroll's following is, of course, international, and many significant foreign language items, particularly items published in Europe are similarly overlooked.

Currently the standard bibliographical reference work is *The Lewis Carroll Handbook,* edited by Sidney Herbert Williams and Falconer Madan and revised by Roger Lancelyn Green (London: Oxford University Press, 1962; rpt. London: Dawsons of Pall Mall, 1970). This bibliography contains entries dated only through 1960, the year the recent, sustained Carroll boom can be said to have begun with the publication of Martin Gardner's *The Annotated Alice.* Unfortunately, the *Handbook*'s list of works about Carroll is not exhaustive, and its impressive compilation of bibliographical information about editions has become slightly dated through recent discoveries. A comprehensive Carroll bibliography for 1960–75 is currently being compiled.

Good selective bibliographies that help fill some of the current gaps are contained in *Alice in Wonderland,* edited by Donald Gray (New York: W. W. Norton, Inc., 1971) and Peter Heath's *The Philosopher's Alice* (New York: St. Martin's Press, 1974). The former is more comprehensive and is conveniently organized; the latter is a somewhat more up-to-date catalogue of commentators and contains an extensive list of philosophical studies that treat Carroll's work.

Much has been done to improve the state of Carroll bibliography by the Lewis Carroll societies that have been founded in both England and America in the last decade. Both societies publish newsletters to keep members abreast of most recent publications (including ephemera). The British society publishes a quarterly journal of Carroll studies: critical, biographical, and bibliographical articles as well as in-depth reviews of all relevant and significant new books. The American society publishes a chapbook series of articles on various aspects of Carroll's life, work, and influence. In 1975, as part of this series, the American society began publishing an annual Carroll bibliography (beginning with 1974). Information about the societies can be obtained by writing to their respective secretaries: in England, c/o 55 Heath Cottages, Chislehurst Common, Chislehurst, Kent, England; and in America, c/o 617 Rockford Road, Silver Spring, Maryland 20902.

Notes on Contributors

HAROLD BEAVER is a Reader at the University of Warwick, England. He has completed five annotated editions for the Penguin English Library: Melville's *Moby-Dick, Billy Budd, Sailor and Other Stories,* and *Redburn;* Poe's *The Narrative of Arthur Gordon Pym* and *The Science Fiction of Edgar Allan Poe.* He is a regular contributor to the *Times Literary Supplement* and has also published two novels.

MORTON N. COHEN is Professor of English at the City College and Graduate School of the City University of New York. He is the author of books on H. Rider Haggard and Rudyard Kipling. With the assistance of Roger Lancelyn Green he has prepared an edition of Lewis Carroll's letters which will be published by Macmillan in 1977.

ERNEST COUMET is Professor of Philosophy (logic and the history of science) at the University of Paris. With Jean Gattégno he produced *Logique sans peine,* a French edition of *Symbolic Logic* and *The Game of Logic,* illustrated by Max Ernst.

MARTIN GARDNER is the author of *The Annotated Alice, The Annotated Snark,* and *The Snark Puzzle Book* as well as many other books and articles on Carroll. He has published extensively on several other subjects and is an editor of *Scientific American.*

JEAN GATTÉGNO is Professor of English at the University of Paris–VIII. He wrote the first French doctoral dissertation on Carroll and has published two books on Carroll: a critical study, *Lewis Carroll;* and a biography, *Lewis Carroll une vie,* published in English as *Lewis Carroll: Fragments of a Looking-Glass.* He has published translations of Carroll's work and recently published a critical book on Charles Dickens.

ROGER LANCELYN GREEN is an eminent British Carroll scholar. He has edited *The Diaries of Lewis Carroll* and *The Works of Lewis Carroll.* He has published biographies of Carroll and is one of the compilers of *The Lewis Carroll Handbook.* In addition, he has published numerous books on other writers and subjects.

EDWARD GUILIANO teaches in the English Department of the State University of New York at Stony Brook and writes regularly on Victorian literature. He is currently compiling a comprehensive annotated Carroll bibliography for 1960–75.

MICHAEL PATRICK HEARN is the author of *The Annotated Wizard of Oz* and *The Annotated Christmas Carol.* He is an editor of *Cricket: The Magazine for Children.*

PETER HEATH, translator, is Professor of Philosophy at the University of Virginia and the author of *The Philosopher's Alice.* A British citizen, he has published many translations of philosophical works and, with Edward Guiliano, is putting together a collection of translations of European Carroll studies.

ROGER B. HENKLE is Associate Professor of English at Brown University and is the associate editor of *Novel: A Forum on Fiction.* He writes regularly on nineteenth- and twentieth-century literature. Added to his published writing on Carroll will be a section in his forthcoming book on comedy in nineteenth-century England.

EDMUND MILLER has a doctorate in British literature and has published scholarly articles on Carroll's *A Tangled Tale* and on the nonsense songs of Edward Lear. He is a poet widely published in little magazines. His most recent book is *The Nadine Poems.*

DONALD RACKIN is Professor of English at Temple University, where he has taught Victorian literature and modern fiction since 1962. He has published several essays on Carroll, including his 1966 *PMLA* article, "Alice's Journey to the End of Night," which won the *PMLA* Prize for 1966. He is also editor of *Alice's Adventures in Wonderland: A Critical Handbook.* Currently he is writing a book about the symbolic uses of the child figure in modern British and American literature.

DAVID H. SCHAEFER is a well-known American collector of Carrolliana. His collection of film adaptations of Carroll's work is the most complete in the world.

ELIZABETH SEWELL, formerly a British citizen, makes her home in North Carolina, where she is Joe Rosenthal Professor of Humanities at the University of North Carolina at Greensboro. She has published several books and many articles, including several studies of Lewis Carroll's art. She is perhaps best known for her seminal study of the nonsense of Edward Lear and Lewis Carroll, *The Field of Nonsense,* and for *The Orphic Voice: Poetry and Natural History.*

JEFFREY STERN completed his doctorate at the University of York, England, with a dissertation entitled "Approaches to Lewis Carroll." At present he is a director of a firm of antiquarian booksellers with interests both in the U.K. and the U.S.A.

Index

Page numbers of illustrations are in italics.